Lend-Lease, Loans, and the Coming of the Cold War

Westview Special Studies
in International Relations

Lend-Lease, Loans, and the Coming of the Cold War:
A Study of the Implementation of Foreign Policy
Leon Martel

This is the first study to discuss in detail the implementation phase of policy decisions. Dr. Martel examines several related foreign policy decisions that contributed significantly to the coming of the Cold War: President Truman's order to cut back lend-lease to the USSR after the defeat of Germany, the termination of lend-lease to the USSR after Japan's capitulation, and the delayed response to two Soviet requests, made in 1945, for long-term credits for postwar reconstruction. He demonstrates how the outcome of these decisions was greatly influenced by the process of their implementation, a process that led to both a less favorable treatment for the Soviets and a stronger signal of U.S. attitudes than was intended by the Truman administration. From this point of view the onset of the Cold War is seen less as the result of the deliberate intentions of U.S. and Soviet leaders than as the consequence of the actions of those who processed their decisions. Dr. Martel concludes with recommendations for making policy outcomes more consistent with policy goals.

Leon Martel is executive vice-president of the Hudson Institute and director of its Research Management Council. He previously was on the political science faculty at Hofstra University.

Lend-Lease, Loans, and the Coming of the Cold War: A Study of the Implementation of Foreign Policy

Leon Martel

Westview Press / Boulder, Colorado

Westview Special Studies in International Relations

Copyright © 1979 by Westview Press, Inc.

Published in 1979 in the United States of America by
  Westview Press, Inc.
  5500 Central Avenue
  Boulder, Colorado 80301
  Frederick A. Praeger, Publisher

Library of Congress Cataloging in Publication Data
Martel, Leon
  Lend-lease, loans, and the coming of the Cold War.
  (Westview special studies in international relations)
  Bibliography: p.
  Includes index.
  1. Lend-lease operations (1941-1945). 2. United States—Foreign relations—Russia.
3. Russia—Foreign relations—United States. 4. World War, 1939-1945—Influence and results. I. Title. II. Series: Westview special studies in international relations and U.S. foreign policy.
D753.2.R9M37   327.73'047   79-13678
ISBN 0-89158-453-6

Printed and bound in the United States of America

To the memory of my father

Contents

Preface

In the study of the making of public policy, and particularly
of foreign policy, the final step of implementation has been
largely ignored. Elaborate conceptual frameworks have been
developed by some analysts for an idealized model of policy
implementation,[1] while others have focused on limits to
effective implementation.[2] But there has been no systematic
effort to examine the influence of the implementation phase of
the policy-making process on the final output of that process,
nor has there been attention paid to the possible improvement
of policy making that might result from greater attention to
this phase.[3] Yet much of the activity of the making of any policy
is carried out during its implementation and it is often the case
that success or failure of a policy rests on what is done during
this final step. Graham Allison has estimated that the
percentage of work done when a policy alternative has been
identified ranges from only about 10 percent (in the normal
case) to perhaps about 50 percent in some cases. He has written
that what remains "—namely the gap between preferred solutions and the actual behavior of the government—we label the
'analysis gap' or 'missing chapter' in conventional analysis."[4]

The purposes of this study are, first, to help fill that gap with
a better understanding of why and how foreign policy decisions
are affected by their implementation and, second, to suggest
what can be done to make implementation more consistent

with desired outcomes—a goal made ever more urgent by both the growing power of nation-states and the increasing complexity of their bureaucracies. The means for accomplishing these purposes will be an examination of the formation and implementation of four important and closely related U.S. decisions at the end of World War II concerning aid to the USSR. The first of these decisions was made after Germany's surrender in May 1945, when President Harry Truman signed an order—subsequently modified—that sharply cut back lend-lease to the USSR. The second decision—also subsequently modified—followed Japan's capitulation in mid-August 1945 and resulted in the abrupt cessation of lend-lease to Russia, while assistance to other nations continued until September 2, the date officially proclaimed for the termination of the war in the Pacific. The third decision was the long-delayed American reply to a January 1945 Soviet request for $6 billion in long-term credits for postwar reconstruction; and the fourth was the U.S. response to, and subsequent handling of, Russia's second request for assistance—for a sum of $1 billion—made at the end of August 1945. Taken together these decisions constituted an important departure from the American wartime policy of giving all possible aid to Russia without any questions asked. Thus, many have considered them an important turning point in U.S.-USSR relations, and some have concluded that they show evidence of U.S. responsibility for the coming of the Cold War.

These four foreign policy decisions were chosen for several reasons. First, each was importantly affected by its implementation. Excessive zeal in the execution of the first lend-lease decision made it appear coercive and punitive; implementation of the second lend-lease decision resulted in different treatment for the Soviet Union than that accorded other lend-lease recipients; and long delays in implementing the loan decisions—which finally made them negative replies to Russia's credit requests—altered both their meaning and purpose. Second, what finally emerged in all four decisions differed significantly from the policy preferences of those who had initiated them. The lend-lease decisions produced effects that were not intended and, in part, they had to be repudiated.

The loan decisions, instead of furthering the goals for which they were undertaken, caused confusion, uncertainty, and an undesired exacerbation of U.S.-USSR relations. Coming at a very sensitive time for American foreign policy, the implementation of these decisions thus created new difficulties for U.S. policy makers. As a result, many participants and close observers have been among their severest critics. Harry Truman, Dean Acheson, and Charles G. Ross retrospectively judged the lend-lease decisions to have been mistaken; others, such as Edward R. Stettinius, Jr., Albert Z. Carr, and Philip E. Mosely, have seen in the failure to provide postwar economic aid lost opportunities to influence Soviet policy in directions favorable to the United States.[5]

Finally, these decisions were chosen because they have occupied a central place in the debate concerning the World War II and post–World War II origins of the Cold War. Some have seen in them evidence of the use of economic pressure by the American government as part of a deliberate policy to get tough with Russia in the closing months of the war, while others have denied the existence of such intentions and have attributed these decisions to strict interpretations of existing laws and the rapid dissolution of America's wartime bureaucracy following Japan's surrender.[6] Thus, a careful account of their formation and implementation should shed further light on the intentions and alleged responsibility of those who participated in them.

This examination of the formation and implementation of these decisions will be developed principally from primary sources. They include the voluminous records of the Foreign Economic Administration, successor in 1943 to the Office of Lend-Lease Administration (OLLA), and the Central Decimal Files and relevant office files of the archives of the Department of State. These have been augmented by reference to the records of the President's Soviet Protocol Committee, the War Production Board, the War Shipping Administration, the Office of War Mobilization and Reconversion, the Export-Import Bank of the United States, and the departments of Commerce, the Treasury, the Army and the Navy. In addition, the available papers, manuscripts, and diaries of all major participants in the policy-making process have been examined. Finally, to make some effort to overcome the unavoidable absence of the contents of countless telephone conversations, unrecorded visits, and informal communications, interviews have been sought and correspondence has been exchanged with all major (and many minor) living participants in these decisions.

The limitations on the above are obvious. Public records only rarely reveal private thoughts, and archival sources, while often more revelatory, are subject to the whims of diverse filing systems and the organizational procedures of the numerous agents through whose hands they pass from the moment of creation to the date of final deposit. The all too frequent accidental discovery of a noteworthy document in an unlikely place quickly stirs visions of unfound troves and deflates pretensions to definitive research. Likewise, the memories of participants—three decades after the events—are often imperfect, skewed by the human tendency to remember best what was done best, or bent by the better judgment of hindsight, or simply softened and dulled by the passage of time.

Finally, there is one further limitation. This is a study of American policy making. It is based, therefore, on a thorough examination of American primary sources. The actions and attitudes of the other major participants in this story, the policy makers of the USSR and the United Kingdom, have been examined only through their secondary sources. Access to their primary sources would undoubtedly enrich this account, though most likely not enough to alter its major conclusions. However, this was not attempted. In the former case, for well-known reasons it was impossible; in the latter, it was simply beyond the scope of this study.

Within the above limitations it is felt that enough has been discovered to accomplish the two ultimate goals of this work. The first is to contribute to the study of the foreign policy-making process by utilizing four American decisions as a case study to examine in depth the implementation phase of this process. Such an examination should yield new insights into the nature and importance of implementation and its influence on the output of the policy-making process. This, it is hoped, will provide new material for those, like the present writer, who believe that the foremost prerequisite for the improvement of future foreign policy decisions is the critical examination of those made in the past.

The second ultimate goal of this work is to deepen and enrich understanding of the decisions to end aid to Russia at the end of World War II by looking more closely at their formation and implementation. This understanding should provide a new perspective for examining a set of issues that have figured importantly in the continuing debate fueled by orthodox and revisionist interpretations of post–World War II Soviet-American rivalry. As such, it is hoped that it will supply additional information and analysis with which to address the questions of responsibility for the results of these decisions and hence of attribution of blame for the coming of the Cold War.

Leon Martel
Tinerhir, Morocco

Acknowledgments

The completion of this study would not have been possible without the support and generous assistance of many people. I would like first to express my gratitude to those who encouraged my research and commented on earlier versions of this manuscript. Of these my greatest debt is to Warner R. Schilling, who suggested the topic of lend-lease to Russia and gave wise and useful counsel on the original manuscript. I am also extremely grateful to John N. Hazard for reading and commenting on this work, and especially for giving me access to his "Day Journal," a detailed record of his Russian lend-lease activities which proved to be an immensely valuable primary source. In addition, I would like to thank Lynn E. Davis for her lengthy and perceptive comments which aided me greatly in my subsequent revisions, and Roger E. Hilsman and Henry F. Graff for their critique and helpful suggestions to the original manuscript. Finally, I owe a special debt to two teachers who, though not involved in this work, provided the impetus that led to its undertaking: the late Philip E. Mosely, who first sparked my interest in the study of the Soviet Union, and William T. R. Fox, who inspired me to undertake the study and teaching of international politics.

I am also grateful to the many persons who assisted me in identifying and locating source material for this study. First, I am indebted to three scholars whose works on lend-lease not only provided models of scholarship on the subject but also saved me many hours in finding important documents: Warren F. Kimball, Raymond H. Dawson, and George C. Herring, Jr. Next, I wish to thank Arthur G. Hogan of the Historical Office of the Department of State who gave generously of his time and expertise in helping me locate the widely scattered documents that tell the story of the lend-lease program. I am also very grateful for the courteous and tireless response given my many requests by the professional staff personnel of the National Archives and Records Service, notably those in the Washington National Records Center, the Franklin D. Roosevelt Library, and the Harry S Truman Library, and to the personnel of the Office of Assistant Secretary for International Affairs of the Treasury Department and the Export-Import Bank of the United States for granting me permission to examine records in the custody of their organizations. In addition, I wish to thank—for their patient and expert service—the curators and manuscript division librarians of the following institutions: the Library of Congress, the Houghton Library of Harvard University, the Yale University Library, the Princeton University Library, the University of Virginia Library, the University of Kentucky Libraries, and the Robert Muldrow Cooper Library of Clemson University.

I also received invaluable assistance from those who shared with me—in interviews and correspondence—their own experiences as participants in the formation and implementation of Russian lend-lease policy, including: the late Dean Acheson, Hawthorne Arey, the late Charles E. Bohlen, Benjamin V. Cohen, the late Leo T. Crowley, Elbridge Durbrow, John N. Hazard, William McChesney Martin, Walter C. Sauer, Sidney P. Spaulding, and John Y. York.

Lastly, there are several to whom I owe very special thanks. I am indebted to Elsie Reynolds of the Hofstra University Library for diligently searching out elusive published materials, to Anne Marie Hampson, who rapidly and accurately typed the final manuscript, and to Daniel Raymond Stein, who helped promote the publication of this study and whose expert editorial guidance led to its being restructured in its present form. My greatest debt is to my family: to my two sons, Christopher and Jonathan, who stoically accepted the long hours their father was away on research trips or locked in his study and patiently inquired with curious if not equally comprehending interest of the progress of his work; and, above all, to my wife, Marilee, who not only typed the early drafts of the manuscript and made valuable suggestions which improved both its form and content, but also endured with fortitude and characteristic grace its long gestation and gave support and encouragement when it was needed most.

All of the above have helped make this a better book. The faults that remain are mine alone.

L.M.

1
The Creation and Renewal
of Lend-Lease

Lend-lease was an ingenious solution to a major problem facing Franklin D. Roosevelt as he prepared to begin an unprecedented third term as the nation's chief executive. FDR and his key cabinet officers, particularly the newly appointed Republican secretaries of War and the Navy, Stimson and Knox, felt with growing conviction that the security of the United States required maximum assistance to a Great Britain that was then standing alone against the Nazi conquest of Europe. Roosevelt had already traded over-age destroyers for bases, diverted to England orders for arms placed for U.S. forces in U.S. plants, and explored every possible device for circumventing the restrictive provisions of American neutrality legislation. These efforts buoyed British courage but they were hardly enough for the long struggle that lay ahead. England would need more of everything—planes, tanks, guns, bullets, eventually even food—but the dollars to purchase for her needs on a cash-and-carry basis were dwindling rapidly. As Britain's ambassador, Lord Lothian, candidly admitted to the press on his return to the United States from England in November 1940, "Well, boys, Britain's broke; it's your money we want."[1]

Supplying that money was not easy. There were the restrictions of the Neutrality Act to overcome, as well as the Johnson Act's prohibition of loans to countries in default on debts to the United States (which included every World War I ally except Finland). Even if these restrictions could have been overcome, there was still the vivid memory of the legacy of the last war's debts: a cycle of worldwide economic crises that had helped spin Europe once again into armed conflict. Finally, if the United States was to increase its supply to England it was inevitably going to move closer to the status of belligerent itself. This raised two further questions: what means of aiding Britain would be acceptable to an American people and their Congress that repeatedly had been promised they would not have to fight in this war, and how, while the United States steadied Britain, could it ready itself for the unforeseen consequences of its act of assistance?

The answer to these questions evolved slowly during the second half of 1940.[2] In June Congress passed the Pittman Resolution, which authorized the sale of surplus defense equipment to Latin American nations. In August Secretary of Interior Harold Ickes wrote Roosevelt in support of the destroyers-bases deal and used the picturesque analogy that Americans who did not want to aid Britain were acting like a householder who refused "to lend or sell his fire extinguisher to help put out the fire in the house that is right next door." A few days later Roosevelt tried this story on his old friend, the ambassador to France, William Bullitt, and several months later, in November, he broached to his cabinet the idea of building ships and then lending them to England for the duration. As an afterthought he added that "any other property that was loanable, returnable, and insurable" might also be leased.[3]

The catalyst for these seemingly disparate utterances came one month later. On December 2 Roosevelt departed for a two-week cruise on the U.S.S. *Tuscaloosa*, ostensibly to inspect the newly acquired British base sites in the West Indies but more likely, as Robert Sherwood described it, for "fishing, basking in the sun and spoofing cronies."[4] Behind him in Washington FDR had left an anxious cabinet. Meeting repeatedly in groups of two and three they could find no answer to the problem of Britain's rapidly diminishing dollar reserves, and with increasing urgency they awaited the return of their chief. Meanwhile, on the morning of December 9, Roosevelt had received by courier from Winston Churchill a letter that the British prime minister later described as "one of the most important I ever wrote." In 4,000 words Churchill candidly assessed Britain's situation on the eve of the new year. He estimated that the danger of German invasion had for the time being passed, but he stressed the vulnerability of Britain's lifeline across the oceans and emphasized the need for naval and air support to protect that lifeline. Then he described England's financial straits, concluding, "You may be certain that we will prove ourselves ready to suffer and sacrifice to the utmost for the Cause . . . The rest we leave with confidence to you and your people."[5]

As Roosevelt cruised in the Caribbean and mulled over this extraordinary message, the bits and pieces of the past months coalesced into a plan. Immediately upon his return to Washington he lunched with his treasury secretary, Henry Morgenthau, and laid out a proposal that would "get away from the dollar sign" by having the United States increase its own production and then lend or lease to England the supplies it needed. At the end of the war Britain would return, in good repair, what it still possessed and replace in kind that which had been consumed. That same afternoon Roosevelt revealed his plan to the press, embellishing it with Ickes's "fire extinguisher" analogy; twelve days later, in one of his famous fireside chats, he put it before the American people, asserting that in the face of the Axis threat the United States must be "the great arsenal of democracy."

On January 2, 1941, drafting of the Lend-Lease Bill began, significantly, in the office of the general counsel of the Treasury Department. Officials in the Department of State, including Secretary Cordell Hull, were consulted and did participate, but their roles—in keeping with Roosevelt's general use of the department—were strictly subsidiary. The key man in the drafting process was Oscar S. Cox, a bright young lawyer from Maine who had come to the legal department of the Treasury from the office of the Corporation Counsel of New York City. Cox, who was later to become the general counsel for the lend-lease administration and play a leading role in the program until its termination, enlisted the aid of John J. McCloy of the War Department and coordinated his work with Congressman Sol Bloom, Democrat of New

York, and Senator Walter George, Democrat of Georgia, chairmen respectively of the House Foreign Affairs and Senate Foreign Relations Committees.

President Roosevelt presented the lend-lease concept to Congress in his State of the Union message on January 6, and four days later the majority leaders of the Senate and House, Alben Barkley, Democrat of Kentucky, and John McCormack, Democrat of Massachusetts, introduced the Treasury's bill in their respective chambers. In the House, because of McCormack's sensitivity to the anti-British feelings of his South Boston Irish constituents, the bill was not tagged with his name but became known instead by its fortuitous number, H.R. 1776.[6]

According to the partially completed and unpublished official "History of Lend-Lease," this piece of legislation "undoubtedly represented the greatest grant of authority to the President in American history."[7] While allowing for a certain degree of hyperbole to the enthusiastic civil servant who authored this statement, it is nonetheless true that seldom in the history of the United States has a president been granted in one piece of legislation such wide discretion in the making of economic and foreign policy. Under the terms of the Lend-Lease Act the president could first designate for receipt of aid any country whose defense he deemed to be vital to the defense of the United States.[8] For the government of the designated country he could then at any time, in the interest of national defense, authorize the secretary of War, the secretary of the Navy, or the head of any other department or agency to manufacture or otherwise procure any defense article (including agricultural and industrial materials), to "sell, transfer title to, exchange, lease, lend, or otherwise dispose of" any such manufactured article or any similar defense articles already on hand, to "test, inspect, prove, repair, outfit, recondition, or otherwise place in good working order" any defense article, and to "communicate . . . any information pertaining to any defense article furnished." In addition, appropriations were authorized to carry out the above provisions and the president was empowered to set as "terms or conditions upon which any . . . foreign government receives any aid . . . payment or repayment in kind or property, or any other direct or indirect benefit which [he] deems satisfactory."

For two weeks lengthy hearings on the bill were held by the House Foreign Affairs Committee, and though most observers felt the measure would pass with votes to spare, the testimony was intense and heated and reports of it received nationwide attention. The issues were nothing less than war and peace and the power of the presidency, and everyone who felt strongly about these issues—and in early 1941 there were few who did not—wanted to be heard by the committee. Testifying for the bill was a solid phalanx of cabinet heads and military chiefs. Not only had they accepted the argument that the best defense for the United States was assistance to Britain, but increasingly they also had come to realize that the Lend-Lease Bill would help to organize the lagging American defense industry. Against them were arrayed a veritable who's who of the nation's leading isolationists, anglophobes, pacifists, and Roosevelt haters. However, the efforts of these groups were largely in vain. H.R. 1776 was reported out of committee essentially as it had been introduced, and after several days of vigorous debate it passed the House by the generous margin of 260 to 165. Hearings in the Senate Foreign Relations Committee were shortly followed by passage, 60 to 31, by the senior house of a slightly amended version of H.R. 1776. House conferees then accepted the Senate's amendments, repassage occurred on March 11, and that afternoon a triumphant President Roosevelt, surrounded by executive and legislative leaders and a crush of news photographers, presided over the ritual signing that made the Lend-Lease Bill law. A brief struggle followed over the appropriations legislation, but attempts to cut it below the $7 billion requested by the administration failed, and on March 24 FDR had the funds to put his program into action.

Thus was created what two French historians have called "the profoundly new, not to say revolutionary, Lend-Lease arrangement" and what an American political scientist labelled "the most extreme interpretation of the American Mission, in terms of a tangible commitment, ever suggested by anyone charged with the conduct of America's foreign affairs."[9] In one act the U.S. government had become both treasury and production facility for the Allied cause, taken a long and probably irrevocable step toward becoming itself a belligerent, given its president unprecedented economic powers, and established a program that was in effect a precursor of the worldwide foreign aid commitment it was to undertake in the years following the defeat of the Axis.

But the program was undertaken—as undoubtedly it had to be—in great haste, and little thought was given to the repercussions, wartime and postwar, that such a massive unilateral effort would have in the sensitive interlocking structure of international politics. Lend-lease assistance could be expected to aid considerably the economies of those countries to whom it was extended, relieving them somewhat from the burden of manufacturing not only their own weapons but also many nonmilitary supplies necessary to sustain their war efforts. In a long war—and most expected it to be long— this would establish an economic dependence on the United States that would surely cause pains of dislocation when it was finally terminated. This raised the additional question of just when lend-lease should be ended: Abruptly and completely when the last shot was fired? Slowly and gradually during a specified number of months or years following surrender? Or even before the war's end, in incremental steps, when victory seemed assured? Finally, lend-lease was an act "further to promote the defense of the United States and for other purposes." Did that defense end when hostilities ended, or did it include at least some repair of those conditions that might cause a new threat to U.S. security? And what, if anything, did "other purposes" include?

Although these questions were occasionally raised in the minds of those who drafted and passed the original Lend-Lease Act, they were put aside in deference to the more pressing business of getting the legislation enacted and establishing an organization to implement it. Only one section of the Lend-Lease Act dealt with its termination. This was Section 3-c, which set the life of the act as two years—unless ended earlier by a concurrent resolution of both houses of Congress—and protected against the default of contracts existing at the time of termination by providing a three-year grace period to clear up any contracts made before July 1, 1943, or before the earlier passage of a concurrent resolution. Beyond these stipulations there were no other provisions concerning the pace and conditions of ending lend-lease or the possibility of its continuation for purposes other than the "defense" of the United States.

First Renewal of Lend-Lease

In 1943 the Lend-Lease Act, having run its statutory two-year life, came up for extension. The original two-year time limit was proposed by the House Foreign Affairs Committee (after rejecting shorter periods) apparently to conform with the constitutional limitation of two-year appropriations for the armed forces. In 1943 Lend-lease Administrator Stettinius decided to ask for only a one-year extension "because it was impossible to ascertain at the present time what world events would be, and that the Congress, perhaps, could have a second look."[10] This became the established extension period for the life of the act, a circumstance that pleased most congressmen but was only reluctantly accepted by the State Department.[11]

During the four weeks of hearings held by the House Foreign Affairs Committee on the extension of lend-lease several critical matters were discussed. The most important of these for the eventual termination of the program was whether lend-lease would continue after the cessation of hostilities. The novelty of the lend-lease idea had been acclaimed in many circles and some saw it as a natural instrument for postwar rehabilitation and reconstruction. In the *Washington Post* on January 25, 1943, Walter Lippmann argued first for the wartime continuation of lend-lease, then added, "What is more the underlying principle of lend-lease will for the same compelling reasons be extended into the period which follows immediately upon the armistice and lasts until order has been restored." Congress, however, was not yet ready to go into the peacetime foreign aid business and committee members questioned lend-lease officials closely on this matter. When Stettinius was asked by Rep. William Fulbright, Democrat of Arkansas, if he cared to express his views "as to whether or not the lend-lease program might not be a proper vehicle for planning perhaps not only the winning of the war but of dealing with the peace," he enthusiastically replied: "I would absolutely agree with you, sir. There is no question about that. That is the case. The lend-lease mechanism I am sure would be of great value to this government and the State Department specifically at the time of peace."[12] Oscar Cox, general counsel for the lend-lease organization (then known as OLLA) and principal author of the original bill, was less willing to commit himself. "The job of lend-lease," he said, "is primarily a war job and we have no primary concern with the postwar job"; but he added, "Now it may very well be that the habits of cooperation as distinct from any words on paper may have a predominant force on whatever happens after the war."[13] Cox's view that lend-lease was primarily a war job was quoted with approval on the floor of the Congress, but no one in OLLA was at that time ready to commit himself to the position that lend-lease was *exclusively* a war job. Here the matter rested, leaving uncertain the fate of the program upon the cessation of hostilities.

A second matter that occupied the attention of congressmen was the related question of using lend-lease funds for relief and rehabilitation in reoccupied areas. In December 1942 Stettinius wrote in a memorandum to Roosevelt that there was no question about the legality of using lend-lease funds for civilian needs in such areas because it could be justified as fulfilling a defense purpose; and FDR quickly gave his approval to this policy.[14] But rehabilitation to assist in the prosecution of the war also helped in the recovery from the damages of the war, and Congress tried hard to draw a line between the two. Stettinius was asked in the House committee's hearings what the relationship would be between lend-lease and Herbert Lehman's recently created Office of Foreign Relief and Rehabilitation Operations (OFRRO, the forerunner of UNRRA, the United Nations Relief and Rehabilitation Administration). He replied that OFRRO would be considered in the same category as other lend-lease claimants making requests for materials and that no supplies would be specifically earmarked for its use.[15] This reply did not really clarify the matter since it only foreclosed advance designation of lend-lease for rehabilitation purposes; but for the time being this was as far as Congress wished to pursue the issue.

On other matters—the extraction of permanent concessions in exchange for lend-lease aid and the fear that the administration would use lend-lease agreements with foreign nations to make postwar committments—several legislators expressed strong opinions, but all amendments covering such matters were defeated. The land-lease extension was over-whelmingly approved by both houses in time for presidential signature on March 11, 1943—the second anniversary of the original act.

Two months later Congress had another opportunity to consider lend-lease when Roosevelt submitted a fourth request for appropriations for the program. This time considerable interest was occasioned by the inclusion in one of the appropriations categories of a sum specifically programmed for supplies for OFRRO. This resulted in close questioning of Stettinius by members of the House Appropriations Com-mittee, particularly about the use of these funds to rehabilitate public utilities and other industrial installations that would have a postwar use. Stettinius assured his questioners that such facilities would be restored only if they were also required for the prosecution of the war. This seemed to satisfy the congressmen, but they did demonstrate their fiscal prerogative by a token excision of $150 million from the appropriation category in question, a move in which the Senate concurred. Other than petulant individual criticisms of the management of lend-lease and a continuing anxiety over possible postwar commitments, passage of the fourth lend-lease appropriation evoked little of moment.

By the end of 1943 lend-lease had thus been renewed without amendment and almost all the funds requested for it had been appropriated by the Congress. But this seeming unanimity masked important differences of opinion regarding its operation and temporarily concealed the unanswered ques-tions of key legislators concerning its future and eventual termination. In March, during the debate on the extension of lend-lease, Senator Vandenberg, Republican from Michigan, elicited audible cheers from his colleagues on the Senate floor when he said, "Of course, the final equities depend on the final settlements," and shortly afterward Senator Ellender, Democrat from Louisiana, concluded the debate by urging, "Let us bargain now while the war is on and not wait till the war is over."[16] During the following months these views attracted increasing support, and in October, following extensive publicity of the criticisms of five senators who had inspected overseas lend-lease operations, Acting Secretary of State Stettinius reported to the absent Secretary Hull on a meeting with Walter Lippmann in which the latter had warned of the "changing congressional attitude on lend-lease."[17]

Second Renewal of Lend-Lease

In the spring of 1944 lend-lease again came up for extension. With the war one year further along and eventual victory a virtual certainty, congressmen in both houses raised with increasing intensity the questions they had asked at the time of the first extension. Under the consolidation of all foreign economic activities that had taken place the previous fall with the creation of the Foreign Economic Administration (FEA), Leo T. Crowley was the new chief of lend-lease operations. He had been selected in part because of the excellent record he had made in dealing with Congress while chairman of the Federal Deposit Insurance Corporation, and he proved to be a most cooperative witness in congressional hearings. In response to requests for reassurance that when the war was over lend-lease would be over, Crowley told the House Foreign Affairs Committee, "I agree that lend-lease is a war emergency measure." Later in the testimony Assistant Secretary of State Dean Acheson added his own assurances when he said, "As a matter of broad principle, I should think it was clear that lend-lease was a wartime measure."[18] On the question of using lend-lease funds for the relief and rehabilitation of occupied areas Crowley was much more specific than his predecessors. While the Army was in control of a liberated area, Crowley said, FEA would assist in the provision of supplies needed as a matter of military necessity for the civilians in that area; but as soon as the Army vacated its control, FEA would step out and it would be UNRRA's job to take care of emergency relief needs in that territory.[19]

Congress continued to express its interest and reassert its prerogatives in the related areas of settlements and postwar benefits to be obtained from lend-lease. In an effort to insure that no final settlements would be made without congressional approval, the House amended the original act with a proviso that nothing in the final settlement of the terms and conditions upon which a country received lend-lease assistance would authorize the president to incur any obligations on the part of the United States with respect to postwar policy "except in accordance with established constitutional procedure."[20] Other more restrictive amendments were defeated, but only by narrow margins, thus testifying to the growing boldness of the House's efforts to reassert its control over the lend-lease program. In the Senate, Arthur Vandenberg moved to strike the words "in any final settlement" from the House amendment, thus broadening it to apply to *all* arrangements that might be made under lend-lease agreements with respect to postwar policies. In arguing for his amendment the Michigan Republican stated that it not only prohibited the president from undertaking obligations outside his constitutional jurisdiction, "but that it also is intended to confine lend-lease absolutely to the military operation of this war, that it does not extend it one minute or one dollar into the postwar period."[21] With the Vandenberg change the Senate passed the bill 63-1. The House concurred with the amended Senate version, and in mid-May the second one-year extension of the Lend-Lease Act became law.

While the Senate was debating and extending lend-lease, the House Appropriations Committee was beginning work on the fifth lend-lease appropriation, incorporated as Title I of the Defense Aid Appropriation Bill for 1945. In extensive hearings lasting almost two weeks the committee received the most unequivocal commitment thus far that lend-lease would end at the war's end. "My own thought about lend-lease," said Leo Crowley, "is that it is strictly a war measure and as soon as possible after the war is over lend-lease will be terminated."[22] A few weeks later, before the Senate Appropriations Committee,

Crowley's general counsel, Oscar Cox, agreed that lend-lease was a war measure but qualified its termination when he said that it would end "in all probability with the war, and subject to ordinary liquidation which is efficient and economical."[23] The difference was slight, but it reflected a growing division of opinion that was to be more fully expressed when the program was cut back and terminated the following year.

Third and Final Renewal of Lend-Lease

Early in 1945 the Lend-Lease Act was again before Congress, this time for what would be its third and final extension. In 1943 and again in 1944 Congress had extended lend-lease by overwhelming majorities. By the end of 1944 it had also made five direct appropriations for the program totaling over $28 billion and had authorized, with very little discussion, the War and Navy departments to use almost $36 billion of their appropriations for lend-lease transfers of arms and munitions. But in committee and in debate on the floors of both houses senators and congressmen had made clear their intention to monitor the program carefully to insure that it did not stray beyond the boundaries that they felt should limit such a novel enterprise. By amendment in 1944 they had restricted the president's power to use lend-lease to incur postwar policy obligations, and by close questioning of lend-lease managers in committee hearings they had extracted increasingly explicit assurances concerning the prohibition of lend-lease for rehabilitation and reconstruction activities and the prompt termination of the program upon the cessation of hostilities. Nevertheless, in the spring of 1945 many members of the new Seventy-ninth Congress found these reactions and adjustments inadequate protection against abuses they felt were already dangerously extending the program. In the context of imminent victory in Europe and their own renascence as an active branch of the government they therefore moved, in the third and final extension of lend-lease, to put into law limitations that would provide the protection they wanted.

Amendment and Passage in the House

Hearings on the bill (H.R. 2013) to extend the Lend-Lease

Act for the third time began in February before the House Committee on Foreign Affairs. For the first two days the major witnesses were FEA Administrator Leo Crowley and Oscar Cox, recently promoted to deputy administrator of the FEA. Crowley and Cox came with their usual collection of charts and tables, all neatly packaged in individual binders for the members of the committee. Their reception was generally friendly and they patiently answered innumerable queries— some picayune and uninformed—about every aspect of the program. Toward the close of the second day Crowley enthusiastically responded at length to a question (perhaps suggested in advance to Committee Chairman Sol Bloom) about lend-lease and postwar reconstruction. "Now, it is our understanding . . ." said the FEA administrator, "that lend-lease is entirely military aid, . . . and that after the war lend-lease will cease and will not be used for postwar rehabilitation purposes or have anything to do with postwar economic aid to these governments."[24]

During hearings the following week the committee took testimony from the assistant secretary of the Navy, Secretary of War Stimson, an Army colonel in charge of reverse lend-lease in England, and Admiral Emory Land, administrator of the War Shipping Administration and chairman of the Maritime Commission. Again, apart from some questions critical of what was perceived as the low amount and inflated evaluation of reverse lend-lease from the Allies, the atmosphere was relaxed and the questions fairly routine. In fact, Stimson recorded in his diary that the hearing in which he participated was "quite a love feast."[25] The secretary of War also testified to the committee that "lend-lease was initiated as a military measure . . . and it should not be carried further after the war is over without the full consent of Congress to every step." He added, though, that in the good will it had achieved it was the kind of example Congress might consider helpful for the postwar years, and in his diary that evening he expressed the hope that it would influence Congress particularly in meeting the problem of "the furnishing of food supplies to civilians for the purpose of rehabilitation after the war."[26]

The House Committee on Foreign Affairs recessed after these six days of hearings in February and did not resume

consideration of the third lend-lease extension until early the
following month. In the meantime, on the last day of February,
three agreements had been signed with France making that
nation the latest recipient of lend-lease assistance. One of these
agreements, the first to be completed under Section 3-c of the
Lend-Lease Act, profoundly affected the House committee's
further consideration of H.R. 2013. The French 3-c agreement
was similar in its general provisions to one that had been
offered the USSR the previous fall. It contained two schedules,
one for raw materials, food, and short-life manufacturing
equipment amounting to $1,675 million; the other for
locomotives, railroad cars, and heavy industrial equipment
valued at $900 million. Under the agreement these supplies
were to be transferred to France under regular lend-lease terms
until such time as the president determined they were no longer
necessary for the prosecution of the war. After that date, and
within the time period permitted by the Lend-Lease Act, these
supplies would continue to be transferred, but France would
have to pay for them with dollars under the provisions of a
long-term credit requiring annual payments during the next
thirty years and carrying an interest charge of 2-3/8 percent on
the unpaid balance.[27]

This agreement was reported in the *New York Times* on
March 1 and its full text was released to the press three days
later. To certain members of the Republican opposition in the
House Foreign Affairs Committee it seemed to confirm the
rumors that had appeared in the press earlier of similar long-
term arrangements already completed or under consideration
with Britain and Russia. Hearings were thus resumed in a
much chillier atmosphere and Crowley and Cox faced a barrage
of critical questions. The FEA administrator, determined to
blunt the expected attack, reassured the committee again in his
opening statement that lend-lease was strictly a war measure,
that it would not be used for postwar reconstruction, and that it
would "end and be liquidated" when the war was won. The
French agreement, he told the committee, was not a "long-term
program of post-war aid," but strictly a means to supply France
with the supplies and services needed to wage war. It took
advantage of the three-year "clean-up" period provided in

Section 3-c of the Lend-Lease Act for contracts made before the end of hostilities and thus, Crowley added, it minimized U.S. financial liabilities during the liquidation of the program and meant that "French taxpayers will assume a burden which might otherwise be borne by American taxpayers."[28]

Rep. John M. Vorys of Ohio, who led the Republican opposition, was equally determined. He welcomed Crowley's assurances that lend-lease was purely a war measure and would end with the war, but he felt that the broad wording of the statute—an act "to promote the defense of the United States" and not specifically just "a war supply measure"—combined with the three-year clean-up period of Section 3-c, meant that it could be used by the president for a great variety of purposes, including postwar economic aid.[29] Crowley and Cox, with the aid of Assistant Secretary of State Dean Acheson, replied at length to Vorys and to similar questions from Representatives Chiperfield, Mundt, and Jonkman, Republicans from Illinois, South Dakota, and Michigan. The majority of the committee, including six of its eleven Republican members, were apparently convinced by the testimony they heard and reported the bill favorably to the House floor, adding only the necessary changes that would extend the act to June 30, 1946, and its clean-up period to June 30, 1949. In their report the majority discussed the recent French agreement and justified it as "in keeping with the administration of the Lend-Lease Act as a war supply measure"; but they also added the admonition that when the war was won, "lend-lease should end and be liquidated as promptly and efficiently as possible, in accordance with the intention of Congress and the provisions of the Lend-Lease Act."[30]

This, however, was not sufficient for Congressman Vorys and four of his Republican colleagues on the committee. Vorys and Representatives Chiperfield, Mundt, Jonkman, and Smith of Wisconsin filed a minority report expressing dissatisfaction with the committee's failure to write limitations into the law that would prohibit the use of lend-lease as a postwar mechanism. They presented an analysis of the French agreement, arguing that the type of supplies, the probable end of the war, and the method of long-term payment made it "by its very terms a postwar agreement." They spoke also of the press reports of possible multibillion dollar arrangements with Britain and Russia and warned that these and others could be made by the president under the broad provisions of the act. To prevent lend-lease from being extended into the postwar period and to have Congress take a "coordinate place" in making the foreign policy of the country, the minority intended—their report concluded—to submit new amendments when the bill came up on the floor of the House the following week.[31]

This threat was sufficient to galvanize the FEA into action. During the ensuing weekend Oscar Cox and FEA General Counsel Alfred Davidson spent several hours with Vorys working out a compromise amendment acceptable to him and his group as well as to the majority leadership of the committee. The new amendment, added to Section 3-c of the original act, had two provisions: first, it provided that nothing in the section could be construed "to authorize the president to enter into or carry out any contract or agreement with a foreign government for postwar relief, postwar rehabilitation, or postwar reconstruction"; and second, it declared that a contract entered into for lend-lease assistance for the war that provided for the payment of such assistance by the recipient after it was no longer necessary for the defense of the United States would not be deemed to be for postwar relief, rehabilitation, or reconstruction. By the first part of the amendment Vorys hoped to limit future lend-lease to contracts that were specifically related to military purposes; by the second part the FEA representatives hoped to continue making 3-c agreements that would give them a postwar period to clean up, for payment, contracts still incomplete at the time of the cessation of hostilities. To Vorys this represented an important new protection in the law, to Cox it was "a harmless amendment."[32]

In executive session the following Monday the Foreign Affairs Committee gave its unanimous consent to the new amendment, and that afternoon it was read on the floor of the House by Committee Chairman Sol Bloom. Debate was conducted on the entire bill the following day and leaders of both parties rose to defend the continuation of lend-lease and to explain and support the new amendment. Toward the end of the debate two further restrictive amendments were offered from the floor, one that in effect would have prohibited contracts of any kind under Section 3-c and another that would have required congressional approval for all final lend-lease settlements. Both were opposed by Bloom and Vorys and both were defeated by voice vote. The House then proceeded to approve the new amendment to Section 3-c and, in a roll call immediately following, passed H.R. 2013 by a vote of 354 to 28. The margin of victory, as in past extensions, was again very large; but to one well-informed observer of the Washington scene—Arthur Krock of the *New York Times*—the quick approval of the bill was the direct result of the committee amendment. Without it, he wrote, the extension of lend-lease might have failed.[33]

Debate and Passage in the Senate

The Senate Foreign Relations Committee held hearings on H.R. 2013 on March 28 and April 4. FEA Administrator Crowley began the first day of testimony with an explanation of the new House amendment and a detailed justification of the French 3-c agreement, then sat back for questions. The first queries mainly requested further amplification of the three-year liquidation period for contracts made before the termination of hostilities, and Crowley, assisted again by Oscar Cox, patiently obliged. One question, from Senator Bridges, Republican from New Hampshire, brought forth the most detailed explanation to date of what would actually happen to lend-lease on the day hostilities ceased. Crowley outlined several steps he thought should be taken: first, all new contracts should cease immediately unless there were 3-c agreements in force with the countries involved; second, contracts in process should be reviewed to see which ones should be cancelled and which ones recipients would be willing to pay for; and finally, an effort should be made to make arrangements with non–3-c agreement countries for the disposition of materials with a postwar use.[34]

At this point Senator Vandenberg interrupted to ask Crowley if he knew of any commitments contrary to the steps he had outlined. When he received a negative reply Vandenberg began to read something he described as "confidential" and of unknown authenticity, though emanating from what he considered "a highly reliable source." What Vandenberg read was a general description of the understanding reached by Roosevelt and Churchill at the OCTAGON Conference in Quebec the previous November concerning lend-lease for Britain during the period following the defeat of Germany (known as Phase II, and in the United States called Period I). In its original form this understanding, which had never been made public, provided for $3.5 billion of military lend-lease and $3 billion in non-war materials to Britain for the period between Germany's surrender and victory over Japan. In reply to Vandenberg's query as to whether there was "any truth" in what he had read, Crowley's initial response was something less than candid. "Senator," said the FEA administrator, who had heard about the understanding directly from Secretary Morgenthau, "to the best of my knowledge I would say there is no truth to it."

Crowley then went on to explain the modifications later made in the original arrangement during the British-American negotiations that followed the Quebec Conference. These had reduced the total to $5.5 billion, a figure that Vandenberg still found very high and for which he wished to know if there had been a definite "commitment" to the British. There then followed a long colloquy during which Crowley sought to convince Vandenberg that the British Phase II figures were simply for planning purposes and covered supplies exclusively for the war against Japan. There was neither a commitment nor an intent to aid British reconversion, the FEA administrator insisted. Vandenberg, however, found the distinction between "commitment" and "figures for planning purposes" unconvincing, and the hearing ended with Crowley promising a detailed written explanation of the understanding with Britain.[35]

Shaken by Senator Vandenberg's revelations, and remembering the furor created in the House committee by the French 3-c agreement, the Roosevelt administration decided it would be politically prudent to delay further action on other pending 3-c agreements. On April 5, the weekly "Digest of Problems

Before the State Department" reported the president's decision that no such agreements would be signed "until after the bill for the renewal of the Lend-Lease Act has been passed by Congress."[36] In the meantime, Crowley had sent his promised letter to Vandenberg giving the particulars of Phase II lend-lease and the Senate Foreign Relations Committee had held its second and final day of hearings on H.R. 2013. Crowley and Cox again appeared before the committee. Vandenberg questioned them at length, especially concerning the need for a three-year liquidation period, and speculated aloud about the possibility of reducing it to one or two years at the most. He did not press the matter, however, and in the end agreed—though somewhat reluctantly and perhaps in deference to his recent cooptation into the inner circle planning for postwar international organization—that the testimony of Crowley and the new House amendment provided protection against the unwarranted extension of lend-lease. With the doubts of its members thus satisfied, the committee unanimously reported the bill on April 4 without further amendment.[37]

While Senator Vandenberg may have felt restrained by his recent conversion to the cause of internationalism (dramatically expressed in a major address to the Senate on January 10) and his interest in working for a bipartisan foreign policy, no such restraints hindered his Republican colleague from Ohio. Like most other members of the senior house, Senator Taft was surprised when the Democratic leadership, in the midst of finishing work on the controversial Mexican Water Treaty on April 9, suddenly brought up for consideration H.R. 2013. He quickly recovered, however, and announced that he would shortly introduce an amendment he believed would correct a major deficiency in the amendment added by the House. After a long interlude in the debate, during which Senator Langer of North Dakota and several of his Midwest colleagues bitterly animadverted on the continued lend-lease transfer of box cars and farm equipment to Europe while orders for their constituents went unfilled, Senator Taft rose to offer his amendment. The influential Ohio Republican proposed to strike out the entire second part of the House amendment. The effect of such a deletion would have been to retain the prohibition against contracts for postwar assistance while depriving the president of the exception that allowed continuation for up to three years after the war, upon payment by the recipients, of contracts for war-related supplies made before the termination of hostilities.[38]

Taft argued that the first part of the House amendment ruled out contracts for postwar relief, rehabilitation, or reconstruction, but that the exception of its second part "absolutely kills" the amendment. The result, he felt, was the creation of a large loophole in Section 3-c of the original act through which the administration could make huge loans for postwar purposes, and he pointed to the French 3-c agreement as an example of just such a loan. Taft was upset that such agreements could be made outside of what he conceived as the scope of the Lend-Lease Act and without congressional approval, but his objections went even deeper. They extended to the very core of his economic philosophy and they touched particularly on the role he felt foreign commerce should play in the postwar economic life of the nation. Taft believed that the French agreement (with its provision for repayment over thirty years), the "understanding" with Britain for $5.5 billion during Phase II, and the rumored consideration of a $6 billion loan for Russia were all based on the assumption that they would be needed to generate sufficient American business to maintain high employment and prevent depression during the period of postwar demobilization. He profoundly disagreed with this assumption and the increased government activity and public spending that would necessarily accompany it.

Taft felt that the real danger after the war would be inflation and not depression. He pointed out that Series E bonds, excess currency, and deposits in savings banks and checking accounts would put $89 billion of liquid spending power in the hands of individuals alone, and that this sum would be swelled by large state unemployment compensation funds and liberal provisions for loans to veterans enabling them to buy homes, farms, and businesses. Coupled with these ready funds, Taft went on, there would be a great unleashed public demand for goods unavailable during the war emergency as well as an enormous need for repairs and capital replacements of all kinds throughout the country. The nation's economy would thus have little need for any stimulation that would result from large loans to enable foreign countries to buy U.S. goods. Beyond this, Taft noted that during lend-lease most U.S. exports had in fact been free, while the United States continued to pay for its imports. The result was that the total resources of foreign nations in the United States, in cash, gold, and negotiable short-term securities, had accumulated to $25 billion. With these kinds of reserves available he felt there was certainly no need for extensive loans to spur foreign trade. Finally, Taft held no brief for what he called the "very strong nationwide propaganda deliberately promoted by the State Department and other Government agencies to sell the American people on the importance of foreign trade." The country was largely self-sufficient, he argued; exports in recent decades had never brought in more than 6 percent of the country's national income and an export trade based on lending large sums of money would create "a wholly artificial activity bound to collapse in time with the most dangerous results." The sum and substance of Taft's opposition to the provision permitting the executive to make 3-c agreements for the postwar liquidation of lend-lease contracts was that it was unwise, unsound, and unnecessary.[39]

Taft's amendment and his subsequent defense of it concluded the Senate's legislative business on April 9. When debate resumed the following day it was clear that a large number of senators were coming over to his side, enough perhaps to pass his amendment. To be sure, not many who supported him did so with the comprehensive and cogently articulated economic arguments he had offered. Some were for the amendment simply because they feared the executive would use the Lend-Lease Act to provide postwar aid not authorized by Congress; others supported Taft because they were disappointed that the administration had not made adequate use of the bargaining advantages inherent in lend-lease to acquire postwar base rights and other facilities; and a growing and mixed group, including Democrat Tydings of Maryland, Republican Ball of Minnesota, and the Senate's lone progressive, La Follette of Wisconsin, rose to speak for the amendment to restore the balance of power between the executive and legislative branches of the government. Senator Vandenberg's position was particularly unique. He agreed with the need for a lend-lease liquidation period, but not one that was to last three years; thus, he declared, he would vote for the Taft amendment so that the conference committee it would require could explore the whole matter further. Overall, the Taft amendment provided a unique opportunity for those who had been uneasy with lend-lease for a variety of reasons, but felt constrained to vote for it because not to do so would jeopardize the war effort. Here they were able to register dissent against the program while still continuing it as a war measure.

Throughout the debate Majority Leader Barkley and Senator George of Georgia, second ranking Democrat on the Foreign Relations Committee, vigorously rebutted Taft and his supporters. Barkley argued that their position constituted a "total misconception" of the language they wished to eliminate in Section 3-c. These words, he insisted, merely provided the means by which the president could, at the termination of hostilities, sell supplies committed to recipient nations rather than attempt to reclaim them and return them to the United States. Barkley went on to defend the French agreement as serving just this purpose and he averred that the administration did not intend to use lend-lease for postwar purposes or to extend it beyond the cessation of hostilities. To these points Senator George, in a long emotional speech, added the argument that the excision proposed by Taft would tie the hands of the president and deprive the country of an orderly and economical liquidation of the lend-lease program.

At this point, with all the arguments stated and restated and only impassioned rhetoric filling the chamber, the Senate had heard enough; from the floor came shouts of "vote!" "vote!" The yeas and nays had been ordered on the amendment, and the presiding officer, Vice President Harry Truman, directed the clerk to call the roll. When the vote had been taken the count stood thirty-nine for Taft's amendment and thirty-nine against. According to the rules of the Senate this defeated the amendment, but it also gave the vice president a chance to vote. This Truman did, and in the one vote he cast in his short term as vice president, he voted nay.[40]

The rest of the debate was anticlimactic. The question was called on the entire bill, and H.R. 2013 was passed by voice vote. It was then enrolled and signed and sent to the president on April 12. As it turned out, it was the last bill to be formally presented to FDR, and one of several left to his successor to sign. This Truman did five days later, making the third and final extension of lend-lease the first public law to bear his signature as president.[41]

On the surface it would appear that the administration came through the final extension struggle unscathed. It accepted and partly arranged an amendment that only made explicit what it had promised to do anyway, and it escaped another that would have been much more restrictive and limiting on its activities. But it just barely escaped, and the close call was a bright caution signal the administration was careful to heed on its way to the termination of lend-lease. The executive had held up signature on two completed 3-c agreements (with Belgium and the Netherlands) pending legislative action on the extension. These, both small, were signed on April 17 and 30; but with the exception of the special case of China one year later (involving a small sum to cover the disarmament and repatriation of Japanese troops), no other 3-c agreements were negotiated, and plans for the offer of a second one to Russia were abruptly dropped. As will be seen, the Phase II understanding with Britain was modified, emasculated, and finally terminated in confusion. No other such arrangements were made after April 1945.

Congress's Influence on the Lend-Lease Program

Lend-Lease was an exceptional program—a wartime expedient hastily assembled for an uncertain duration, its bureaucratic structure a jerry-built jumble of overlapping agencies and committees. But it was also a means by which some of its creators and supporters hoped to realize in the postwar period their vision of a free-trading world dominated by a strong and prosperous United States. To the public still entwined in the cocoon of isolationism and only vaguely aware of the responsibilities of great-power status, lend-lease was largely a mystery—a sleight of hand conjured by the master magician in the White House. They applauded the trick, but it was a nervous applause that betrayed a suspicion of what lay hidden by the illusion.

Congress had little choice but to approve lend-lease, for it sent to war American matériel instead of American men; but Congress regarded it with suspicion because it gave much in return for little, and because it encroached on congressional powers while swelling those of an already strong chief executive. Thus, through questions in committee, and through amendments and proposed amendments to the several renewals of the Lend-Lease Act, it slowly and successfully shaped and modified the administrations's program. While Congress took no direct part in making policy for the ending of lend-lease, it did nonetheless clearly convey its opinion that the termination of the program should be as immediate as possible and at minimum further cost to the U.S. taxpayer. In addition, in the debates over the extensions of lend-lease influential members of Congress had begun making known their preferences for postwar reconstruction arrangements that would be limited, specific, and not detrimental to the postwar economic interests of the United States—interests that they increasingly expressed in national rather than international terms.

2

Organization and Operation of the Special Lend-Lease Program for Russia

The administration of lend-lease to the forty-seven countries eventually made eligible for it was an immense and complex task. It was carried out by an untried ad hoc organization that often cut chaotically across well-established operational lines; it employed procedures that were unfamiliar and often unnerving to civil servants long accustomed to punctiliously filling forms and following regulations; and the breadth and pervasiveness of its impact on the American economy and the economies it aided stirred uneasy fears of unknown future consequences. Yet lend-lease worked and largely achieved its goals. It did so because those who were involved understood that the common cause demanded uncommon cooperation. Thus, differences that normally would have imperiled the program were sublimated, postponed, or simply forgotten.

This was least true, however, in the administration of lend-lease to Russia. The legacy of suspicion and distrust was so high and the level of mutual understanding was so low that aid to Russia always appeared to be extended grudgingly and received diffidently. Only occasionally—when prompted by prodding from higher up or when inhibitions were loosened by rounds of euphoric toasts—did officials of either side testify to the contribution made through mutual collaboration. More often they dealt with each other warily, concerned mostly it seemed with the advantages that might be taken of their actions rather than given by them. From the beginning lend-lease to Russia was—and had to be—a special program, with a special organization and special procedures.

The Nazi-Soviet nonaggression pact of August 1939, followed by the Russian attack on Finland, had brought a distinct chill to Soviet-American relations and had all but drained the small reservoir of good will toward Russia that had gradually accumulated in the public mind since American recognition in 1933. Nevertheless, during 1940 the changing facts of international life were slowly provoking a reconsideration of U.S. interests regarding the USSR in the inner circles of the government. As Hitler subjugated the European continent and posed a growing threat to the British Isles and U.S. commerce, continued isolation of the USSR seemed less and less desirable, and tentative steps were taken to improve relations. Roosevelt discussed with his cabinet the possibility of a trade arrangement with Russia, steps were taken to lift restrictions that had frozen Soviet orders for strategic goods in the United States, and in January 1941, the Soviet ambassador to Washington, Constantine Oumansky, was officially informed of the lifting of the "moral embargo" imposed in December 1939, against the export of military-related equipment to the USSR.[1] But these were halfway measures, often tangled in a thicket of priority regulations and export license controls erected by well-meaning but uncoordinated Washington bureaucrats. Only a dramatic turn of events could sweep such obstacles aside. Hitler obliged on Sunday morning, June 22, 1941, when at last he made his move to the east and launched Operation Barbarossa.

Official U.S. reaction to the German invasion of Russia was mixed. Military chiefs, basing their estimates on observations of the Soviet armed forces in the Finnish war and speculating on the loss of morale and expertise inflicted by the purges of the Russian high command in the 1930s, predicted a war of short duration capped by a German victory before the end of the summer. Their civilian superiors, Secretaries Stimson and Knox, agreed and concluded logically that while aid to Russia might thus be wasted, assistance to Britain—with Germany so occupied in the east—was even more vital. Stimson expressed the view that "Germany's action seems like an almost providential occurrence," and Knox wrote to FDR: "I feel very deeply that I ought to say to you that, in my judgement, this provides us with an opportunity to strike and strike effectively at Germany."[2] Former ambassador to and strong friend of the Soviet Union, Joseph E. Davies, and Henry Morgenthau and Supreme Court Justice Felix Frankfurter led a move toward greater confidence in Russia's staying power and advised direct material assistance to the Soviets.[3]

In the summer of 1941, Roosevelt was keenly aware of the strong support still commanded by isolationist spokesmen in America, and he knew, too, that with certain groups—notable Catholics and East European émigrés—aid to Russia would hardly be popular. Such groups could coalesce and bring strong pressure on a war-shy Congress that was about to consider another multibillion dollar lend-lease appropriation. In addition, Roosevelt looked for signs from the east. First, he sought some indication of how Stalin's troops would fare against Hitler's Panzers, and second, further east, what reaction there would be from Tokyo to the Russo-German war. In the wake of the German attack FDR thus moved cautiously. Soviet funds in the United States, which had been conditionally frozen in mid-June in a move to block German and Italian assets, were unfrozen. At the same time the president told a press conference that Britain would continue to have first claim on U.S. assistance and that while ready to aid the Soviet Union he had no idea what the Russians needed, adding, "When we get a list it will probably be of such a character that you can't just go around to Mr. Garfinckel's and fill the order." To a reporter's query as to whether the defense of the USSR was "essential" to the defense of the United States (meaning eligibility for lend-lease aid), Roosevelt quipped, "Oh, ask me a different type of question—such as 'how old is Ann?' "[4]

In the following days the president declined to issue a proclamation of neutrality in the Russo-German conflict (thus effectively leaving Russian ports open to U.S. shipping), and directed Acting Secretary of State Welles to reassure Soviet Ambassador Oumansky concerning his requests for assistance and to set up a special State Department committee to expedite purchasing operations and export clearances for the Soviet embassy and Amtorg, the Soviet state trading corporation in the United States.[5]

In reponse to these overtures Oumansky hastily submitted a general list of Russian requirements that showed by its emphasis on plant equipment a Soviet determination to fight on, certainly through the coming winter. Cheered by this, Welles requested a detailed breakdown of Soviet needs, which he received a week later. With some of his earlier doubts removed, FDR then began to move more decisively. He told Welles he wanted substantial aid sent to the USSR before October 1; then he received Ambassador Oumansky at the White House (his first visit since before the outbreak of the war in 1939) and told him of U.S. intentions to expedite the supply, pending only the availability of shipping, of those orders that the Soviet government desired to place in the United States.[6]

Turning to his own administrators Roosevelt then bore down hard. He alerted the ever ready Harry Hopkins to pay special attention to the Russian aid program, and he bombarded his administrators with a series of directives that reflected the urgency with which he viewed Soviet assistance. At the end of July he demanded "within forty-eight hours" a complete list of items recommended for shipment before October. Upon receiving this list he passed it on to his military aide, General Edwin "Pa" Watson, with this penned note: "To take up this morning with the Secretary of War, the Acting Secretary of State, the Secretary of the Navy (if the latter is involved) and get the thing through because there is some mix-up on it and I would like the thing gotten through by tonight."[7]

The Commitment to Aid the USSR

Roosevelt's persistence paid off. Within the next two months a commitment was made to supply Russia with maximum assistance and a procedure was established that gave aid to the USSR a unique status that lasted almost until the end of the war. The decisive events that produced these results began in early August. On the first day of that month Roosevelt lectured his cabinet for forty-five minutes about the Russian aid program, expressing with Olympian fury his anger over the lack of progress thus far. Morgenthau noted in his diary that

FDR "went to town in a way I never heard him go to town before. He was terrific. He said he didn't want to hear what was an order; he said he wanted to hear what was on the water." To Secretary of War Stimson's well-founded explanations of the problems that had bottlenecked the procurement and shipment of supplies Roosevelt was curt and unsympathetic: "Get 'em" he said, "even if it is necessary to take them from [U.S.] troops."[8] Shortly afterward he set forth his immediate wishes in a directive to Wayne Coy, newly appointed as a special assistant to expedite Soviet aid: "Frankly the Russians feel that they have been given the run-around in the United States. Please get out the list [submitted by Oumansky in July] and please with my full authority use a heavy hand and act as a burr under the saddle and get things moving." After specifying items and dates, the president concluded, "Step on it."[9]

Having thus energized his own administration, Roosevelt decided that the time had come to make formal his promises to assist the USSR. In an exchange of notes on August 2 Soviet Ambassador Oumansky was informed that the United States had decided to give the USSR "all economic assistance practicable," that it welcomed orders for goods urgently required for Soviet defense, and that it would give "priority assistance" in handling such orders.[10] Coming at one of the darkest hours of the war for Russia, when the full force of the Nazi blitzkrieg had just fallen on the Ukraine, this was a formidable commitment. It was so regarded at the time by the Russians and has since been acknowledged by Soviet historians.[11]

Two weeks later Roosevelt's actions were reinforced by the news his special assistant, Harry Hopkins, brought with him from Moscow. While in the Soviet capital Hopkins had received personally from Stalin a candid briefing on the military situation and a forthright assessment of Russia's most urgent material needs. As a result of this trip, W. Averrell Harriman, lend-lease representative in London and a businessman already experienced in dealing with Soviet leaders, was named by Roosevelt to head an Anglo-American delegation to Moscow to work out a long-range supply program for the USSR. When the Harriman mission arrived in Moscow at the end of September the Russians had their backs to the wall. Leningrad was encircled, the Ukraine had been overrun, and the battle for Moscow was about to begin. Nonetheless, the Russians were holding on and they conveyed to the members of the mission every sign of willingness to continue the fight. For three days, in an atmosphere that was alternately friendly and hostile, representatives of the three nations worked to bridge the gap between Soviet desires and Anglo-American offers. In the end the Russians were forced to accept some reductions in their requests, but the final agreed commitment was nonetheless considerable. For each of the following nine months the Russians were promised 400 planes, 500 tanks, 152 antiaircraft guns, 1,256 antitank guns, 5,000 jeeps, 2,000 tons of aluminum, and 66 other kinds of munitions, tools, and raw materials. Altogether some 1,500,000 long tons of supplies were to be made available, a vivid contrast to the 128,038 tons that had been shipped from June through August.[12]

These undertakings were enumerated in a formal protocol that was duly signed by the representatives of the three powers on October 2, 1941. This was the first of four such protocols to be signed with the Soviet Union during the war (the Third and Fourth Protocols were also signed by Canada).[13] Each protocol—considered by its signatories to be a binding diplomatic agreement—set down the supplies to be made available to the Soviet Union by its Western allies for a specific period (nine months for the First Protocol, one year for each of the other three). These documents, as will be discussed further, thus gave aid to Russia a unique status not enjoyed by other recipients of U.S. wartime assistance.

Special Lend-Lease Organization and Procedures for the USSR

To speed aid to Russia and fulfill the commitments made by the protocols, an organizational structure was set up that partly overlapped and largely overrode the established lend-lease administration. This began with the special committee set up in the State Department in late June 1941 to expedite orders for munitions and other goods and to assist the Soviets in obtaining export licenses. However, the State Department was not well equipped to handle such a task; in addition, as the commitment to Russia grew it was apparent to Roosevelt that organizational changes were needed to keep it firmly under his personal direction. He therefore directed Harry Hopkins to instruct Maj. Gen. James H. Burns, executive officer of the Division of Defense Aid Reports (the lend-lease agency at the time), to take charge of Soviet supply. Burns set up a special section within his division for this purpose and, following the advice of one of his aides, General Sidney P. Spalding, he chose Col. Philip R. Faymonville to head it. Faymonville had been the military attaché to the Soviet Union in the 1930s during most of the ambassadorship of Joseph E. Davies and, like Davies, had developed a strong admiration for the Soviet regime. In fact, his unremitting support of the Russians raised strong doubts in both the State and War departments about his selection for the new position and later plunged him into a maelstrom of controversy that abated only upon his retirement from the Russian aid program.[14]

Faymonville selected as his chief assistant Professor John N. Hazard of Columbia University, a specialist in Soviet law whom Faymonville had met in the 1930s when Hazard was studying at the Moscow Juridical Institute. This new section served initially as the home secretariat for the Harriman mission, which negotiated the First Soviet Protocol in October 1941. Faymonville accompanied Harriman to Moscow on that mission, then took up residence there to coordinate the program at the Russian end while General Spalding took over Faymonville's position as head of the Soviet supply section back in Washington. When the Division of Defense Aid Reports was abolished at the end of October 1941, Spalding's section then became the Division for Soviet Supply in the new lend-lease organization, continuing its function of coordinating the supply program under the terms of the protocol. Finally, when the Foreign Economic Administration was established two years later in September 1943, the Division for Soviet Supply became the USSR Branch of its Bureau of Areas. Professor Hazard stayed with the organization throughout its various transformations and eventually became director of the

USSR Branch at the end of the war.

This organizational evolution took aid to Russia further and further from the hands of the president, a development that increasingly frustrated him as he vainly sought during the first ten months of 1942 to stimulate the lagging Soviet assistance program. Finally, he conceived a new organizational device designed to put the whole operation clearly under White House control. In a letter at the end of October 1942, addressed to each department and agency concerned with Soviet supply, Roosevelt announced the creation of the President's Soviet Protocol Committee "to be responsible," as he later declared to Secretary Hull, "for the overall coordination of the Russian Protocol through action by appropriate existing agencies and in conformity with policies approved by me."[15] The new committee included representatives of all interested departments and agencies, with the Division of Soviet Supply of the Lend-Lease Administration (later the USSR Branch of the FEA) supplying the committee's secretary and acting as its secretariat. Roosevelt named Harry Hopkins as chairman, reflecting the importance the president attached to this new organization.

While still within the lend-lease organization, Hazard became the committee's secretary. To act as executive of the committee under Hopkins's direction Roosevelt named General Burns, whom he had once tapped to be the next ambassador to Moscow but had later decided to keep in Washington where he would be more useful in lend-lease work. Burns remained in this position until September 1944, when illness forced his retirement, and was succeeded by Brig. Gen. John Y. York, an officer who closely shared Burns's views of the importance of aid to Russia. It should also be noted that the executive of the protocol committee carried added weight in that he was "double-hatted" as executive of the Munitions Assignment Board, also chaired by Hopkins.

The President's Soviet Protocol Committee met only irregularly to discuss general policy matters, but its two subcommittees, one on supplies and the other on shipping, met frequently and exercised close and constant supervision over the whole Russian aid program. Through the operations of the

Soviet Protocol Committee Roosevelt was thus able to wield much tighter control over lend-lease to the USSR than he could have through the more cumbersome bureaucratic structure of the regular lend-lease organization. As Dean Acheson, who was the State Department's representative on the committee, put it, the protocol committee was a group "which Harry Hopkins gathered together to hear orders from the White House about what must go to the Soviet Union."[16]

To this outline of organizational developments must be added a few words about the Americans who were initially involved in lend-lease to Russia and the changes that occurred in their influence over decision making in the program. First, the key personnel involved—especially Hopkins, Burns, and Spalding—had been with lend-lease from its beginning and were the first to be chosen to organize the Soviet supply program. These men, and those they later selected to assist them, not only believed strongly in lend-lease but were also determined supporters of aid to Russia. Yet, when the program was drawing to a close in 1945 many of them were no longer in a position to be influential. Hopkins was too ill to be continuously involved; Burns, ill also, had retired, and Spalding was far away in Moscow, where he had been sent in October 1943 to head the lend-lease mission of the newly created U.S. Military Mission to the USSR. Second, although military representatives sat in important positions in the organization, those associated with the program in its formative stages did not always play the roles of spokesmen for the military that were played by their counterparts elsewhere in the lend-lease organization. Several had been called from retirement to fill unglamorous desk jobs while their younger colleagues, with reputations still to be made, sought commands in the field; some developed stronger loyalties toward Roosevelt, Hopkins, and the larger vision of the world these men perceived and promoted; still others simply felt powerless in an organization that seemed to them to be responding more readily to the pleas of foreign forces than to the needs of its own soldiers. But in the last year of the program such idiosyncratic behavior by the organization's military representatives increasingly gave way to more traditional positions that put

America and the needs of its military first. For these and for other reasons to be explored more fully later, the President's Soviet Protocol Committee, which had often served as a court of last resort for supporters of aid to the USSR (including the Russians themselves), became much less so as the program neared its termination.

The procedure for lend-lease supply to non-Russian recipients split requests into military and nonmilitary categories and mandated a separate gauntlet of departments and agencies for each to run to gain approval and an eventual firm commitment. Furthermore, requests for lend-lease aid had to be accompanied by evidence indicating financial inability to otherwise obtain such assistance (including the disclosure of gold and dollar assets) and full justification of the need for the materials requested. But under the protocol system that governed lend-lease to the USSR procedures were quite different. Throughout the summer and early fall of 1941 Roosevelt had demanded with increasing vigor higher and higher priority for aid to Russia. The First Soviet Protocol served to institutionalize these expressed preferences.

Regarded by the three signing parties as a firm commitment, the Moscow protocol of October 1941 stated simply in its brief preamble that the parties had unanimously agreed that the list of supplies appended "will be made available at British and U.S.A. centers of production for the Soviet Union by Great Britain and the United States of America" within the nine-month period of the protocol, and it added: "Great Britain and the U.S.A. will give aid to the transportation of these materials to the Soviet Union and will help with the delivery."[17] No information was requested from the Soviet Union and no conditions of any kind were set, a practice that was followed in the subsequent three protocols. To assure that preferential treatment for supplies to Russia would be forthcoming, lend-lease authorities agreed in mid-November 1941 to give Russia a production priority equal to that given the British and American armed forces. Known first as A-1-a and later as AA-1, this priority was continued for the Russian aid program throughout the war. It was also decided at this time that the most important factor governing the programming of Russian aid was not to be the need for any given article, "but the need to meet the protocol and shipping dates."[18]

These early decisions provided guidance for the supply of lend-lease aid to the USSR throughout the four protocol periods and contributed importantly to the unique status of the Russian program. They insured that all major initiatives came from a White House committee chaired by the president's chief assistant, that priorities were assigned which guaranteed the production and procurement of Soviet needs, and that constant pressure was exerted from the highest levels to assure the fulfillment and delivery of Russian orders. Arrangements were made from time to time to give consideration to the interests of the military and other agencies competing for materials, but as the historians of army logistics put it, "the basic protocol agreements transcended military authority. The guidelines for military policy on supplying the USSR emanated from the president himself."[19]

In its organization lend-lease for Russia was thus by necessity and by design a special program. It was begun outside the regular framework of lend-lease for fear that it might weaken that unique and newly conceived operation. It was funded below its needs in tentative ad hoc steps until finally the dollar sign was removed and Russia was granted the financial status of its corecipients. But from the very beginning the program carried a special seal of presidential approval. This gave it eventually its own organization and unique procedures that for most of its life put it beyond the reach of the many administrative hands that shaped and altered other programs in wartime Washington. However, these unique characteristics gave those who influenced the granting of aid to Russia a double-edged sword: swung in one direction it was a splendid weapon against bureaucratic red tape to speed aid to the USSR; swung in the other, it could with equal dispatch help cut the program to a fraction of its size.

Operation of Lend-Lease to the USSR

In its operation the special lend-lease program for Russia was at first an embarrassing failure and later an overwhelming success. Its shortfalls early in the war were the casualties of overoptimistic expectations, and its later overfulfillment was in part an effort to make amends; as it turned out, the lessons of both periods figured in the formation and implementation of policy to terminate the program.

First Soviet Supply Protocol

The signing of the First Soviet Protocol in Moscow in October 1941, and the declaration of Russian eligibility for lend-lease one month later had not suddenly opened the floodgates to a vast outpouring of material for the embattled Red Armies. Aid to Russia did eventually increase from a thin trickle to a veritable river of supplies, but in the first critical months of the war the flow was constantly hindered.[20]

The reasons for this were readily understandable, but that did not make them any the more acceptable to a Soviet leadership long locked in dogmatic certainties that interpreted with deepest suspicion the acts and motives of capitalist nations. First and foremost, the huge American defense production establishment, which eventually would make an enormous contribution to the war effort, was still in its infancy, and like most infants it had not yet mastered its functions. Responsibilities were divided among many agencies, priorities crossed and conflicted in a flood of requisitions, and only a trickle of production spilled into a military organization whose component parts were unprepared to receive it but nonetheless competed noisily for every last nut and bolt. Second, the Russians set detailed specifications for their orders and insisted on critical inspections of the finished products, all the more so since under the initial conditions of their eligibility for lend-lease they had an obligation for eventual payment in full for the goods they received. (The inspection problem was further compounded because of hasty and inadequate packing by shippers inexperienced in handling such supplies. Thus, much of what was landed arrived damaged.) Finally, Russian requirements had been levied on a production capacity already fully committed to British and American orders. Satisfaction of the former could come only at the expense of the latter, and thus the Russian program prompted a series of intramural skirmishes in which each American official fought bitterly to protect the interests of his organization or client. The outcome of these struggles usually satisfied no one and often left a residue of ill will that made future cooperation even more difficult. The frustrations of the time were well illustrated by a response from the normally taciturn Secretary of War Henry Stimson to a request by a theater commander for more aircraft: "There ain't no Kitty Hawks for the poor army to give you. The British and the Russians have them all!"[21]

In addition to problems of production and supply there was the even more serious problem of shipping. Since there was virtually no Soviet merchant marine at the time, most cargo had to be carried in British and American bottoms; but these vessels had long been designated for shipments to England, and thus painful diversions were necessary. In addition, routes to the Soviet Union were long, roundabout, and subject to the vagaries of the weather and the dangers of enemy action. When ships did arrive they had to put up with the delays of inadequate port and inland clearance facilities. In late November 1941, on the eve of the decisive battle for Moscow, the Russians complained bitterly about the inadequacy of shipping and Roosevelt sought by every device to respond to their pleas. He directed the Maritime Commission "to provide ships to transport aid to Russia in accordance with protocol schedules subject only to insurmountable physical limitations" and he even suggested the use of an aircraft carrier to deliver planes to the USSR. When told in a note from Hopkins that this was not possible and that only merchant ships could be used, FDR penciled in the margin, "OK but say to them from me: Hurry, Hurry, Hurry!"[22]

These efforts from the chief executive were of little avail against the insurmountable obstacles of low production, competing demands, and insufficient shipping. During the final months of 1941 aid continued to move to Russia at a snail's pace. While Soviet officials asked for eighty ships a month to transport cargoes promised in the protocol, only fifteen sailed in October, thirteen in November, and twenty-five in December, and of the total of fifty-three, five were lost at sea. In all, only 180,000 tons of lend-lease supplies reached the

USSR during the first three months of the protocol period. In terms of critical items promised in the protocol for these months, this meant a supply of 750 out of 1,200 aircraft (including only 5 of 300 bombers), 501 of 1,500 tanks, and 4 of 50 antiaircraft guns.[23] While the Russians fought back from the walls of Moscow during the most perilous days of the eastern front they were virtually unaided by the West. There and then they stood alone. The self-congratulatory praise of statesmen like Sumner Welles, who wrote, "it should never be forgotten that the arms and airplanes he [Stalin] received from the then limited resources of the United States helped greatly to make possible the victory at Moscow" must therefore be replaced by the more judicious conclusion of the official historians of the U.S. Army in World War II: "The impact of U.S. aid to the Soviet Union was as yet insignificant and played no role in the repulse of the German attack before Moscow."[24]

On December 7, 1941, the Japanese struck at Pearl Harbor, and immediately the whole supply situation was dramatically altered. With the United States formally at war, its massive economic potential began to move into high gear and, as Winston Churchill well understood at that very moment, this meant that the war would be won. But December 7 also required an urgent husbanding of American resources for defense, and on the following day an immediate halt was ordered to all lend-lease shipments. This suspension of lend-lease assistance and the subsequent diversions of materials and vessels to meet U.S. needs put protocol shipments even further in arrears. It seemed to many in the military that the protocol must now be revised in the light of expanded American requirements. But Roosevelt and his close advisors remained persuaded by the compelling logic of the argument that the greatest contribution to the defeat of enemy forces on the battlefield was then being made by the Russians and that they therefore needed all the assistance they could be given. At the end of December FDR directed that "the Soviet aid program as provided in the protocol agreement be reestablished beginning January 1" and that "existing deficits . . . be made up and shipped from this country no later than April 1."[25]

Partly because of Roosevelt's urgent pleas, but mostly

because the impact of actually being at war was finally accelerating all types of defense production, the Russian supply situation slowly began to improve. Forty-three ships sailed for Russia during the first two months of 1942. The same number sailed in March alone, and seventy-nine embarked in April. But in the early spring a new danger cast a long shadow across the brightening picture of Soviet supply. Because the Pacific and Persian Gulf routes were lengthy and uncertain, most supplies were traveling to Russia over the northern sea route. Not only was this the shortest route to the front, but it also had the advantage of easier access and unloading during the warmer weather of spring and summer. Hitler, too, realized these advantages and increasingly directed his raiders and U-boats to the vulnerable and lightly escorted convoys of merchantmen plying these waters. Three of the nineteen ships that sailed the route in February were lost to weather and enemy action; of the forty-three that left the following month, seven were lost, and of the total of seventy-nine that sailed in April, nineteen were lost, the highest loss of monthly sailings of the entire war. Included in the April sailings was the ill-fated convoy PQ-17. Precipitately dispersed on orders of the British admiralty because of an incorrect estimate of German surface ships in the area, the scattered merchantmen were easy prey for German submarines and aircraft. Only eleven of the convoy's thirty-three vessels successfully completed the icy passage and reached their destination of the Russian port of Archangel.[26]

In the face of such formidable difficulties it was surprising that as much cargo arrived in Russia as actually did. During the First Protocol period (October 1, 1941–June 30, 1942) 282 vessels sailed from the Western Hemisphere with 1,420,000 tons of cargo. Two hundred and nine vessels with 984,000 tons of cargo actually reached their Russian destinations, the rest being either lost at sea (51 vessels) or forced to discharge their cargo in England (22 vessels).[27] It is much more difficult to determine how many of the individual items promised in the First Protocol actually arrived. Although abundant statistics exist in published and unpublished documentary sources they are difficult to compare because they are expressed variously in ships, tons, and dollars and for materials committed, made available, and actually shipped; furthermore, changes were frequently made during the protocol periods and there is little evidence available to indicate what precisely was landed in the Soviet Union. However, an examination of U.S. and Soviet sources taken together does give an approximate indication of the record of fulfillment, and it shows that for the First Protocol it was at best spotty: glaring deficiencies in some cases and surprisingly large overfulfillment in others. A few examples will suffice to illustrate this. Eighteen hundred planes were promised in the protocol; 1,727 were made available for shipment; 1,285 were actually exported; and approximately 900 were received by the Russians. More than the promised 2,250 tanks were made available; 2,249 were shipped; and approximately 1,600 reached their destination. In some categories very little of what was promised was even made available (4 of a total of 152 antiaircraft guns, 63 of 756 antitank guns), while in others the amount made available and exported equalled or far exceeded the protocol commitment (1.6 million pairs of army shoes promised, 1.8 million made available, and almost all shipped; 1 million yards of army cloth promised, 1.8 million made available and shipped).[28]

Second Soviet Supply Protocol

For the Second Soviet Protocol (to cover the period July 1, 1942 through June 30, 1943), a projected offering of 7.2 million short tons of supplies was presented to Roosevelt in May 1942. Along with the British offering of 1 million short tons this made a grand total of approximately 8 million tons—a vast increase over the amount offered in the First Protocol. Of this amount the Combined Shipping Adjustment Board estimated that about 4 million tons could actually be shipped during the designated period.[29]

These were the figures Roosevelt gave to Soviet Foreign Commissar Molotov, at the time of his secret mission to Washington in May 1942, in a statement of the resources that the United States and Great Britain were in a position to make available to the USSR during the Second Protocol period. However, even as these figures were being presented they were being sharply challenged by the Joint Chiefs of Staff (JCS). Not only did they appear unduly optimistic in the light of the 20 percent loss rate of U.S. merchant ships from March through May, but they also ignored the heavy drain on shipping that would be made by Operation BOLERO, the build-up of U.S. forces and supplies in England for a cross-Channel attack.

When the JCS opinion was finally brought to Roosevelt's attention he proposed at his last meeting with Molotov that shipments of all supplies except munitions be reduced so that a total of only 2.5 million tons would be sent to the Soviet Union during the Second Protocol period. The president assured Molotov that this reduction would release a large number of ships for supply to England, which would in turn hasten the opening of the much-desired second front in Europe. Molotov strongly objected to Roosevelt's suggestion, and even though FDR admonished him that "the Soviets could not eat their cake and have it, too," the Russian commissar not only insisted on fulfillment of the protocol, but also requested a monthly American convoy to Archangel and additional deliveries of aircraft and trucks. "What would happen," Molotov asked with barely concealed sarcasm, "if the Soviets did agree to cut down their requirements and then no second front eventuated?"[30]

The outcome of this meeting saw no acceptance by the Russians of a reduction in the tonnage of supplies to be shipped during the Second Protocol period, but it did bring a verbal assurance from Roosevelt, later incorporated in a widely publicized press release of June 11, 1942, concerning the creation of a second front in Europe in 1942. Roosevelt thus saddled himself with the impossible burden of trying to increase supplies for both BOLERO and Russia with shipping that was probably inadequate to fully accomplish either mission.

Events soon proved that the fears of the JCS planners concerning the availability of shipping to fulfill the Second Protocol were well founded. A series of German successes in North Africa and the Caucasus, collectively referred to as the "midsummer crisis" of 1942, began developing shortly after Molotov's departure and soon dictated a drastic readjustment of plans and a reordering of priorities. In order to stem the Axis tide emergency steps were taken to bolster the British position, and supplies were diverted from BOLERO. Under these circumstances plans for SLEDGEHAMMER, the limited cross-Channel attack in 1942, were all but dropped and attention was turned to the previously shelved GYMNAST, the plan for an invasion of northwest Africa to strike at the German rear.

Close on the heels of these developments came the full report of Convoy PQ-17. Shocked by this disaster, and unable to sustain such losses in the future, the British—in charge of assembling and escorting the northern convoys to Russia—reluctantly decided to suspend them entirely for July and August. This was then followed by a British-American decision for a North African invasion (with the new code name TORCH), finally killing any possibility of a cross-Channel attack in 1942. The Russians thus had to face another winter without a European second front to draw off a substantial number of German troops and without the full amount of assistance promised in their supply protocol. As Churchill told Roosevelt in September, this promised to be "a formidable moment in Anglo-American-Soviet relations."[31]

Roosevelt continued during the Second Protocol period to put heavy pressure on the Russian supply program. At the end of July he wrote to Stimson, Knox, Stettinius, Hopkins, and Admiral Land: "The one essential criterion is not pages and pages listing commitments under the Moscow Protocol. The real criterion is the ability to deliver materials into Russia. We must make every effort to make deliveries by any and all practicable means."[32] But the means available in mid-1942 were severely limited. Not only were large numbers of ships being diverted to deliver material to the British in the Middle East and to build up supplies for TORCH, but each of the three main supply routes to Russia was still severely constricted. The quickest and most direct route, the northern, was closed for the months of July and August because of the menace of German attack; the Pacific route, limited to Russian vessels with nonmilitary cargoes, was long and required extended overland transportation across the USSR; and the Persian Gulf route, the freest from the hazards of weather and enemy attack, was twice as long as the northern route with only one-sixth its cargo-clearing capacity.

At the end of 1942, the Russians thus found themselves once again on the short end of estimates that had proven too optimistic. With half the Second Protocol period over, only a little more than 25 percent of its projected 4 million tons of supplies had been delivered, and the prospects for the second half did not appear bright. The Western Allies for their part faced the agonizing dilemma of having to choose between reducing supplies shipped for the protocol and postponing again the much-desired and long-promised second front in Europe. In the end they had to do both.

When the leaders of Britain and America met at the Anfa Hotel on the outskirts of Casablanca in January 1943, the Soviet aid program was high on their list of critical problems. Even higher, though, was the long-smoldering dispute between British and American military chiefs over grand strategy in the war against Germany, and it was the decision in this matter that set the priority to be given to future aid to the USSR. The dispute on grand strategy was finally resolved in the decisions to proceed immediately with the planning for Operation HUSKY (the invasion of Sicily) while continuing the build-up of men and supplies for ROUNDUP, the plan for a cross-Channel attack in 1943. Although no one apparently wanted to admit it at the time, such an ordering of priorities meant that ROUNDUP could not be launched before the end of the summer, and possibly not even before the end of the year. Since the further postponement of a major second front against Germany would continue to leave the major burden of ground combat with the Russians, the conferees at Casablanca logically had to give high priority to continued assistance to the USSR. This they did by making aid to Russia second only to the complementary goal of overcoming the submarine menace in the Atlantic.[33]

Roosevelt and Churchill jointly telegraphed the results of the conference to their absent third partner, Joseph Stalin. They noted their agreement to launch a large-scale amphibious operation in the Mediterranean (HUSKY) "at the earliest possible moment" but promised only to prepare themselves to reenter the continent of Europe (ROUNDUP) "as soon as possible." They also stated their desire to deliver to Russia "the maximum flow of supplies," and they pledged: "We shall spare no exertion to send you material assistance by every available route."[34] In accordance with this pledge a new schedule of ship sailings to Russia for the rest of the calendar year was drawn up that would almost completely eliminate the deficit in the Second Protocol by its June 30 termination date and more than overcome it by the end of the year.[35]

In the wake of these decisions at Casablanca, which augured well for future supplies but uncertainly for drawing off the full force of German armies, a diplomatic "incident" occurred in Moscow involving lend-lease to Russia. Although it had no lasting political consequences it did reflect the tensions and conflicting opinions that coursed through the whole Soviet aid program. In early March 1943, U.S. Ambassador to Moscow William Standley—an admiral turned diplomat at the behest of FDR—gave vent to accumulated frustrations in dealing with the cumbersome and often enigmatic Soviet bureaucracy with a verbal blast against Soviet ingratitude for American assistance. "It's not fair," said the admiral in the forum of what a moment before had been a humdrum news conference. "The American people are giving millions to help the Russian people and yet the Russian people do not know where the supplies are coming from. . . . The Soviet authorities apparently are trying to create the impression at home and abroad that they are fighting the war alone and with their own resources."[36]

This outburst, which Standley clearly stated could be used for publication, resounded discordantly against official claims of Allied harmony. From the press, from the halls of Congress, and from U.S. diplomats in other capitals came a chorus of comment. Some praised the admiral for his candor, others feared the damage such diplomatic indiscretion might do to the delicate Soviet-American alliance. The *New York Times*'s Moscow correspondent commented: "Though undoubtedly made with the best of intentions, Ambassador Standley's criticisms of the manner in which the Soviet government is handling internal propaganda is likely to undermine the painstakingly built-up confidence between the Allies."[37] On the Senate floor Sen. Tom Connally deplored the possibility "that there should be any incident to provoke friction between the United Nations" and said he could not understand "why he

[Standley] should make such a statement," and Senator Vandenberg confessed to being "amazed by Admiral Standley's remarks."[38] But from London, lend-lease representative Averell Harriman—soon to replace Standley in Moscow—wrote Harry Hopkins, "Many of my friends here, both British and American, seniors and juniors, are secretly pleased at the way Standley spoke out in Moscow even if this was an indiscretion. The feeling is growing here that we will build trouble for the future if we allow ourselves to be kicked around by the Russians."[39]

In all, very little was changed by the incident, but it did serve to bring briefly to the surface attitudes that had been carefully hidden before, revealing for a moment true feelings toward the Russian aid program and providing a foretaste of some of the views that would influence the program's terminal phase. For Admiral Standley, the repercussions of the incident and the continuing arrival of "Very VIP's" (as he called them) who undercut his role as chief U.S. representative in the Soviet capital, all amounted to a burden he could no longer bear. On May Day 1943, Standley records in his memoirs, he made up his mind to ask the president to relieve him. Roosevelt acceded to his request, sought to reappoint Joseph E. Davies, who was unable to serve because of ill health, and finally chose W. Averell Harriman to be the next U.S. envoy to the Soviet Union.

In mid-March 1943, a few days after the Standley "incident," came the first setback to the optimistic shipping schedule drawn up at Casablanca. Convoys over the northern route had been resumed the previous December, but in March the renewed German naval concentration in northern Norway presented such a danger that at the end of the month Churchill informed Stalin that the convoys over this route once again had to be halted. Stalin replied that he considered this action "a catastrophic diminution of supplies . . . which cannot fail to affect the position of the Soviet troops."[40] Churchill and Roosevelt had hoped to compensate by increasing deliveries via other routes, especially through the Persian Gulf, but the demands of HUSKY and BOLERO, plus very slow progress in expanding the capacity of the Persian Gulf route soon made

this an unwarranted hope. The Casablanca schedule had called
for 126 vessels to sail this route during the first half of 1943, but
actually only 75 made the voyage. On the other routes the
picture was just as bad, and of the projected total of 376 vessels
for the last six months of the Second Protocol, only 322 sailed
and only 280 reached their destinations.[41]

At the end of the protocol period deliveries were thus more
than one million tons short of original commitments. The
Second Soviet Protocol had been only 75 percent fulfilled, and
although the Allies had landed in North Africa and were about
to embark on the invasion of Sicily, there was still no major
second front on the Continent and there would not be one for
another year. Yet in the spring of 1943—though it was not then
fully realized—the balance had shifted; the worst was over.
North Africa had been cleared of Germans. At Stalingrad the
enemy had been stopped, stalemated, then routed; the red tide
of the Soviet armies was sweeping back through the Caucasus.
There were more U-boats in the Atlantic, but there were also
more Allied planes and ships, with improved detection devices
and better weapons. The battle of the Atlantic was not won, but
Hitler had lost the strategic initiative, and more and more ships
were able to cross the northern route unmolested. Above all,
there was more of everything needed to fight the war. American
defense production was at last in high gear, and from its
assembly lines came growing numbers of tanks, trucks, planes,
guns, bombs, and bullets, and along with these tools of war
more ships to carry them. The Second Protocol indeed had not
been fulfilled, but it was the last to suffer that fate. The sources
of supply were wide open and from them poured a flood of
materials, too late to halt the Germans—for the Russians had
already done that—but soon enough to help push them back to
Berlin.

Third Soviet Supply Protocol

For the Third Protocol (to cover the period July 1, 1943 to
June 30, 1944) a total offering of 7,080,000 tons of supplies,
including undelivered Second Protocol commitments, was
made to the Russians. From this they could select whatever they
wished up to a total of the 4,500,000 tons of shipping capacity

that would be available during the protocol period. The Soviet government insisted, however, that its war effort required more than 4.5 million tons of supplies, and after prolonged discussion it finally accepted a compromise total of 5.1 million tons plus a 500,000 ton standby stockpile. After further changes and additions during the summer and early fall the final version of the Third Protocol was drawn up and formally signed in London in October 1943, by Great Britain, the United States, the Soviet Union, and—for the first time—Canada. Although signed late, like its predecessor it had immediately gone into effect on July 1.[42]

Soviet requests for the Third Protocol, and subsequent selections for shipment from supplies made available, clearly indicated the changed Russian military situation. Tanks, artillery, and ammunition, all of which had been urgently requested earlier, were no longer so vital. In fact, of 3,000 tanks offered, the Russians requested none! The one military item to which they still gave high priority was aircraft of all types, but especially fighters. In addition, they emphasized specialized types of transportation and communication equipment, military clothing, medical supplies, and bulk explosives. In the sector of civilian supplies there was a marked emphasis on agricultural products and on industrial equipment and other materials for reconstruction and rehabilitation in the territories being liberated by the advancing Red Army.[43]

While the Russians became more selective in their needs, the ability of the United States to supply them steadily improved. In September 1943, shipments via the Persian Gulf route finally reached the planned goal of over 200,000 tons per month, and Brig. Gen. Donald H. Donnolly, head of the Persian Gulf Command, reported that a continuing capacity of 242,000 tons per month could be anticipated on that route. In the same month shipments over the Pacific route reached a new high of 345,000 tons, and in November supply via the northern route—cut off since late March—was finally resumed. With all routes running with capacity to spare, it was possible to make adjustments that could not be made before. Thus, when difficult winter navigation slowed Pacific transit and when preparations for OVERLORD (the cross-Channel invasion of

Europe, rescheduled for 1944) made heavy demands on the North Atlantic route, additional shipments were made via the Persian Gulf. The net result of this great increase in shipping capacity was that by the terminal date of June 30, 1944, the Third Protocol commitment of 5.1 million tons was exceeded by approximately 25 percent.[44]

Fourth Soviet Supply Protocol

While the Third Protocol was being overfulfilled, planning was underway for a Fourth Protocol. In February 1944, FDR circulated a memorandum similar to that of the previous two years stressing the high priority of aid to Russia. "We must . . . continue to support the USSR," the president wrote, "by providing the maximum amount of supplies which can be delivered to her ports. This is a matter of paramount importance." Roosevelt went on to state that the USSR had been requested to state requirements for a Fourth Protocol to cover the period July 1, 1944, through June 30, 1945, and he urged the agencies involved to make every effort to meet these requirements.[45] The initial American supply offering was just under 7.4 million tons, including a carry-over of stockpiles from the Third Protocol. The shipping commitment was initially set for 5.4 million tons, equally divided between the Atlantic and Pacific. Again the Soviets felt this was too low. They pressed for a total commitment of 7 million tons, but finally settled for an increase of just 300,000 tons via the Atlantic route. The Russians also received the promise that more would be shipped if possible, and in fact the FEA made plans to procure the entire 7.4 million tons in the event excess shipping materialized.[46] After prolonged discussion and many alterations the Fourth Protocol was finally signed in Ottawa on April 17, 1945. However, as was the case with Protocols Two and Three, it had already gone into effect on July 1 of the previous year.[47]

Soviet requests under the Fourth Protocol maintained the trend noted in the Third Protocol away from munitions and war materials toward agricultural products and supplies for reconstruction. The Russians continued to ask for large numbers of aircraft, including fighter planes and medium bombers, and they sought heavy bombers as well as the new, larger types of transports. Some tanks reappeared on the Soviet list, but trucks, jeeps, and artillery pieces were considerably reduced, as were naval stores of all kinds. Foodstuffs and related products made up almost 25 percent of their request, while industrial equipment comprised almost 10 percent. In the latter category, construction equipment and power generation and transmission equipment were heavily represented, testifying to the high priority given to supplies for rebuilding.[48]

A unique feature of the Fourth Protocol was a supplementary program (code-named MILEPOST) added in the fall of 1944 to build up supplies for Soviet forces in the Far East for use against Japan. The United States had been trying since very early in the war to enlist the support of the USSR in the contest against Japan and had finally received a commitment from Stalin in late 1943 that the Soviet Union would enter the war at an appropriate time after the defeat of Germany. A year later, in a conference with Churchill during the prime minister's October 1944 visit to Moscow, Stalin reaffirmed his commitment and stated that the Soviet Union could take the offensive against Japan three months after Germany's defeat, but that to do so it would require U.S. assistance in building up necessary reserve supplies in Siberia. Soviet representatives then presented Ambassador Harriman with a list of requirements for semimilitary types of supplies (equipment, fuel, and food) amounting to 860,000 tons of dry cargo and 206,000 tons of liquid petroleum products to be delivered via the Pacific route before June 30, 1945. After a series of adjustments, agreement was reached on totals of 568,000 and 231,000 tons in the two categories of cargo, and in early April 1945, the final revised MILEPOST list was added to the Fourth Protocol as Annex III.[49]

During the period of the Fourth Protocol shipping availibility on all routes continued to increase and, despite a worldwide shipping crisis in the fall of 1944, the monthly average of vessels sailing to the USSR from Northern Hemisphere ports rose steadily throughout that year.[50] Along the northern route the British proved able to maintain convoys from August 1944 to the end of the war without interruption and with inconsequential losses. Shipments via Vladivostok and the few Arctic ports open during the summer months were pushed vigorously and the normal winter reduction due to weather conditions was less during 1944-1945 than the previous year. The Persian Gulf for the first time had more than sufficient port capacity and inland clearance facilities to handle all incoming traffic, and when the Russian Black Sea ports were finally cleared of Germans in September 1944, the direct Mediterranean route rapidly replaced the longer Iranian passage for shipment of goods into the southern USSR. Under these favorable conditions shipping was no longer the limiting factor on Soviet supply it had been throughout the war, and in May 1945, when the Fourth Protocol was terminated short of its estimated closing date, its original commitment of 5.7 million tons (excluding MILEPOST) had already been surpassed.[51]

Planning for a Fifth Soviet Supply Protocol

In January 1945, Roosevelt sent a new memorandum to departmental secretaries and agency heads concerning the Soviet aid program. In almost identical language to that used at about the same date on the three previous years, FDR urged continued support of Russia by the maximum amount of supplies that could be delivered to its ports and stated that every effort should be made to meet the requirements for a Fifth Protocol to cover the period July 1, 1945 to June 30, 1946. He received the usual letters of compliance, and planning dutifully went forward for a Fifth Protocol. But in January 1945 even the most pessimistic observer did not expect the war with Germany to continue until mid-1946, and since Russia was not yet at war with Japan there seemed little need for a binding protocol of the type that had served during the past three and a half years. Accordingly, a movement began among those who felt most sorely tried by their dealings with the Russians to do away with the protocols entirely at the end of the period of the one then current. Although this movement never reached fruition while the war with Germany was still on, it did provide the basis—as will be seen later—for the dissolution following V-E Day of the protocol system that had governed the Soviet aid program since October 1, 1941.

The Record of Lend-Lease to the USSR

If lend-lease was an exception, then lend-lease to Russia was an exception to the exception. A legacy of cool relations and cooler attitudes, an atmosphere of mutual mistrust and suspicion, and a widespread negative assessment of Russia's chances against Germany all dictated that FDR proceed slowly and deliberately in aiding the USSR. The result was the establishment of a special program with its own organization and procedures—all under close White House supervision—to direct lend-lease to Russia. In practice this meant that Russia's unique needs would receive a ready response, but it also meant that once these needs lessened it would be increasingly difficult to justify the continuation of special treatment for the USSR.

In operation, the special lend-lease program for the USSR during World War II mirrored the deep differences between America and Russia—of ideological, economic, and political origin—that not only made their alliance "strange," as Gen. John Deane of the U.S. Military Mission in Moscow called it, but also continually uneasy. It reflected an ambivalence toward the Soviet Union, born in America almost in the first moments of the Bolshevik Revolution, that created partisan camps in almost all branches of the government dealing with Russia. For some in the executive branch, in the Congress, and in the military, the appropriate posture to assume toward the new socialist motherland was the extended hand of friendship, proffered with a readiness to overlook the vast ideological differences that separated them in the interests of mutual cooperation. As Henry L. Stimson mused at the war's end, "Might not trust beget trust; as Russian confidence was earned, might not the repressive—and aggressive—tendencies of Stalinism be abated?"[52] For others the appropriate posture was to respond in kind with the clenched fist that symbolized international communism. Since the only thing the Russians understood was power, this argument went, the United States could best gain their respect by a firm display of its own power. As General Arnold put it in a memorandum to Harry Hopkins in September 1944, "The Soviets, who have a reputation of being tough realists, may be more inclined to play with us if we adopt a policy matching their own."[53]

Those who supported a policy of friendship toward the Soviet Union also believed, almost as an article of faith it sometimes seemed, that in 1941 the Soviet Union would do what no other nation on the continent of Europe had been able to do in the previous two years: it would withstand the German onslaught, it would stop it, and it would finally turn it back. Former Ambassador Joseph Davies, former Army Attaché Col. Philip Faymonville, and others argued in the face of strong opposition from experienced diplomats and soldiers that there would be no separate peace on the Russian front, no eastern Vichy in Moscow. Harry Hopkins was persuaded, especially after his visit to Stalin, and Roosevelt in turn was persuaded. Both, to be sure, were more receptive by temperament and previous belief to this view than the opposite. Nevertheless, their conversion to full support of the Soviet military effort—in the firm belief it would endure—marked a critical turning point in the war against Germany.

Roosevelt backed his conviction with sweeping promises of full material support from America's still unbuilt "arsenal of democracy." In the months of Russia's agony, while Hitler's Panzers burned their way into the Soviet heartland and the Red Army fell back under the hammer blows of the Wehrmacht and the Luftwaffe, Roosevelt gave highest priority to supplies for the USSR and spurred his administrators to deliver. No questions were asked of the Russians, and unlike other lend-lease recipients, they were not required to justify in advance their need for the equipment they requested. To American warriors, short on supplies and soon desperately at war themselves in the Pacific, such largesse at the expense of one's own needs was painful indeed; to render it without either reciprocal benefits or at least information concerning its use seemed like folly bordering on treason. This privileged position accorded supply to Russia produced ill will and a strong desire to end its special status as soon as possible.

In the first months of the war, however, FDR's unlimited efforts on behalf of the Soviet supply program were of little avail. During Russia's darkest hour there was precious little in the way of promised material aid that actually reached the

Russian front. The leaders in the Kremlin may indeed have been able to appreciate the excuses offered: slow production, disorganized supply, inadequate shipping; but these were of little solace while their land, their people, and their weapons were being relentlessly engorged by the bloody maw of war. Their ready explanation was an ideology that depicted capitalism as the main enemy, and a quarter-century of experience seemed to confirm this. In this context the true motives of the capitalist allies seemed further proven by the evident duplicity of their promises to open a second front in Europe. Such an invasion, demanded by Russia in 1941, strongly indicated for 1942, and promised several times for 1943, was finally achieved in mid-1944. Only a Russian of extraordinary detachment could have attributed these successive postponements to the complex impedimenta of competing strategies, insufficient equipment, and required margins of safety. Were there any in Stalin's entourage who perceived these realities, it is doubtful that they would have received much of a hearing.[54]

The failure to supply Russia with all the goods promised in the first two protocols was clearly evident to President Roosevelt; he more than anyone else felt acutely the brunt of Stalin's criticism and the responsibility for nonfulfillment of agreed commitments. Thus, during the First and Second Protocol periods he worked unceasingly to speed deliveries to Russia. By the beginning of the Third Protocol the immediate danger to Russia had passed and with it, seemingly, the urgent need for supplies. Yet Roosevelt kept up pressure to get goods to the USSR. In part, he may have been trying to make up for the shortages during the first months of the war when Russia's need was so great. In part, too, he wanted to win the war against Germany as quickly as possible, and aid to the USSR would serve that purpose. It also might help stifle any lingering inclinations to make a separate peace, troubling signs of which still appeared occasionally in Soviet public statements during the second half of 1943. In addition, Roosevelt earnestly desired Soviet entry in the war against Japan, and reducing aid to Russia would hardly serve that goal. Finally, FDR knew that the postwar world order he had in mind to prevent future wars would require the cooperation of the USSR, and so, in the general way in which American politicians bank good will with both supporters and opponents by doing them favors, Roosevelt sought to make just such a deposit with the Soviet Union by maintaining an undiminished flow of supplies to its shores.

These purposes were neither fully perceived nor fully shared by many of the civilian and military officials who dealt with the Soviet aid program. They looked at supply to Russia from the narrower perspectives of their own responsibilities: to support and protect their troops or to deal on a daily basis with their enigmatic counterparts in the Soviet bureaucracy. For many of them, the strenuous effort to supply Russia when U.S. need was so great was a mistake, and the later equally strenuous effort to continue that supply when the need was no longer so great was equally mistaken. From early 1943 onward each of the military chiefs of the Joint Chiefs of Staff at one time or another expressed his displeasure at the apparent effort to "placate" Stalin with further high priority deliveries of supplies.[55] These views were echoed by military and civilian representatives in the FEA and other agencies dealing with lend-lease who had long urged a "firm" policy toward Russia. During the closing years of the war tensions grew between such officials and those who continued to profess a "friendly" policy toward the USSR.[56] From Moscow similar critical attitudes were expressed by Ambassador Averell Harriman, Military Mission Chief General Deane, and Counselor of Embassy, George F. Kennan. Typical of such views were the following comments in a telegram by Harriman to the secretary of state on January 15, 1944:

> I can see no reason why we should deprive ourselves of urgent requirements unless we are reasonably satisfied that the supplies are put to good use here. . . . Now that the military crisis in Russia is passed and the volume of our shipments is attaining such tremendous proportions I see no reason why reasonable supporting evidence at least should not be expected from the Soviets.[57]

Despite such pleas the policy of all possible aid to Russia continued unchanged. In a memorandum to the president on January 18, 1945, FEA Administrator Leo T. Crowley summed up the then-current policy on lend-lease to the Soviet Union in these concise words: "to provide everything the USSR asks for that can be produced and is lend-leasable and possible to ship."[58]

The response of the Russians to the continuing high priority accorded the Soviet supply program further agitated the program's U.S. critics. In September, 1941, Molotov had told Polish Ambassador Stanislaw Kot, "Great Britain and America must realize that we are shedding our blood for them, that we are bearing all the burden of the sacrifice. In exchange for their peace they must provide us with arms."[59] This view persisted even after U.S. entry into the war and throughout the four protocols. As one observer has written, "The Soviet concept of lend-lease remained quite simple; they forwarded their requirements and the Anglo-Americans filled them."[60] In the beginning these requirements were the items most desperately needed to stop the Germans. Shipping was so limited that the Russians truly had to choose only that which was essential. As the crisis at the front passed and shipping and supply improved—and priorities remained high—the Russian appetite became more varied and more voracious. Supplies were chronically overordered, specifications became "silver-lined," and esoteric nonessential items appeared with increasing frequency in Soviet lists of requirements. Typical of these was a request in May 1945, on the very eve of the German surrender, for P-80 jet aircraft that were still not operational for U.S. forces.[61]

Other problems with Soviet lend-lease also added new irritants during the final years of the program. Most persistent among these from early 1944 onward were the increasing Soviet transfers of U.S. supplies to third parties (the nations they were conquering and liberating in eastern Europe) without prior consultation. Although these actions probably had no serious long-term consequences, they were in opposition to Soviet assurances given earlier and they did conjure up fears of misuse of lend-lease assistance for political purposes and interference in U.S. foreign trade.[62] There were also cases of mistreatment of foreign liaison personnel, instances of missions stranded for weeks for reasons that seemed either inadequate or incomprehensible, and there were all the difficulties of dealing with Soviet officials. They were often inexplicably moody and suspicious to the point of noncooperation and seemingly could not make decisions of any kind without referring to Moscow for instructions.[63] It is little wonder that in these circumstances mutual aid brought not mutual trust but rather a vicious circle of misunderstanding and suspicion, and that by the end of the war the two sides in the alliance found themselves enclosed by an iron ring of hostility.

The story of the organization and operation of the Russian lend-lease program thus makes a melancholy tale. When the Russians were in greatest need they received little material assistance and absorbed largely unaided the worst blows of the enemy. When their need became less acute, supplies became more abundant and their appetite grew in proportion. Their suppliers faced dilemmas of their own. The period of greatest Soviet need corresponded with the period of greatest U.S. need and greatest U.S. insufficiency. The overwhelming effort made to supply Russia at that time reinforced the desire to reduce supply later when its need was no longer so great. Overall, aid to the USSR was assailed by the Russians as too little too late, and by most American military leaders as too much too soon. Under these circumstances it was not unnatural for some Russians to view the late-burgeoning supply program as part payment for earlier Soviet sacrifices, while some Americans saw it as the garnering of means for a Russian conquest of Eastern Europe. This was the atmosphere of mutual suspicion and mistrust in which policy was formed to cut back and terminate lend-lease to Russia.

Policy Formation for the End of Lend-Lease

The United States was not at war when Congress passed the Lend-Lease Act, and its title proclaimed only the general purpose "to Promote the Defense of the United States." Nonetheless, it was thought of almost from the beginning as a war measure with a limited life. It was a war measure because it provided the United States with a means to aid nations who were actually in combat, and it was limited because it was given a life of only two years, with a provision for one-year renewals. During hearings that preceded the act's successive renewals members of Congress repeatedly stressed these points. They insisted that lend-lease was to be strictly a wartime measure, and with increasing force they demanded assurances that it would end with the war. On the sidelines they were cheered on by numbers of economists, businessmen, and foreign traders— all concerned at the disruption to international trade wrought by this unique program.[1]

Administration spokesmen, reluctant to renounce early in the war any future means to influence events, responded cautiously at first. Then, with the evident backing of President Roosevelt, they too averred that lend-lease would not extend into the postwar period. During hearings on the second extension of lend-lease in the spring of 1944, both FEA Administrator Crowley and Assistant Secretary of State Acheson asserted that lend-lease was a wartime measure. Later in the summer, during appropriations hearings, Crowley went a step further and stated that the program would be terminated "as soon as possible after the war is over." Finally, at the end of the year, the new secretary of state, Edward Stettinius, gave his personal assurance to Congressman Vorys of the Foreign Affairs Committee that lend-lease "comes to an end with the war." There were still differences of opinion in the lower levels of the FEA and the State and other departments, but by the end of 1944 the major spokesmen for the program were agreed on its termination with the war's conclusion. Henceforth this was the position Crowley maintained both within his own organization and before Congress.[2]

Although it was clear to many that lend-lease should terminate at the end of hostilities, there was very little discussion of how this would be done. It was obvious that a sudden termination—with partially filled contracts in process and material still in the supply pipeline—would be unnecessarily costly to the United States. To some extent the original act had attempted to solve this problem by providing for a three-year period during which a contract made before the ending of the program could be carried out. There were other problems not foreseen or covered by the act, and as allied fortunes on the battlefield steadily improved while relations with Russia became more troubled, two of these problems increasingly influenced the formation of policy for the end of lend-lease, particularly with regard to the special program for Russia. One issue was whether to use lend-lease as a bargaining tool to extract economic and political concessions; the other was the matter of obtaining payment for lend-lease supplies that had a postwar use.

Lend-Lease as a Bargaining Tool

On the eve of the German attack against Russia in June 1941 the State Department adopted a firm policy toward Russia, demanding appropriate return for any favors given. Point three of a six-point policy statement on relations with the USSR read: "To reject any Soviet suggestions that we make concessions for the sake 'of improving the atmosphere of Soviet-American relations' and to exact a strict quid pro quo for anything which we are willing to give the Soviet Union."[3]

In the aftermath of the Nazi invasion this policy was quickly abandoned. The Soviets were not asked to disclose their gold and dollar assets as a condition for material assistance as Britain and other lend-lease recipients were required to do, nor were they required to provide more than the most cursory justification for their requests. William H. McNeill has ably summed up the reasons for this policy: Russia, fighting with her back to the wall, needed all the military supplies she could get; there was no problem of reexport as there had been with goods sent to England; haggling over statistics would only complicate Russian resistance; demands for information and justifications would probably not be met anyway and would only serve to heighten Soviet suspicions of western motives; and above all else hung the ever present fear of a separate Soviet peace that would enable Hitler to redirect his entire war machine westward. The policy therefore was to give aid with no questions asked and to regard Soviet requests as prima facie evidence of Soviet needs.[4]

This policy dovetailed with another that had evolved at about the same time concerning the question of making political arrangements—particularly regarding territories and boundaries in Eastern Europe—while the war was still being fought. Within weeks of Hitler's attack Soviet representatives had raised with British and American diplomats their desire for Allied guarantees of Russian acquisition of the Baltic states as well as certain territorial changes along their western frontiers. At the urging of the State Department, Roosevelt sent a strong message to Churchill stating that he thought it was much too early to make any territorial or other postwar political commitments, and several months later, as Foreign Secretary Eden was about to depart for Moscow to discuss "both military questions and the field of war aims and postwar aims," he was informed orally that the United States considered that as far as postwar policies were concerned, these had been delineated by the Atlantic Charter, and that "it would be unfortunate were any of the three governments . . . to express any willingness to enter into commitments regarding specific terms of the postwar settlement."[5]

The Administration's Policy of Unconditional Aid

Once in the war the United States continued to maintain this policy. In spite of differences of opinion on the question of political concessions within the administration—and wavering at times even by Roosevelt himself—Secretary Hull, the Joint Chiefs of Staff, and others steadfastly insisted that winning the war was the first and paramount priority. When that had been accomplished the victors could then meet at the peace table and make whatever postwar settlements seemed appropriate. From this policy, and the previously stated position that no questions would be asked in extending aid to Russia, it was a logical leap to the view that lend-lease should not be used as a bargaining tool to extract concessions from the Soviet Union on either wartime or postwar policy. Except for an abortive effort by Roosevelt in the late summer of 1941 to get a statement on religious tolerance from the Russians to aid passage of the lend-lease appropriations bill, this was the policy followed from the inception of the Soviet aid program. It was given formal expression, in conformity with FDR's views, by Harry Hopkins, chairman of the President's Soviet Protocol Committee, at the first meeting of that newly created group in November 1942.[6]

Lend-lease was thus not to be used directly as a quid pro quo for concessions desired from its recipients, but Secretary Hull and his supporters at the State Department, as well as other high officials in the administration, realized that the postwar settlement of lend-lease accounts would have a great influence on future international economic relations. It was for this reason that they had sought through the Master Lend-Lease Agreements (which were eventually concluded with each assisted nation, and which set forth the principles that were to govern the extension of lend-lease aid as well as the benefits the United States would receive in return) to commit recipient nations to principles that they believed would promote free international trade in an environment that would be in the best interests of the United States. The particular section of these agreements on which they relied to achieve this goal was Article VII, with its broad promises of international and domestic measures to eliminate discriminatory treatment in international commerce and reduce tariffs and other trade barriers. This goal was clearly endorsed by FDR when he wrote in his report to the Congress on the first year of lend-lease operations that "the third direct benefit received in return for our aid [in addition to aiding the fight against the Axis and receiving reciprocal aid from recipients] is an understanding with Britain (and prospectively with other of our allies) as to the shape of future commercial and financial policy."[7] With regard to the Soviet Union, it was specifically hoped that Article VII would oblige it to become a full participant in a new postwar international order of American design. The high hopes held for the use of Article VII were well illustrated by one State Department historian who wrote during the war that the "degree to which [the nations] are willing to cooperate in achieving the objectives set forth in Article VII will determine whether the U.S., and the other united nations, will be repaid for their sacrifices in this war by having achieved a secure peace."[8]

But while Hull was interested in using eventual lend-lease settlements for agreement only on general economic principles, others, particularly in the Congress, wished to go further and make use of currently extended aid to obtain specific commitments that would not only aid the U.S. economy but also enhance U.S. security. In January 1943, Vice President Wallace warned FDR of the strong congressional sentiment for obtaining postwar use of air bases in exchange for the renewal of lend-lease, and during hearings and debate on the first extension of the Lend-Lease Act, Wallace's impression was borne out. Several times in committee testimony administration spokesmen were pointedly asked if the United States was making appropriate use of its bargaining position under lend-lease to acquire postwar base rights. On the House floor Rep. Robert B. Chiperfield, Republican from Illinois, asserted that the United States should seek solutions to its postwar problems before the war's end, including the taking of steps to assure control of naval bases, air bases, and trade routes; and in Senate debate Senator Ellender of Louisiana went even further, demanding not only bases but also "in sovereignty" the bauxite and tin mines owned by the British and the Dutch.[9]

These strong expressions of congressional opinion did not cause any quid pro quo conditions to be written into legislation extending lend-lease, but they did serve notice on the administration that influential members of the Congress regarded lend-lease as a bargaining tool and did expect that the United States would use it, at least in its settlement phase if not sooner, to obtain important concessions in a number of areas. This served to strengthen the opinions of those in Roosevelt's government who tended toward similar positions, and it gave officials like Navy Secretary Knox and Assistant State Department Secretaries Acheson and Berle an opportunity to air their views on the more general question of obtaining postwar benefits in the final settlement of lend-lease obliga-tions, particularly through Article VII of the Master Agreements.

Opposition to the Administration's Policy

While the State Department and the Congress debated the possible bargaining implications of lend-lease aid, others in the administration were chafing under Roosevelt's no-questions-asked policy regarding aid to the USSR. When U.S. Ambassador to the USSR Admiral Standley returned briefly to Washington in October 1942 to discuss his trying relations with the Russians, he expressed to the president and Hopkins his strong disagreement with the policy of demanding nothing in return for American generosity with lend-lease supplies. "Stop acting like Santa Claus, Chief," Standley urged FDR, "and let's get something from Stalin in return. . . . My advice is to treat Stalin like an adult, keep any promises we make to him, but insist that he keep his promises, too. And if he doesn't make good within a reasonable time, hold out on him until he does."[10]

Among the military chiefs in Washington there was strong support for this position, especially from General Arnold, Commander of the Army air corps. Arnold's differences with the Soviet assistance program had become particularly acute over the question of aircraft, the military item that was in greatest demand and shortest supply. Anxious to exercise stricter control over deliveries to Russia—and thus increase the number of planes for his own forces—Arnold pointed out that the United States was furnishing Russia with military supplies but did not know Russia's actual military needs nor, more important, the use that was being made of these supplies. He suggested that because of a lack of information and analysis the policy then being followed in relation to Russia might not be in the best military interests of the United States and he recommended that joint U.S. staff planners undertake a study of that policy. After examining the matter, the Operations Division of the War Department General Staff concluded that no useful purpose would be served by giving the problem to the joint staff planners at that time; nonetheless its Policy Committee did comment that "the United States should continue to furnish lend-lease supplies to Russia to the full extent of our capacity, provided—and provided only—that Russia cooperates with us and takes us into her confidence. . . . The time is appropriate for us to start some straight-from-the-shoulder talk with Mr. Joseph Stalin."[11]

In line with these sentiments Army and Navy representatives to the President's Soviet Protocol Committee proposed in April 1943 that a clause be inserted in the Third Protocol calling for all authorized military attachés and observers in the USSR to be given the same rights of visit and access to information as those extended to their Soviet counterparts in the United States. In addition, the British chiefs of staff sought a pledge of Russian assistance in defending the northern convoy route. But these proposals did not meet with widespread approval and were turned down by the protocol committee with the observation that "in the experience of those engaged in the execution of previous protocols, the Soviets are very difficult to deal with on a bargaining basis, but respond most satisfactorily in performing their share of an understanding when a generous offer is made, and which does not force the Soviets into a bargaining position."[12]

The policy of unconditional aid to the Soviet Union was sustained through 1943 by a coalition of supporters who held important positions in the Russian aid program in both

Washington and Moscow. Prominent among these in the U.S. capital were Harry Hopkins, chairman of the President's Soviet Protocol Committee, and Maj. Gen. James H. Burns, his executive on the committee, both of whom enjoyed the strong support of the president and Secretary Hull. In Moscow the key man was Col. Philip R. Faymonville (later promoted to Brigadier General), head of the Supply Mission to the USSR and chief lend-lease representative in Russia. Faymonville was a firm advocate of all possible aid to the USSR without any strings attached. His strong admiration for the Russians and the almost complete autonomy of his mission from any embassy control had been a source of great irritation to Admiral Standley and stood high on the list of reasons for his request in mid-1943 to be replaced as ambassador to the USSR.

By the end of 1943 this coalition of supporters of unrestricted aid to Russia began to break up, and its influence slowly weakened. In Washington serious illness reduced the activities of both Hopkins and Burns and finally forced the latter into retirement. Their supporters in the lend-lease administration continued to promote their views, and these still received, when needed, the backing of the White House, but the lack of day-to-day attention by someone with the considerable influence of Hopkins gradually eroded their position and left the field open to the entrance of those with opposing views. In Moscow a complete overhaul occurred when Ambassador Standley was replaced by Averell Harriman—already committed to a "firm" policy toward the Soviet Union, though not as dogmatic as the man he succeeded—and a new military mission was established under Maj. Gen. John R. Deane. Faymonville was returned to the United States for non-lend-lease duties and Maj. Gen. Sidney P. Spalding was appointed to handle lend-lease functions within Deane's mission.[13]

This new political-military team gave much greater cohesion and unity to U.S. representation in Moscow. It arrived in October 1943, with Secretary Hull, to participate in the Moscow Conference; it was impressed by the good will generated by that event, and it began its work in expectation of an atmosphere free of many of the difficulties that had troubled the previous staff. However, it quickly discovered the same secretiveness and suspicion and the often impenetrable Soviet bureaucracy that had beset its predecessors. Its impatience in the face of these obstacles, combined with a realization that the military tide had turned and was now definitely running in favor of the Allies, caused it to look with an increasingly critical eye at Soviet supply demands and American largesse in fulfilling them. From the arrival of this group in Moscow can be dated a steadily growing effort—with increasing support from various quarters in Washington—to reverse the policy of unconditional aid to Russia and to substitute a definite quid pro quo for continued American supply.

In January 1944, two months after he became ambassador to the Soviet Union, Harriman summed up for the president and the secretary of state developments since his arrival. He reported that the contacts he and the members of the military mission had had with Molotov and other top Soviet leaders had been cordial and friendly, but in getting action on or even detailed discussion of proposals approved in principle they had received a "complete runaround." He was particularly disturbed that information to support lend-lease requests had not been forthcoming or had been so vague as to be valueless, and he stated that after discussing these matters with General Deane and members of his mission he had reached the conclusion that "the time had come for us to demand action."[14]

The first demand for action came within a few days. General Deane had learned that the Russians were requesting additional diesel engines for patrol craft despite the fact that of the 126 already sent to them only 3 had been installed while 45 were designated for known hulls and at least 50 more were rusting out in the open. With Harriman's concurrence Deane sent a message to the War Department asking for a change in the policy of acceding to Soviet requests with few questions asked. He suggested that the Russians be required to provide justification for their requests, particularly of items in short supply, and that these requests first be cleared by the Supply Division of the Military Mission in Moscow. If the Soviets failed to provide sufficient information, Deane added, they should be told "to give it to us or else." He argued that this would cause the Russians to calculate their needs more closely and that in addition, firmness in this regard would "give the Soviets much more respect for us." He did not feel that lend-lease should be used as a lever to force Soviet acquiescence to any operational proposals, but he felt that the respect gained would "carry over into the settlement of other war problems."[15]

Deane's proposal ran headlong into the opposition of Gen. John York, acting executive of the President's Soviet Protocol Committee. York immediately fired off a memo to the secretary of the JCS recommending that no action be taken by the Joint Chiefs pending solution of the problem by the president himself or the protocol committee and another memo to Admiral Leahy reminding him that "General Burns has always felt that if we are to get ahead with the Russians we must act in a spirit of sincere friendship toward them, without a direct request for something to be given to us as a quid pro quo for our generosity." Finally, after several weeks of discussion, an answer was cabled to Moscow. Harriman was told that "after careful consideration it has been decided that it is inadvisable to subject USSR requirements to screening in Moscow or to reject Soviet requests because of failure to provide operational or other justification to your mission." No position was taken on the arguments put forth concerning the potential long-term effects of policy in this matter on Soviet-American relations in general; instead, the message simply stated that a change in procedure "might cause the Russians to withdraw a large part of the Soviet Purchasing Commission which would not be understood by the public here or elsewhere."[16]

The Deane-Harriman proposal did not succeed, but it did stimulate the thinking of others in Washington who felt that American economic assistance was a powerful tool that could be used either to promote policies the United States desired or prevent those that were against its interests. In February of 1944 Elbridge Durbrow of the Division of Eastern European Affairs of the Department of State prepared a long memorandum entitled "Certain Aspects of Present Soviet Policy." In this paper he stated that the Soviet Union, through the use of various front groups, was building up a communist organization capable of exerting considerable influence and even dominant control over many countries in Eastern and Western

Europe. He then argued that the Russians' fear of the basic weakness of their country after the war gave the United States its "best lever" to combat this policy and that the United States should therefore point out to the Russians that "they will have to drop their 'Comintern Foreign Policy' if they want our aid and cooperation after the war."[18] When Harriman received Durbrow's memorandum he immediately cabled the department his approval of the argument it made that economic assistance was one of the most effective weapons to influence European political events and avoid a Soviet sphere of influence over Eastern Europe and the Balkans. Harriman expressed his concurrence with Durbrow's ideas in these words:

> The granting of economic assistance should be in accordance with our basic policy vis-à-vis each country and subject to withholding if individual countries do not conform to our standards. This policy would include economic assistance to the Soviet Union which as I have expressed in other cables is one of our principal practical levers for influencing political action compatible with our principles.[18]

During the remainder of 1944 these sentiments were increasingly seconded by U.S. military leaders in Washington. In March, General Marshall, in a memo to President Roosevelt, argued that if Russia were deprived of lend-lease Germany could probably still defeat the USSR, and thus, "lend-lease is our trump card in dealing with the USSR and its control is possibly the most effective means we have to keep the Soviets on the offensive in connection with the second front."[19] General Arnold went further and in September proposed that the United States play its "trump card," urging Harry Hopkins to direct the protocol committee to take a "stiffer attitude" toward the Soviets and regard any requests by them over and above the amounts specified in the protocol to be on an "inferred quid pro quo basis" to be "used as 'bargaining points' to further our own interests in pursuing the war, both in Europe and the Far East."[20] Two months later the Navy added its weight to the argument when its new secretary, James V. Forrestal, who advocated a "firm" policy toward the USSR and supported the

use of lend-lease for bargaining, raised again the matter of
Soviet requests for diesel engines for patrol craft and demanded
full justification before any more were shipped.[21]

In the War Department the tactic of bargaining with the
Soviets in order to obtain changes in their policies was also
being considered by Secretary Henry Stimson. However,
Stimson's bargaining tool was not economic power, but the
power of S-1, the code name for the atomic bomb, about which
only he and a few others were fully informed at that time.
During the winter of 1944-1945, Stimson several times wrote in
his diary of his thoughts about using S-1 to obtain major
changes in Soviet policy. On December 31 he recorded a
conversation with FDR in which he told the president that the
United States would not gain anything by further easy
concessions to Russia and that it should be more vigorous in
insisting on a quid pro quo. In particular, nothing should be
told them about S-1 until such a quid pro quo was
forthcoming. In February 1945, following the Yalta Conference, Stimson returned again to this theme and expanded his
views further. He was sympathetic, he said, with Dr. Vannevar
Bush's desire "to be very chivalrous to the Russians" on the
subject of S-1, but he was "still inclined to tread softly . . . until
we have some much more tangible 'fruits of repentence' from
the Russians as quid pro quo for such a communication to
them."[22]

The attitude of Roosevelt himself throughout most of this
controversy is much more difficult to discern. From the support
he gave the decisions of Hopkins, Burns, and York it can be
inferred that he continued to back the policy of unconditional
aid to Russia that he had set at the beginning of the Soviet lend-
lease program and that he did not favor using economic aid as a
lever for concessions of any kind. Yet Roosevelt often sided
with conflicting advisers, encouraging them to develop their
arguments as fully as possible until he settled the ensuing
controversy by selecting the position he favored. That he was
not averse to using lend-lease as leverage to achieve other
objectives was seen in his authorization of a sharp note to
Portuguese Premier Antonio Salazar threatening "immediate
curtailment" of economic aid when Salazar stalled on the

construction of an air base in the Azores.[23] But it was not until mid-January 1945, that any clear indication appeared of Roosevelt's evaluation of the economic leverage the United States had vis-à-vis the Soviet Union. Reporting to Secretary Stettinius on a meeting Roosevelt had with seven senators from the Foreign Relations Committee, Dean Acheson told the secretary that in the context of a discussion of Russian policy in Eastern Europe Roosevelt had replied to a question from Senator Vandenburg by arguing that "our economic position did not constitute a bargaining weapon of any strength because its only present impact was on lend-lease, which to cut down would hurt us as much as it would hurt the Russians."[24]

In early April 1945 another effort was made by General Deane in Moscow to use economic aid as a bargaining tool. Deane had been unsuccessful in his efforts to obtain Russian permission—as he had been promised at Yalta—to visit the recently captured German submarine base at Gdynia to obtain information on new developments the Germans had made in underseas warfare. Very bitter over this refusal of cooperation on what he considered a vital and legitimate military matter, Deane proposed to the Joint Chiefs of Staff that Convoy JW-67, then being formed for dispatch to north Russia, be cancelled and that further convoys be halted until the Soviets agreed to honor their promises. But again General York reiterated established policy in this matter and strongly recommended to the JCS that no action be taken without express approval by Hopkins or the president.[25] No such approval was sought or given and preparations continued on the formation of the convoy.

This proved to be but a temporary cap—and the last one—on the head of pressure that had been steadily building for a change in the policy of unconditional lend-lease aid to Russia. As relations with the USSR became more strained on a wide variety of matters in the closing months of the war the continuation of such a policy seemed to many less and less justified. Some, like Counselor George Kennan in Moscow, argued that lend-lease to Russia simply should be ended; others adhered to the view that its continuation should be used to extract political, economic, or military concessions; fewer and fewer believed it should be maintained as before. The culmination of this growing discontent came in a long telegram from Harriman on April 4. This message, and one that followed two days later, were widely circulated among high officials in Washington; together they marked an important turning point in wartime Soviet-American relations.

Harriman was replying to a State Department telegram concerning relief supplies for Europe. He began by contrasting what he described as the humanitarian motives of the United States and the political objectives of the Soviet Union. This distinction suggested to Harriman that the United States should take care of the Western Allies and those areas under its control first, allocating to the USSR whatever was left. Harriman explained that in justifying his suggestions he recognized that he was going beyond the requirements for information in the department's message, but he felt that this was necessary to support his final recommendation, which was "to adopt a more positive policy of using our economic influence to further our broad political ideals." This meant, first, assisting countries that were "naturally friendly" toward American concepts. Second, toward the Soviet Union it meant a policy still based on developing friendly relations and cooperation, "but always on a quid pro quo basis." Harriman concluded: "This means tying our economic assistance directly into our political problems with the Soviet Union. This should be faced squarely in our consideration of the Fifth Protocol."[26]

This message arrived in the midst of mounting difficulties in U.S. relations with Russia. It was therefore read and pondered in a context of events which to many appeared to fully support its analysis; this in turn lent weight to its recommendations. Those who had long been dubious about the policy of unconditional aid to Russia could say their doubts were confirmed; others who had gone along with this policy because of its White House support, but who were never wholly convinced, could slip easily into the role of its opponents. The few who remained staunch supporters of all-out aid to Russia without any questions asked became less vocal and less influential, and from April 3 onward this policy was never again formally advocated. For many of those involved in the formation of policy for the end of lend-lease the ground had thus been cleared for an attempt to use its cutback and termination as a means to influence both wartime and postwar Soviet policy.

Payment for Lend-Lease Supplies with Postwar Use

The second important problem facing lend-lease policy makers concerned arrangements to be made—when lend-lease was cut back and finally terminated—for compensation for those supplies (such as equipment for factories) which were not consumed in the war effort, could not sensibly or easily be returned, and clearly had a postwar use. As success in the war favored the Allies and the victorious outcome of the contest increasingly seemed assured, this became a growing concern for those who sought to keep lend-lease separate from reconstruction and assure the Congress that the former was being used strictly for war aid. For the special program of lend-lease to the Soviet Union, where proof of need and information requirements were virtually nonexistent while the recipient was regarded with growing suspicion, it was a particularly acute problem.

In the early days of the Soviet supply program there had been a reluctance on the part of American officials to commit themselves to provide assistance that did not have immediate and direct war use. In July 1941, when Soviet Ambassador Oumansky requested that the question of the ultimate use of equipment sent to Russia not be raised in advance, Assistant Secretary of State Dean Acheson replied that this question must be raised and added, according to the department's memorandum of the conversation, that "it did not seem advisable at this time to give consideration to long-term projects which would take several years to complete and which were not directly connected with the war effort."[27]

Acheson's initial caution undoubtedly reflected in part the widespread uncertainty at the time as to whether the Russians could hold out against the Germans. To help them do so, the reasoning went, they should be provided with materials that had an immediate war use; to supply them for long-term projects would not help them in the imminent crisis, and if they failed, such supplies might well fall into the hands of the Germans. As it turned out these early fears were unfounded, for the Russians did hold out and their early requests were mainly for materials with an immediate war use. However, once the military crises of the first eighteen months had passed and the Russians settled down to the long task of driving back the Germans, the composition of Soviet requests for assistance began to change. As has been shown, between 1942 and 1943 Russian desires for goods shifted from an emphasis on munitions for war to an emphasis on materials and tools for reconstruction.

This change in priorities occasioned a sharp debate within the Lend-Lease Administration. From London lend-lease representative Averell Harriman wrote in April 1943, in a private letter to OLLA administrator Stettinius, that he had heard about "the long-range projects of one type or another for which the Russians are pressing" and wanted to express himself "as unalterably opposed to granting these requests." Assaying the possible effect of his recommendation on Soviet-American relations, Harriman added, "my experience is that the Russians are brutally and bluntly frank with us, and we can well afford to be equally so."[28] A few days later Gen. Sidney P. Spalding of the Division for Soviet Supply of OLLA wrote a memorandum to Harry Hopkins expressing his view on the matter and seeking a clarification of policy in advance of Stettinius's forthcoming appearance before the House Appropriations Committee. Spalding argued strongly for a favorable response to Soviet requests for long-range industrial projects, opposed determining their acceptability for inclusion in the protocol on the basis of a fixed time by which they would be in operation, and concluded, "we can gain Russian good will probably more by being generous with industrial equipment than with any other item except airplanes."[29] After some weeks of discussion, Stettinius proposed that no project be approved unless it was believed that it would definitely contribute to winning the war, and that emphasis be placed on projects which could be fabricated, shipped, and put into operation in less than eighteen months and could be readily used in the United States or in other lend-lease countries in the event shipping was interrupted. To this policy, which became known as the "eighteen-month rule," FDR gave his approval, subject only to the reservation that he could make exceptions for diplomatic considerations.[30]

In accordance with this policy, and in view of the increasing number of Soviet requests for long-range industrial projects, a clause was inserted in the Third Protocol whereby the United States undertook to consider the approval of orders for industrial equipment totaling not in excess of $300 million for delivery after June 30, 1944. As long as the termination of the war remained in the indeterminate future such a commitment appeared to fall within the terms of the Lend-Lease Act; but the successful Allied offensives of the summer and fall of 1943 raised the possibility of an early Axis defeat and created several thorny problems. If the war were to end before promised long-range industrial equipment could be produced and shipped, would the United States still be obliged to deliver? If so, who would pay? It seemed to many that neither the Congress nor the public would countenance the continued supply of goods to the USSR on lend-lease terms after hostilities with Germany had ended. But if Russia did not pay, huge cancellation costs would be involved since, in spite of Stettinius's expressed wishes, most of the equipment was specifically designed for Russian use and would be of little value elsewhere. Such equipment could be justified for use against Japan—with whom it was felt war would continue for many months following Germany's fall—but the USSR was not yet at war with Japan. Some, like Generals Burns and Spalding, did feel that a generous aid policy toward Russia might encourage its early entry into the contest in the Pacific, but there was no firm prospect of this in mid-1943. Beyond these questions there were important conflicting views regarding postwar domestic and foreign policy. Oscar Cox, and Donald Nelson of the War Production Board, among others, argued that the USSR's need for reconstruction assistance was acute and that provision of long-term use industrial goods would not only insure postwar Soviet good will but would also provide business and employment in U.S. factories when war work was cut back. Others, particularly Leo Crowley and Gen. Charles Wesson, director of the FEA's USSR Branch, were not so convinced, and a combination of lingering suspicion of Russian motives and reluctance to extend assistance not specifically meant for war purposes persuaded them that the United States should adhere strictly to the letter of the Lend-Lease Act and not use it for purposes for which it was not intended.

Proposed Agreement with the USSR

In November 1943, the ever resourceful Oscar S. Cox, by then counselor of the newly established Foreign Economic Administration, sent a long memorandum to his chief, Leo T. Crowley, in which he raised these related problems and discussed possible solutions for them. Cox pointed out that Section 3-c of the Lend-Lease Act—which set the terminal date of its powers (originally June 30, 1943, later extended for two one-year periods)—contained an exception that gave the president a three-year period following the terminal date during which he could exercise the powers of the act to carry out a contract or agreement made with a foreign government before the terminal date. In accordance with this section of the act, Cox proposed an agreement with the USSR in which the United States would undertake to deliver, after the war had ended, those supplies contracted for but not delivered before the termination of hostilities. For such supplies the Soviet Union would in turn agree to pay the United States in cash, gold, or commodities either upon delivery or in installments over a period of time. Cox argued that this would solve many of the problems raised by Soviet requests for long-range industrial projects that might not be finished before the war's end. In a further elaboration of this proposal to Crowley, Cox added, on the first of January 1944, "this, to my mind, presents a quite important central issue in our present and future dealings with the Russians. It may well set the partial pattern for the postwar rehabilitation and reconstruction problems with the USSR." Two weeks later, in explaining his plan to Harry Hopkins, he was even more explicit: "Using the method I have suggested would start them [the Russians] well on the road to reconstruction."[31] This approach was viewed much more warily by Cox's superiors in the FEA, as well as in the State Department, and though it was recognized that the proposed supplementary agreement would assist Soviet rehabilitation, it was decided to keep lend-lease and any arrangements for postwar assistance as separate as possible by negotiating the former in Washington and the latter in Moscow.[32]

Accordingly, in March 1944, Acting Secretary of State Stettinius and FEA Administrator Crowley submitted a joint memorandum to Roosevelt enclosing a message to Harriman embodying a comprehensive approach to the related questions of reconstruction and war-related lend-lease materials with a postwar use. In their message to Harriman, Stettinius and Crowley expressed their intention to open negotiations with the Russians in Washington for an agreement whereby the USSR would "agree to take any equipment in certain categories not delivered at the conclusion of hostilities under a separate contract calling for regular payments on terms of interest and amortization to be laid down." At first Section 3-c of the Lend-Lease Act would be used to permit such contracts; eventually they hoped that the Export-Import Bank, if it received a congressional extension of its powers, could take over the operation. As for regular reconstruction activities that were not definable was war-essential, the two administrators advised Harriman that in the absence of the establishment of a United Nations Bank for Reconstruction and Development, they were considering the possibility of obtaining authority to use the Export-Import Bank for this role.

In their covering memorandum to the president, Stettinius and Crowley argued that their use of Section 3-c, which they said might also be applied to certain other countries receiving lend-lease aid, would assure an uninterrupted flow of supplies needed for the war and would also contribute to an orderly liquidation of the lend-lease program. But they also cautioned that "certainly these arrangements are not conceived of as in any way a substitute for methods of helping to finance the main job of reconstruction." FDR gave his approval, and in May 1944, an aide-memoire was presented to Soviet Ambassador Andrei Gromyko containing the seven-article draft of an

agreement supplementary to the Soviet-American Mutual Aid
Agreement (the Master Lend-Lease Agreement) of June 11,
1942.

The key provisions of this draft agreement stated that the
United States would undertake to transfer to the USSR, after
active military operations against the common enemy had
ceased, named categories of supplies that had been contracted
for or had been in inventory but were not transferred prior to
the end of hostilities. These supplies (which consisted mostly
of raw materials, machinery, and other miscellaneous finished
equipment) would be paid for in dollars by the USSR
according to the following terms: 5 percent of the total cost of
the supplies to be paid each year, beginning the fourth year
after their transfer, until the entire cost shall have been paid
(in effect, a grace period of three years followed by a total
amortization period of twenty years), and interest on the
unpaid balance beginning immediately at the rate of interest
on the public debt of the United States during the preceding
year, plus a carrying charge of one-eighth of 1 percent. (Under
this formula the rate applicable for 1944 was 2.1 percent.) Items
of war-related capital equipment that required a long period to
produce and that had a long period of useful life would be
included regardless of when they were actually transferred,
provided that they had been contracted for before the
termination of hostilities. The terms of payment for this capital
equipment were similar to those for the named categories of
supplies except that in the case of equipment transferred prior
to the cessation of active military operations against the
common enemy, the date of transfer was deemed to have been
the date of such cessation.[33]

Negotiations with the USSR

At the end of July, in the almost unbearable heat of a corner
room in the old State Department building, negotiations began
on the agreement between Vice Commissar of Foreign Trade
M. S. Stepanov and Assistant Secretary of State Dean Acheson.[34]
The Russians proved to be hard traders: they demanded a
uniform interest rate of 2 percent rather than the sliding scale

suggested; they wanted the period of grace to be ten years rather than three; they desired a long period of amortization; and they wanted to make payment in dollars or in gold with a clause that their payments in gold would be at an equivalent never lower than thirty-five dollars per ounce. Many other subsidiary matters, some of very minor importance, were also raised by the Russians, and the negotiations dragged on through thirteen sessions over a period of six weeks. Although the Soviet negotiators did move somewhat from their initial positions, the final terms submitted to Stepanov on September 14, 1944, by Dean Acheson represented important concessions by the United States—so much so that others in the State Department felt called upon to express their dissent.[35]

In setting forth the final U.S. position Acheson offered the Russians either a fixed rate of interest of 2-3/8 percent over the repayment period or the average rate of interest of the U.S. public debt for each year. Both rates were based on the cost to the government of borrowing money needed to procure the supplies covered by the agreement, and in defense of these figures Acheson argued that Congress would not appropriate money for the credit if the rate was lower than the government could obtain, and that a lower rate for the USSR would set a precedent for other countries that the United States did not want to establish. Payment on the principal, Acheson proposed, would be on a sliding scale of annual installments over a period of twenty-two years beginning after a nine-year grace period. Such payment could be made in dollars or gold valued at the buying price for gold in effect at the time of each gold delivery.[36]

When Stepanov was given these terms he was informed that the agreement could be signed in Washington or, if he desired to proceed to Moscow to discuss the draft with his colleagues, it could be signed there. Stepanov chose the latter course and left a few days later for the Soviet capital. Despite Acheson's request for a prompt reply to facilitate placing orders, no immediate response was forthcoming. Instead, U.S. representatives in Moscow heard from time to time that the Russians objected to certain parts of the agreement, that they wished to make some changes in the draft, and that they intended to offer a counter proposal on the question of long-term credit for industrial equipment.

While these negotiations and discussions were continuing for what by then had become known as the "3-c Agreement" there was a virtual moratorium on procurement of industrial equipment for the USSR. As of March 31, 1944, only $180 million of the $300 million of industrial equipment that the United States had committed itself to in the Third Protocol had actually been approved, and not all of that was in procurement at the time.[37] During negotiations it was decided that the balance of undelivered equipment from the Third Protocol (designated Category I and finally set at $223 million) would be made available during the Fourth Protocol period. Also included in the Fourth Protocol was a second group of equipment and machinery requiring only a short period to produce. This amounted to $300 million and was designated Category II. In effect these were the named categories of supplies of the proposed 3-c Agreement. There was also a third group of industrial equipment in the protocol that required a long period to produce and had a long useful life. This amounted to $481 million, was designated Category III, and was the remaining long-life capital equipment of the draft 3-c Agreement.[38]

While the 3-c Agreement negotiations dragged on without resolution, very little of the industrial equipment in the three categories was procured, and even less of it was actually delivered. In many cases where there was doubt about an item, procurement was simply held up pending signature of the 3-c Agreement. In other cases, perceived political pressures brought about negative action, as seen in the comment of John Hazard of the USSR Branch in a letter to General Spalding in Moscow that "Mr. Crowley and General Wesson feel that politically these [construction industry] plants would be difficult to finance since people might jump to the conclusion that they were solely for reconstruction purposes."[39] General Rudenko and his associates in the Soviet Purchasing Commission in Washington complained bitterly about this development, but to no avail. At the ninth meeting of the President's

Soviet Protocol Committee in November 1944 its Subcommittee on Supplies reported that "no requisitions have been
accepted against the offerings for industrial equipment set
forth in connection with the financial proposals made under
Article 3-c since these proposals have not yet been accepted by
the USSR."[40]

This practice may have caused consternation to Rudenko in
Washington, but it should have come as no surprise to his
associates in Moscow since Harriman had already emphasized
to Vice Commissar of Foreign Trade Krutikov in late June of
that year that one of the consequences of delay in reaching
agreement under the terms of Section 3-c of the Lend-Lease Act
would be a delay in the flow of supplies. In mid-August an even
stronger warning was transmitted to Russia by the State
Department via Harriman. The ambassador was instructed to
"impress upon the Soviet authorities that if this agreement is
not concluded before the German collapse, considerable time
may elapse before either American government credits could be
made available to them or private concerns could conclude
contracts with them to provide postwar items on a credit basis."
Curiously, Harriman did not convey this message at once. He
prepared a brief memorandum for himself on the matter, but
not until the last day of August did he write to Mikoyan.[41] But
by that date, when by his own admission he had become
thoroughly disenchanted with the course of Soviet-American
relations due to what he later called the "startling turn" taken
by the Soviets in the previous two months, he went beyond his
instructions, amending with his own stronger warning the
message he had received two weeks before.

> I have been asked to call your attention to the fact that until a
> financial agreement along the lines proposed is reached it is
> impossible for my government to put into production these
> items, that after the termination of hostilities there is at present
> no legal way that my government can extend credits to the
> Soviet Union to the extent required, *and that unless some
> financial agreement is reached prior to the termination of
> hostilities with our common enemy shipments under lend-lease
> will automatically cease* [emphasis added].[42]

A few weeks later, when he learned that Stepanov had been given the final American offer on the 3-c Agreement, Harriman again wrote to Mikoyan: "I am sure you appreciate the need for prompt conclusion of both the amendment to the Lend-Lease Agreement and the protocol in order that there may be no interruption in the flow of needed supplies to the USSR."[43]

In view of the cutoff of procurement of industrial equipment in Washington and the sharp warnings given the Russians by Harriman in Moscow, there is cause to wonder why the Russians were so intransigent over the terms of the 3-c Agreement. There are several explanations for their behavior. First, Soviet officials shared expectations concerning the probable state of the U.S. economy that indicated to them they could assume a very tough bargaining position. These views, partly rooted in their own ideological assumptions concerning capitalist economies, were expressed several times in private conversations with American officials and also during the course of the negotiations for the 3-c Agreement. In mid-August 1944, John Hazard reported a conversation with Ivan Eremin, assistant chairman of the Soviet Purchasing Commission in the United States, in which (in Hazard's words) Eremin asserted that "U.S. industry was in large measure idle in the types of equipment the USSR wants, and that it is certainly to the government's interest to get business into these plants."[44] During negotiating sessions at the end of that month, Vice Commissar Stepanov similarly indicated that he thought the United States had proposed the 3-c Agreement because it was "most desirous of giving business to American firms to help tide them over from a wartime to a peacetime basis."[45]

A second reason for the intransigence of the Russians over the terms of the 3-c Agreement is that they did not fully understand the legal and political difficulties involved in a grant of large-scale credits by the United States, nor did they appreciate the sensitivity of American officials to these difficulties. From Stalin on down they held a view of governmental decision making in the United States that—though they recognized great differences from their own political system—nevertheless assumed power to be centered in the executive and totally failed to include a notion of accountability other than to the decision makers themselves. In 1942 Stalin had thanked Roosevelt and *his cabinet* for the grant of an additional billion dollar credit. According to Hazard, Eremin "expected after the negotiators had reached their limits and clearly outlined the extent of disagreement, the highest people would make the decisions for both sides," and after a lengthy and futile negotiating session with Stepanov, State Department representatives concluded that despite their detailed explanations they were not certain that the Soviet negotiator fully understood why lend-lease funds could not be used for other than war purposes.[46] These views, too, were conditioned by ideological assumptions concerning the location of power in a capitalist regime, as well as by experience with the Roosevelt administration. FDR had, after all, invented lend-lease and masterminded its passage through what originally had been depicted as a reluctant Congress. He conducted important state business through emissaries like Harry Hopkins who had not been elected to office and were responsible to no one but the president. He had pressed hard for delivery of materials and equipment to Russia, and even after the most severe military crises had passed he continued to give high priority to such supplies. Given these circumstances, in a context of supporting economic and political ideas, it must have been hard to believe the United States would hold out for three-eighths of a percentage point of interest!

Finally, as time passed and the United States failed to make concessions evidently expected by the Soviet leadership, the prospect of alternate and even more attractive financial arrangements loomed steadily larger. Soviet officials in Washington and Moscow had been repeatedly told that the 3-c Agreement was a stopgap measure with a postwar use and that the United States expected to finance more comprehensive large-scale reconstruction aid through the Export-Import Bank and eventually the International Bank as soon as necessary legislation made these institutions available for such purposes. Furthermore, the Russians were undoubtedly aware that there were important differences of opinion within the American administration concerning the terms and amount of economic assistance to be extended to the USSR for postwar reconstruction. In October 1944, Secretary of the Treasury Henry Morgenthau and his director of monetary research, Harry Dexter White, were ready to make a "no-interest" proposal to break the 3-c Agreement deadlock, and three months later—as will be discussed in the following chapter— they proposed to FDR a generous plan for comprehensive reconstruction aid to Russia.[47] Thus, at the end of 1944 it seemed clear to the Russians that there was little point in continuing to haggle over the terms of a 3-c Agreement. As John Hazard wrote in his day journal, "it now seems very doubtful whether the Russians would sign this 3-c Agreement in view of the efforts being made by Mr. Acheson to obtain repeal of the Johnson Act and the expanding of the Export-Import Bank Charter."[48]

Conclusive evidence that the Russians had decided to drop further consideration of the 3-c Agreement came early in 1945. On January 3, Ambassador Harriman was called to the Kremlin to receive from Foreign Commissar Molotov an aide-memoire requesting from the United States a long-term $6 billion credit to finance mainly postwar reconstruction, but also to include war-related materials and equipment ordered under lend-lease but undelivered at the war's end. Harriman replied that he was sure his government would wish to divide this new Soviet proposal into two parts, one covering the lend-lease period and the other the postwar period; that at the time it had authority from Congress to deal only with the former; and that its answer to the wartime lend-lease question would be the final terms that had been submitted to the Soviet government at the end of the 3-c negotiations in Washington the previous September.[49]

The State Department and the FEA confirmed Harriman's view that credits designed for the terminal phases of lend-lease should be separated from those exclusively for postwar reconstruction and that the final terms for the former still stood. A month later, in Washington, Soviet Chargé Nikolai Novikov made it unequivocally clear to Acting Secretary Grew that Molotov's January 3 request for a long-term reconstruction credit was meant to cover machinery and equipment with a postwar use ordered under lend-lease, but was specifically not connected with the master Soviet lend-lease agreement of June 11, 1942. This was interpreted by Grew as a final rejection by the Russians of the proposed 3-c Agreement.[50] During the following weeks Novikov's remarks—later confirmed by Ambassador Gromyko—were discussed extensively in the State Department and the FEA and support grew within these organizations for formal withdrawal of the agreement. From Moscow Harriman gave his enthusiastic concurrence to this course of action and at the end of March, following FDR's approval, Grew handed Novikov an aide-memoire stating that the USSR's request of January 3 for a postwar credit had to be considered apart from lend-lease and that the U.S. government considered that its proposals for a 3-c Agreement stated in final form to Vice Commissar Stepanov the previous September "have lapsed and that the negotiations on these specific proposals have come to an end."[51]

Planning for the End of Lend-Lease

Because the provision of lend-lease aid was ultimately a matter of presidential determination, and because there was nothing in the Lend-Lease Act that required that assistance be terminated at the close of hostilities with a common enemy, the 3-c Agreement withdrawal did not mean that lend-lease to Russia would definitely end when the war against Germany ended; but it did terminate one effort designed to provide a firm legal foundation for the uninterrupted flow of supplies at least through the end of the protocol period, and it did eliminate finally any procurement for the USSR of war-related industrial equipment with a postwar use. Thus, as long as Russia was not at war with Japan there was no unassailable legal basis for automatically continuing aid beyond V-E Day. This meant that within the general terms of the Lend-Lease Act any one of several decisions could be supported when the war with Germany ended, including cutting back, terminating, or continuing aid.

Planning for this eventuality began early in 1944 when U.S. military leaders—anxious to husband their resources for the coming battle in Europe following D Day and the long struggle still ahead with Japan, and always chafing at the imposed sharing forced on them by lend-lease—begin to think of reductions and major adjustments in the entire program for the period after V-E Day. In addition there was the scarcely veiled attitude within the Army Air Corps and the Navy that reduction of lend-lease would be a useful method of limiting British participation in the main drive against Japan, which they intended to be mostly an American show.[52] In early May the Joint Chiefs of Staff received approval from Roosevelt for a directive entitled "Policy Concerning Assignments of Lend-Lease Munitions Following the Defeat of Germany." The major principle of this directive read:

> Upon the defeat of Germany assignment of lend-lease munitions will be limited to the materials which are not available to the Allied nations concerned and which are necessary to support that portion of the forces of such nations, as in the opinion of the United States Joint Chiefs of Staff, can and will be profitably employed against Japan in the furtherance of our agreed strategy.[53]

This gave the military the grant of unilateral authority over lend-lease munitions they had long desired and not previously possessed. They understood that this directive would go into effect automatically upon the defeat of Germany, and during the next several months they used it as a guide for future procurement planning. Other agencies learned of these activities and also began planning for the adjustment of their own lend-lease activities. By early August 1944, memoranda were being circulated for comment in the Office of Economic Programs of the FEA administrator spelling out in detail proposed policies for lend-lease reduction upon the cessation of hostilities in Europe.[54]

Word of this planning, especially in the military where it was well advanced in all the services, reached Gen. John York, executive of the Soviet Protocol Committee and the Munitions Assignment Board, and disturbed him greatly. Although an Army officer himself, he felt that these activities represented a usurpation of authority by the military and a threat to the continuation of the board's machinery then in effect. In mid-

August he set forth his views in memoranda to Harry Hopkins and in a draft memorandum he prepared for Hopkins to address to the president. York pointed out the steps that had been taken thus far and indicated that "although not yet formalized for presentation to the JCS, further restrictive policies are being considered." In the draft memorandum for the president he argued that both the trend in thinking and the examples he had cited were in conflict with FDR's long-range policies, and he recommended that Admiral Leahy be asked to remind the chiefs of the armed forces of the following:

   a. It is [the president's] policy to finish out the war in full partnership with the British, and as a true friend and ally of the USSR, China, France, and the smaller nations to whom we have already supplied so much war material.
   b. After Germany's defeat, continued assignments to nations not actively engaged against Japan may be necessary to carry out and to insure retention by the U.S. of its role as the arsenal of democracy.
   c. Assignments shall continue to be made as a combined undertaking and assignment policies and directives shall not be interpreted to impede or prevent this end.[55]

Either by way of these memoranda to Hopkins or through sources that had been in contact with the British (who were becoming aware of the meaning for them of the new JCS policy), Roosevelt came to understand the policy's implications.[56] On September 9, the eve of his departure for OCTAGON (the Second Quebec Conference), Roosevelt wrote a letter to the chiefs of the Army and Navy, the secretaries of State and the Treasury, and the administrators of FEA and the War Shipping Administration stating that he understood there had been a good deal of discussion relative to lend-lease policy after the collapse of Germany. He went on:

It is my wish that no department of the government take unilateral action in regard to any matters that concern Lease Lend, because the implications of any such action are bound to affect other departments of the government and, indeed, our whole national policy. I am particularly anxious that any instructions which may have been issued, or are about to be issued regarding Lease Lend material or supplies to our allies after the collapse of Germany, be immediately cancelled and withdrawn.

Roosevelt stated that he intended to give instructions to all departments on the government's lend-lease policy "at an early date," and he requested that the bureaus and divisions of each addressee's department be advised of his position "at once."[57]

Upon receipt of this letter all directives and plans on lend-lease policy following the defeat of Germany were withdrawn and cancelled and the departments and agencies involved in the program stood by, awaiting the promised instructions. At the end of September FDR sent to the FEA administrator a public letter that set forth the policies the FEA was to put into effect when German military resistance was overcome. Included was a statement on lend-lease, but the recommendations—as was to be expected in such a communication—were very general. The FEA was told to continue lend-lease until the complete defeat of both Japan and Germany, but guidance on aid following the collapse of the latter was limited to the ambiguous observation that it would be "closely tied up with the strategic plans for the Pacific War, and the programs for reconstruction and for reconversion of industry to civilian needs which we and our allies work out on a basis of mutual understanding."[58] This was of little help to military and civilian planners in the executive departments, and in the following weeks they waited for more specific word. But their wait was in vain, for not until two months *after* V-E Day was there a presidential directive dealing with adjustments to be made throughout the lend-lease program following the defeat of Germany. In the meantime important decisions had to be made concerning the future of lend-lease to the two recipients to whom 94 percent of the program's aid had been transferred, the British Empire and the Soviet Union.

The British Program

It was for the British that lend-lease had been conceived, and by the end of the war the United Kingdom, the dominions, and the colonies of the empire had received 75 percent of its assistance. But the British had also spent a great deal of their own resources, and in mid-1944 their economy was in a parlous state. They were in desperate need of housing to replace that damaged by bombing, their industrial plant and public utilities required extensive capital replacement and maintenance, their traditional lifeblood—exports—had declined to 30 percent of prewar levels while foreign obligations had risen astronomically, and, what was most debilitating, their civilian standard of living was in its fifth year of penurious wartime austerity. Under these circumstances not only would Britain have a slow painful postwar recovery, but it would also find it very difficult to play a leading role in the new freer international economic order devoutly hoped for by Hull and his supporters.

In July of 1944, on a visit to Washington, Richard Law, of the British Foreign Office, suggested an extension of lend-lease to ease England's straitened circumstances and give a boost to its export trade. Two months later this matter was urgently raised by Churchill at OCTAGON when he requested lend-lease for the period from the surrender of Germany to the defeat of Japan in an amount sufficient to continue maximum effort against Japan and permit some steps toward restoration of the British economy. Roosevelt, advised by Secretary Morgenthau, who himself had lately been converted to the view that England was indeed "broke," was swayed by the evidence of his ally's plight and initialed with Churchill a memorandum calling for $6.5 billion in Phase II lend-lease for Britain and a relaxation of restrictions that might jeopardize the recovery of England's export trade.[59]

This unilateral innovation in the lend-lease program, quite out of keeping with previous assurances concerning its future, was warmly received by Churchill—with "tears in his eyes" said Morgenthau—but got a cool reception in Washington. Hull was furious that such an unconditional pledge had cast away the "bargaining position" with which he hoped to crack Britain's system of imperial preferences; Stimson and Crowley doubted that such an accord was within the scope of the Lend-Lease Act as understood and approved by the Congress; and the military chiefs held that lend-lease should be only for materials that would actually be used in the conduct of war.[60]

In the months that followed, opposition to the Quebec accord—and the subsequent statements made in support of it—continued and attracted additional supporters. Restive congressmen received new assurances that lend-lease would be used only for military purposes. Military leaders found excuse in the continuing German resistance to delay procurement of Phase II lend-lease for Britain. Finally, Roosevelt himself retreated from the agreement and told FEA head Crowley to administer lend-lease and consider British requests "without regard to the Quebec agreement." Later, in March of 1945, strongly worded telegrams between Roosevelt and Churchill testified to the widening gap between American supply and British need.[61]

Although the British Phase II arrangements were never scrapped and many of their provisions were eventually fulfilled, they were so continuously altered and so affected by the changing military situation that they never did achieve the goals for which they were designed. Beyond this they were an unexpected and tangential diversion from the main direction in which lend-lease appeared to be moving in the summer of 1944. Taken together with FDR's order of September 9 and his ambiguous public letter to Crowley at the end of that month these arrangements created confusion and uncertainty in the terminal phases of the program. In some they stirred hopes that were unwarranted, in others fears that were unfounded. For the British they raised expectations that could not be fulfilled; in the Congress they were seen as evidence of the need for additional legislative shackles; and to the Russians they were one further sign that in the allied partnership there were special relationships not open to all.

The Russian Program

Concerning the Soviet Union, the proposed 3-c Agreement would have permitted the Russians to continue receiving lend-lease supplies after the termination of hostilities in exchange for payment on the basis of a long-term credit. Withdrawal of the agreement ended this opportunity; however, since it did not cover all types of lend-lease to Russia, the question of the status of the program when the European war would end was still left unanswered. In the case of Russia the question was especially delicate because although there had been intimations that the Soviet Union would join the war against Japan, by early 1944 it had not done so and there was no clear indication of when it would. If hostilities with Germany ended and if the Soviet Union were not at war with Japan at the time, what lend-lease aid, if any, should continue to the USSR? This was the problem that officials of the USSR branch of the FEA began wrestling with in the spring of 1944.

In February Harriman had suggested from Moscow that a clause be inserted in the Fourth Protocol stating that lend-lease commitments would be subject to review by the United States upon the cessation of hostilities "with any of our common enemies."[62] Three months later he suggested more specifically that such a clause provide for adjustment in the program in the event of a German collapse.[63] Harriman's suggestion was finally considered at a special meeting in the office of General York, called to consider changes in the wording of the Fourth Protocol that would make it clear that the termination of the war with Germany would call for review and possible revision of the lend-lease program. Several amendments were suggested, but in the end only a slight and inconsequential change in wording was made.[64] There the matter rested until the beginning of August when the combined pressures of planning for lend-lease reduction underway in other departments and what was widely felt to be the imminent collapse of Germany brought renewed consideration of contingency planning for the future of Russian lend-lease.

The impetus in August was supplied mainly by the director of the USSR Branch of the FEA, General Wesson, increasingly the advocate of a "firmer" position toward the Soviet Union. At the eighth meeting of the protocol committee Wesson called attention to the only slightly amended wording of the Fourth Protocol and submitted for consideration at the next meeting of the committee's Subcommittee on Supplies a proposal regarding Russian lend-lease that would anticipate "major changes in the war situation." Wesson's proposal was "a

program of action . . . in the event of slackening of the war on
the Soviet-German front or termination of hostilities." Its
proposed action covered two scenarios. In one (cessation of war
in Europe and no hostilities against a common enemy of the
United States), all lend-lease to Russia would be cut off except
for that covered by the 3-c Agreement or that in ships loaded or
cleared to sail for the USSR. In the second scenario (cessation
of war in Europe but the continuation or the initiation of
hostilities against a common enemy), supply to Russia would
continue in accordance with the terms of the protocol then in
force and the protocol committee would review future
schedules with the aim of revising them so that only those
materials would be sent which "can and will be profitably
employed against a common enemy in furtherance of the
strategy of the United States."[65]

At the end of the meeting of the Subcommittee on Supplies,
which followed a month later, an off-the-record discussion was
conducted by General York on the substance of General
Wesson's proposal. In this discussion York strongly opposed
Wesson's proposal on the grounds, first, that word of it might
reach the Russians, who would misunderstand it, and second,
that such a policy statement would tie the president's hands.
Wesson replied that it was the duty of the committee to have
such a proposal ready for the president when he requested it.
York was unmoved and insisted that the proposal should not be
adopted and that there should be no further discussion of it.
Wesson then concluded the meeting by stating that since the
Army, the Navy, and the Air Force appeared to have already
developed their plans, he intended to proceed on his own—
through Crowley—to obtain such a program for the FEA. This
he did three days later, transmitting to Crowley essentially the
same proposal he had originally submitted to the protocol
committee in August.[66] By this date, however, Crowley had
received FDR's order of September 9 cancelling all instructions
for lend-lease activities following the collapse of Germany; and
so in the FEA, as elsewhere, contingency planning on the
matter stopped.

At the request of Secretary Hull Roosevelt made one
exception to his September 9 directive. Hull asked whether the

negotiations then being conducted for the proposed 3-c Agreement with the USSR should be interrupted, and FDR replied that it was not intended that his directive apply to these talks.[67] By then, however, the final terms for the agreement had already been given to Vice Commissar Stepanov, who had then left for Moscow for consultations, and the American negotiators were waiting in Washington for a reply. In the interim Churchill went to Moscow to confer with Stalin and there received from the Russian leader his firm commitment to enter the war against Japan three months after the German surrender. Two days after Stalin's talk with Churchill, General Deane of the U.S. Military Mission drew up with Kremlin leaders a list of materials to be shipped to the Soviet Far East to supply Russian armies there for combat against the Japanese. This was the list, code-named MILEPOST, which later became the third and final annex to the Fourth Protocol.

With the war in Europe continuing beyond its originally anticipated terminal date of approximately January 1, 1945, and with Russia committed to enter the contest in the Pacific, Roosevelt had once again sent letters similar to those of past years asking the Russians to state their requirements for a Fifth Protocol for the period July 1, 1945, to June 30, 1946, and urging all departments and agencies to make every effort to meet these requirements.[68] But by the beginning of 1945 support for the Soviet aid program was eroding in almost all offices dealing with it. Russia's demands seemed to grow rather than lessen, while the reverse was true with the patience of its representatives. The 3-c Agreement proposal was unanswered, or, in the light of Molotov's January 3 credit request, at least evaded; the Russians refused to notify the United States when they made retransfers of lend-lease materials to third countries; and although the war was not over, few could doubt that its end was in sight. Notwithstanding White House policy, these circumstances began to affect lend-lease to Russia. At the end of December suggestions had been made to do away with the protocol system and thus eliminate the delays that each year had lengthened the preparation of the program.[69] As discussed above, the absence of a reply to the 3-c proposal had already resulted in the exclusion from the Fourth Protocol of industrial equipment to be offered under the terms of the agreement, and at the end of January General Wesson decided to exclude capital equipment entirely from the advance program for the Fifth Protocol.[70] In February an official of the War Shipping Administration informed its San Francisco office that the Russian program was "in a very hazy state" and that it appeared doubtful that the scheduled delivery of three liberty ships would be approved.[71]

In March the 3-c proposal made to the Russians the previous September was in fact formally withdrawn; at the same time cuts were also planned in the Soviet food program.[72] Finally, in early April, USSR Branch Chief Wesson—who had been a strong supporter of both reduction in Russian lend-lease and withdrawal of the 3-c Agreement offer—decided the time had come to put the Soviet aid program on an entirely new footing. The best way to do this, he thought, was via a memorandum jointly signed by the FEA administrator and the secretary of state. In early April he drew up a draft, expanding it two days after FDR's death to include more detail for the new president. Wesson's memorandum, which foreshadowed the cutback policy instituted a month later, contained two major points. First, it proposed a new 3-c agreement under which lend-lease supplies for Russia on hand or on order on the date of a presidential determination that their shipment was no longer necessary for the defense of the United States would be furnished to the USSR "at a fair price and on reasonable credit terms." In addition, similar provision would be made for supplies shipped from the United States during the ninety days preceding such presidential determination. Second, Wesson's memorandum proposed that the Soviet government be informed that if it did not enter such an agreement, "the United States would be obliged to curtail its offer of such supplies on the usual lend-lease terms after June 30, 1945." In other words, there would be no Fifth Protocol.[73]

Opposition to Wesson's memorandum came from several sources, but again most strongly from the executive of the Soviet Protocol Committee, General York. York immediately wrote two urgent memoranda to Harry Hopkins, then convalescing at his Georgetown home. In the first he referred to

Hopkins's position as "Civilian Chairman" of both the Munitions Assignment Board and the protocol committee and expressed his belief that it was "of utmost urgency to avoid creating a situation in which it will be taken for granted that all basic decisions are being made by U.S. Army and Navy officers (myself included), with the Combined Chiefs of Staff as the only court of appeal." In the second memorandum York referred to FDR's "continue the march" order on lend-lease of the previous September and the subsequent withdrawal by the Joint Chiefs of Staff of papers establishing their own unilateral procedures. He told Hopkins that in the last month several communications had been sent to the White House requesting new instructions and he feared that immediate efforts would be made "to obtain some kind of pronouncement from President Truman, probably along restrictive lines." York then concluded that perhaps Hopkins would want to look into the matter and that "certainly any statement affecting Russia or the assignment of munitions should come to you first."[74]

Two days later Wesson received strong support when Harriman arrived in Washington bent on a much tighter policy for Russian lend-lease and anxious to make whatever use he could of its leverage to gain important economic and political concessions. Harriman strongly supported Wesson's proposal to eliminate the Fifth Protocol and he told the Secretary's Staff Committee, "When the war in Europe ends . . . the Soviet Union should have ample production to meet essential needs in many fields, and our shipments should be reduced accordingly."[75] General Deane concurred with Harriman's recommendation regarding the protocol, as did also FEA Administrator Crowley, and at the beginning of the last week in April Wesson on his own initiative asked the War Production Board to review industrial equipment items and raw materials for the USSR to see whether they could be diverted to other programs.[76]

Following Harriman's visit Wesson also wrote a new, stronger draft memorandum for the president, again to be jointly presented by the State Department and the FEA. This called explicitly for the elimination of the protocol and its replacement by a promise "to make offerings to the Soviet government from time to time of the supplies needed . . . to meet the Soviet government's war requirements . . . on the basis of adequate information regarding their essentiality in the prosecution of the war." It also indicated a readiness to discuss with the USSR the conclusion of a new 3-c agreement.[77] Once again York reacted with a memorandum to Hopkins, warning him that Wesson's proposal was "radically different" from what was then in effect.[78] At this point Harriman intervened with the recommendation that the offer of a new 3-c agreement also be dropped. It would be better, Harriman felt, to let the Russians take the first step in the way of making a definite proposal on this matter. Wesson and the FEA agreed, although there were some misgivings in the USSR Branch.[79] Such a major change, however, required considerable redrafting and a new round of consultation and coordination in the departments involved. This activity dragged on through the following week and was continuing into the next when it was stopped short by the event for which it was so determinedly planning—the surrender of Germany.

Status of Lend-Lease Termination Planning on the Eve of V-E Day

On V-E Day there was thus no agreed proposal and no concerted plan for Russian lend-lease at the end of the war with Germany. On the last day of April John Hazard of the USSR Branch had written in one of his regular letters to General Spalding in Moscow that while everyone understood that the end of the war in Europe could not be very far off, there was still no determination of "how much of cargoes available should continue to go forward and how many additional items should be put into production." Hazard concluded: "We are certainly in a difficult position at the moment. . . . I do not know how this is going to be worked out and regret that we have no directive as yet to follow."[80]

This uncertainty in the USSR Branch one week before V-E Day was a reflection of that felt throughout the lend-lease program. In his last budget message President Roosevelt had told the Congress: "Lend-lease has been and will be an instrument of war; it will be liquidated with the end of the war."[81] In the early months of 1945 FEA Administrator Leo Crowley had given increasingly explicit assurances that lend-lease would end with the war and in his last conversation with Roosevelt the president had advised him that at the end of the war they had to be sure to "put lend-lease to bed" otherwise "we would never hear the end of it."[82] Yet, despite these intentions no further instructions had come from the White House after September 1944. Of necessity, piecemeal—and at times even wholesale—adjustments had been made in the following months to meet changing war plans and variations in procurement, supply, and allocation. These had been brought on especially by supply shortages due to the lengthening of the European war beyond its expected termination, and thus they had cut deeply into plans for Phase II, particularly those made with the British.

By mid-March, when it was clear with the crossing of the Rhine that the spring offensive would bring final victory over Germany, comprehensive planning for continuation of the Pacific war had become a matter of urgency and Acting Secretary of War Robert Patterson wrote to Roosevelt asking for guidance. Referring to both FDR's letter of September 9 and his agreements with the British, Patterson requested that the "War Department be authorized to proceed at once with the planning for lend-lease supply during Period I—Phase II for the British—(an eighteen-month period assuming German collapse on July 1, 1945) under such instructions as you may desire to issue."[83] But the press of other matters, and finally death, prevented a definite reply by Roosevelt. On April 17 the new president, Harry Truman, wrote to Secretary Stimson in answer to Patterson's letter, but he laid down no policy. On the advice of War Food Administrator Marvin Jones, he merely told Stimson to proceed in accordance with the suggestions contained in Patterson's letter (which were general and noncommittal) and to take up with the director of War Mobilization and Reconversion, Fred M. Vinson, any problems that might arise in connection with his planning.[84] Stimson eventually did take up with Vinson certain problems he had in future lend-lease planning, but by the time he did it was May

15, a full week after the cessation of hostilities with Germany.

However, in the proposals that had been made and the memoranda that had been exchanged within the USSR Branch—and endorsed by key members of the State Department—the bits and pieces of a policy for the cutback of lend-lease on V-E Day had coalesced. In the minds of those who would implement it, the thrust of that policy seemed quite clear, but because they had worked without clear direction from those who would ultimately be responsible for it, and because the latter—fully occupied by the demands of conducting war in two major theaters—had given little thought as to how their generally expressed preferences would be carried out, the result was an outcome that was neither desired nor desirable.

The same demands of war fighting that had left little time for the problems of lend-lease termination had also taken top-level attention from another matter which by the war's end had become—in purpose and procedure—closely intertwined with lend-lease. This was the question of postwar economic reconstruction for a world whose major powers—all but one—had suffered wounds so severe that the process of unaided self-recovery appeared interminable, if not impossible. The exception was the United States. Undamaged by the war, it alone had sufficient resources to materially spur recovery; but undamaged, it also felt less urgency to do so.

4
Planning for Postwar
Economic Reconstruction

America has gone to war for many reasons, but in each of its major wars economic issues have been at stake and economic goals have been important war aims. Central among these has been the advocacy of free trade, and appended to that advocacy has been the unproven but oft-spoken assumption that in the long run such a policy would benefit the commercial interests of all trading nations. It is probably no exaggeration to say that most Americans have genuinely felt that in economic matters what was best for America was best for the peace and security of the rest of the world. This view was given succinct expression during World War II by President Roosevelt himself when he wrote in a letter published in September 1944: "Any marked improvement in the economic well-being of the United States will not only improve the economic well-being of the other peace-loving peoples of the world, but will also aid materially in the building of a durable peace."[1]

It followed then that during the war top officials in Washington were just as concerned about the postwar international economic order as the postwar international political order, and just as anxious that the United States exercise predominant influence in its design. Typical of this attitude was a memorandum entitled "A Few Concrete Proposals for the Postwar World" sent to Harry Hopkins by Milo Perkins, executive director of the Board of Economic Warfare, one year after the United States had gone to war. In a series of wide-ranging recommendations Perkins urged that the United States use its economic power to build a stable world that would protect the principles it supported. "This nation from its beginning has stood for certain basic ideals," Perkins summed up; "We must work boldly for their worldwide fulfillment and let the chips fall where they may. Anything less than this will be a cowardly betrayal of our inward greatness and the leadership that the present trend of history is thrusting upon us."[2]

More specifically, these views led to the conclusion that any economic arrangements made for the postwar world had to assure as a first condition the development and growth of American industry, a condition that could easily be rationalized by the predominant position the U.S. economy would have in aiding postwar recovery. But in 1944 there was growing concern that this condition might not be achieved. In August 1944, Roosevelt's administrative assistant, James M. Barnes, warned him that the public was worried and confused about reconversion, particularly the possibility of sudden unemployment, and that this would have "a tremendous bearing on the campaign."[3] Three weeks later, another adviser, Lauchlin Currie, former deputy director of the FEA, reported the consensus of a group of government advisers that the defeat of Germany would bring a net decline in national income of $36 billion.[4]

FDR responded to these and similar warnings by repeatedly pledging to the public during his fourth-term campaign a postwar era of full employment at a level of 60 million jobs. His concern over this matter at this time was further indicated when he queried Secretary Hull on the advisability of making a presidential statement asserting that while the United States would not take advantage of any country it would "see that American industry had its fair share of world markets."[5] Hull concurred, but the suggested statement was never used. However, Assistant Secretaries of State Dean Acheson and William Clayton regularly stated in departmental memoranda and congressional testimony that the United States had to increase its production, its foreign trade, and its foreign markets, and that to do so it had also to extend to foreign nations the financial means to buy U.S. products as well as be prepared to purchase their goods once they got back into production.[6]

Thus postwar reconstruction had been a matter of concern since August 1941, when a meeting of top officials in the State Department had drawn up several broad policy recommendations, including among them the proposal that at the end of the war the United States should take an active part in European recovery.[7] But by early 1944—despite the time and effort expended on postwar economic planning—only limited progress had been made on the goal of helping Europe to rebuild. The United Nations Relief and Rehabilitation Administration (UNRRA) had been founded, but it was severely limited, both in purpose and funding, to the immediate task of relief. Movement toward implementing those provisions of the lend-lease Mutual Aid Agreements (especially Article VII, pledging the elimination of discriminatory treatment in international commerce) that might have aided European recovery was stalled. The International Monetary Fund and the International Bank were about to be established, but it was clear that they would be slow in getting under way and, once in operation, would be of only limited use for European reconstruction. Ernest F. Penrose, economic adviser to U.S. Ambassador to England John G. Winant, has written that in the early months of 1944, in appraising postwar preparations, he became convinced that "planning for reconstruction was at once supremely important and seriously deficient." In a long memorandum written for a visiting State Department mission on postwar planning, Penrose pointed out that little provision had been made for the transition period between relief and the application of long-term economic measures and that the subjects discussed under Article VII had concerned policies that could take effect only in the distant future. "One of the most neglected fields," he wrote, "is that of lending for immediate reconstruction purposes after the war," and he urged that "the time has now come when measures for the transition period must be considered on a comprehensive scale without delay."[8]

Reconstruction Assistance Through Lend-Lease

In Washington, similar apprehensions had led from time to time to the consideration of using lend-lease as a device for immediate postwar reconstruction. In June of 1942, Oscar Cox, the principal author of the original lend-lease bill, proposed amending the act by substituting the words "war, relief, or reconstruction articles" in place of the term "defense article." Six months later he drew up for Harry Hopkins a more comprehensive proposal to meet the same general goal, involving public speeches by the president and other top administration figures, amendments for the Lend-Lease Act renewal, and discussions with key congressional committee chairmen and minority members. In January 1943, the gist of Cox's ideas received the public support of his close friend, the influential Washington columnist Walter Lippmann, and two months later Ambassador Winant also suggested to Hull that the lend-lease machinery might play a role in reconstruction.[9]

From other quarters, however, there was vigorous opposition to such proposals. The strongest expressions of these feelings came, as described earlier, from members of the Congress. Lend-Lease Administrator Stettinius and other officials in the program were closely questioned in committee hearings by legislators who sought assurances that lend-lease was being used strictly to prosecute the war. Speakers in floor debate in both houses warned repeatedly against the use of lend-lease for reconstruction, and some members even went into public print to utter scarcely veiled threats against misuse of the program.[10] Influential journals and certain business and trade organs also featured articles pointing out the deleterious consequences to world trade and other commercial activities of "permanent" lend-lease arrangements.[11] Finally, opinion polls insisting that lend-lease be somehow repaid implied that there was little incipient public support for a continuation of the program for the purpose of postwar reconstruction.[12]

It is difficult to state with absolute certainty what President Roosevelt's opinion was on this matter. The evidence indicates that from 1942 to early 1944 he moved toward a narrower construction of the Lend-Lease Act emphasizing that it was purely for wartime purposes. In early 1942 he apparently toyed briefly with a scheme for a special postwar fund under international trusteeship that could be used for capital construction and would embody the "common pool" approach used in lend-lease.[13] However, there is no record of any further development of this idea and it probably represented simply an early version of what eventually became the Treasury Department's plan for the International Bank. A year and a half later, in discussing with Stettinius the relationship of UNRRA to lend-lease, FDR stated that UNRRA should take over the role of relief and that lend-lease aid should not continue after hostilities. But he admitted that he did not know just what his authority was under the Lend-lease Act for the postwar period. Stettinius confessed to the same uncertainty, but ventured the opinion that the use of lend-lease funds to any large extent after hostilities would cause difficulty in the Congress.[14]

The matter of using lend-lease for postwar reconstruction finally came to a head in the early months of 1944, when consideration of various schemes for postwar recovery intensified and decisions had to be made about the interpretation of Section 3-c for materials with a useful postwar life— particularly those materials being sent to the USSR. A memorandum had circulated in the State Department in early February suggesting that the lend-lease protocol to Russia then being discussed should include supplies meant for reconstruction up to an amount of $1 billion.[15] Roosevelt apparently felt that activities of this kind could not be subsumed under the Lend-Lease Act, and even though he retreated from this position later in the fall, when he briefly acquiesced to a scheme that would have given Britain lend-lease for essentially reconstruction purposes, he told Stettinius in February that he did not wish lend-lease to be used for anything having a postwar flavor. "The line must be drawn very clearly," he added, "so that lend-lease funds are used only if the item concerned has a reasonable relationship to the war."[16]

Reconstruction Assistance Through Loans

This expression of presidential opinion apparently helped spur renewed consideration of other means of financing postwar reconstruction. By the end of February 1944, the general consensus of those dealing with the problem in the State Department was that reconstruction financing for the immediate postwar period should be undertaken in the form of loans with the expectation of full repayment rather than by grants or partial grants.[17] It was also felt that the most suitable vehicle to make such loans was the Export-Import Bank of Washington. The Export-Import Bank was originally chartered in 1934 as a District of Columbia banking corporation to finance trade with the newly recognized government of the Soviet Union. However, when difficulties arose over the settlement of debts of the prior Russian regime to the United States government and its citizens, the bank decided not to enter into any transactions with the USSR. A second Export-Import Bank was chartered to finance Russian trade and when the Soviet debt negotiations broke down in early 1935 this second bank was dissolved and its assets were transferred to the first bank, which continued in operation on the basis of regular extensions of its charter by the Congress. During the following decade the Export-Import Bank made a variety of well-secured long-term loans, mostly to cover the export of heavy equipment such as electric power plants, machinery, locomotives, cars, and similar items. The criteria for such loans, as the bank's president, Warren Lee Pierson, explained in Senate hearings in 1944, was that they aid the sale of U.S. merchandise and help American relations with the countries involved.[18]

In early 1944 there were three factors that inhibited the possible use of the Export-Import Bank for reconstruction financing. First, the Johnson Act of 1934 prohibited loans to foreign governments who were in default in payments of obligations to the government of the United States. Attorney General Homer Cummings had specifically ruled that this prohibition applied to the Soviet Union even while it might be negotiating its indebtedness, and the bank had issued a statement that it would extend no credits to the Soviet government until its obligations to the U.S. government and American citizens had been satisfactorily adjusted;[19] second, the lending authority of the bank was limited to $700 million, clearly insufficient for the huge task of reconstruction that lay ahead; and third, legislation limited the life of the bank to 1947.

State Department experts therefore recommended that the default provisions of the Johnson Act be eliminated and that the lending power and the life of the Export-Import Bank be extended. In May 1944, these proposals were taken before the Executive Committee on Economic Foreign Policy (ECEFP), a new interdepartmental committee formed in April 1944, to make recommendations to the president and the secretary of state concerning problems and developments affecting the long-range economic foreign policy of the United States. The ECEFP concluded that it should be the policy of the United States "to engage in a properly conceived program of foreign investment to aid in financing the reconstruction of war-torn areas and for related purposes including facilitating the export generally of capital goods from the United States" and that "in general reconstruction financing should take the form of loans with expectation of eventual full repayment." The committee went on to recommend "immediate congressional action" to increase the lending powers of the Export-Import Bank "by one billion dollars or so" and to repeal the Johnson Act. These recommendations were promptly sent by the secretary of state to the president, and on June 6, 1944, D Day, Roosevelt noted on Hull's memo, "C.H. O.K. F.D.R."[20]

At this point further action on this measure simply stopped. Perhaps the fear of stirring latent opposition to foreign lending during the coming electoral campaign caused Roosevelt to shelve the matter (though there is no direct evidence to support such a contention); perhaps the administration's attention was diverted by more pressing matters, such as the Allied invasion of Europe and the coming International Monetary Conference at Bretton Woods. More likely it was simply that the matter had a low priority in the swollen wartime bureaucracy that in 1944 was a tangle of overlapping and uncertain jurisdictions, poorly structured to deal with postwar measures. At any rate, for whatever reasons, fourteen months passed and the German surrender occurred before the "immediate" action recommended by the ECEFP finally became law.

Assistance Specifically for the USSR

For one country, the most devastated of the Allied powers, reconstruction had beome a priority interest, an interest second

only to the defeat of Germany itself. As the Wehrmacht had
rolled across Soviet soil in the early months of the war and the
Russian people had scorched the earth in its path, it had been
clear that the toll of destruction in the USSR would be very
great and the cost of recovery very high. Almost from the first
days of the German attack the Russians had thus shown a keen
interest in discussing postwar relief and reconstruction with
their allies. In September 1941 Soviet representatives had
attended an inter-Allied council meeting in London, which
had as one of its purposes the laying of the foundations for
postwar relief and reconstruction. During the winter of 1941-
1942 the Russians had been particularly active in pressing their
own plans for an organization for postwar relief. Later, in 1943,
Soviet representatives participated in the lengthy negotiations
that culminated in the establishment of UNRRA.

It was clear, however, as UNRRA evolved, that its purpose
would be limited to immediate relief, and even were it to aid the
Soviet Union—which was not certain at the time of its
ounding—it would make little contribution to the USSR's
massive need for reconstruction assistance. The Russians
would require more than emergency food and clothing after the
war. They would need the machines and equipment to rebuild,
and the most likely source would be the war-swollen industrial
plant of the United States. Secretary of State Hull and the
architects of the Master Lend-Lease Agreement understood
this, expected increased postwar trade with the USSR, and
hoped to use Article VII of the agreement as a means to guide
that trade along lines they favored. Roosevelt agreed, and
though some suggested that loans of any kind to Russia might
make the Soviet Union dangerously powerful after the war, the
president dismissed such arguments as emanating from "the
Cliveden set of Washington."[21]

However, for the first eighteen months of the war attention
was focused primarily on the supply of materials to fight it, and
very little consideration was given to postwar reconstruction
aid for the USSR. Only in mid-1943, when growing Allied
strength had finally begun to push back the Germans, was the
subject again brought to Roosevelt's attention, this time in a
long candid letter from his lend-lease representative in

London, Averell Harriman. The main subject of the letter was FDR's proposal for a Big Three conference that fall, but in closing Harriman also indicated his willingness to accept the post of ambassador to Moscow offered to him a short time before by Roosevelt and expressed some of his own feelings about relations with Russia. Since Harriman's views were to become very influential in shaping Soviet-American relations, his opinion on reconstruction aid to Russia is worth noting in full. Harriman wrote the president on July 5, 1943:

> As you know, I am a confirmed optimist in our relations with Russia because of my conviction that Stalin wants, if obtainable, a firm understanding with you and America more than anything else—after the destruction of Hitler. He sees Russia's reconstruction and security more soundly based on it than on any alternative. He is a man of simple purposes and, although he may use devious means in attempting to accomplish them, he does not deviate from his long run objectives.[22]

A few months later, shortly before Harriman did in fact replace Admiral Standley as ambassador to Moscow, top Russian leaders had a chance to meet the first of several high-level American visitors who came to talk about postwar Soviet-American trade. Donald Nelson, a prominent business executive who at the time was being eased out of his position as chairman of the War Production Board, arrived in Russia in mid-October 1943, on an official visit sanctioned by the president. He received everywhere the most hospitable and cooperative treatment, and during his visit he had long interviews with Molotov and Stalin in which the subject of U.S. assistance for Soviet reconstruction received more attention than it had in any other conversations to date.

Both Kremlin leaders asked Nelson if he thought Russia could count on receiving machine tools and capital equipment from the United States after the war. Stalin even set forth a brief list of railroad and hydroelectric equipment that he said represented an initial order. Nelson replied that after the war the United States would have surplus equipment and could easily supply the USSR what it would need to rehabilitate the country and its industry, and that, furthermore, orders for such equipment would help in solving America's postwar unemployment problems. When Stalin asked whether the Soviet Union could buy on credit from the United States, Nelson replied that he personally favored an arrangement whereby Russia would make small payments during the early postwar years, when its rehabilitation needs would be great, and increasingly larger payments thereafter. According to the memorandum of the conversation, "Marshall Stalin appeared to be greatly interested in this idea and in obtaining United States goods on credit."[23]

Close on the heels of Nelson came the American delegation to the Moscow Foreign Ministers Conference led by the secretary of state and including the new ambassador, Harriman, and the new Military Mission headed by General Deane. Secretary Hull had come to the Soviet capital with high hopes of gaining Russian participation in his plans for freer postwar world trade. Part of the inducement for this participation, he hoped, would be the promise of U.S. assistance for postwar reconstruction. In fact, he had earlier indicated to Anthony Eden that Soviet failure to cooperate in joint economic efforts would make it difficult "to prevail on the American people to continue to furnish supplies to Russia."[24] Conference agenda item 15, proposed by the United States and entitled "Economic Matters for Reconstruction," thus included both cooperation in rehabilitation of war damage in the USSR and collaboration on an international basis in dealing with a variety of matters including finance and trade. Supporting documents suggested a readiness on the part of the United States to play "a substantial part" in reconstructing the USSR and set forth in elaborate detail Hull's proposals for international economic cooperation.[25]

However, the Russians through 1943 had stood a wary distance from American efforts to involve them in conversations concerning postwar financial and trade arrangements. They had expressed interest in Secretary Morgenthau's proposal for an international stabilization fund, but despite his earnest requests they had not sent representatives to discuss postwar monetary problems. They had also made no reply to an invitation a month before the Moscow Conference to discuss the principles embodied in Article VII of the Master Lend-Lease Agreement. In the face of Soviet reluctance to explore these matters further Secretary Hull had to content himself at Moscow with the simple inclusion of his memorandum on international economic cooperation as an annex to the conference protocol. On the question of assistance in the rehabilitation of war damage in the USSR the conferees were more successful and agreed that "It was considered desirable to start conversations between the People's Commissariat for Foreign Affairs and the United States Embassy in Moscow."[26]

In accordance with this decision Ambassador Harriman raised with the Russians shortly after the conference the question of Soviet needs for postwar reconstruction. In a long conversation with Foreign Trade Commissar Mikoyan in November he explained that the legal status of lend-lease restricted it to the supply of equipment obviously related to the conduct of the war and only for the war's duration. Harriman then pointed out that "while he knew the president and the lend-lease officials in Washington were disposed to give a reasonably broad interpretation to this aspect of the act, it was nonetheless in the interests of both countries to keep within the meaning of the act." He further told Mikoyan that lend-lease would become "an important political question" in the 1944 elections and that the support of both political parties would depend on an honest and clear presentation of the work of lend-lease. Turning to the question of postwar reconstruction, Harriman stated that the American people were desirous of assisting Russia and that it might be possible to begin discussing the question of future credits and financial assistance for that purpose. Not only were Americans sympathetic to the plight of those ravaged by war, Harriman added, but their own self-interest would be aided by full employment during the period of transition from wartime to peacetime economy. Mikoyan welcomed these views and emphasized the Soviet preference for American over European goods because of the former's quality and standardization; but he also added shrewdly that the conditions of the credit terms would necessarily affect Soviet orders and that in any event he expected that prices would go down. Harriman closed the interview by reiterating his willingness to discuss at Mikoyan's convenience any matters relating to postwar reconstruction in the Soviet Union.[27]

During the next few weeks Harriman exchanged views several times with the State Department on the question of postwar aid to Russia, and in these messages he began to sound a theme that he was to repeat with growing insistence throughout his tour as ambassador. Shortly after his talk with Mikoyan he cabled, "we must not lose sight also of the fact that this subject [credits for postwar reconstruction] is of great importance in our overall relations with the Soviet government," and a few days later, in urging that negotiations on this matter be handled by him in Moscow and not by a new independent group in Washington, he added: "I am not sure I have made it clear that this question of reconstruction is considered by the Soviet government as, next to the war, the most important political as well as economic problem that confronts them. Our participation in reconstruction is an important and integral part of our diplomatic dealings with them."[28]

Within two weeks the Big Three met at Tehran and Roosevelt had his first opportunity to talk directly with Stalin about the reconstruction aid that Harriman felt weighed so heavily in the scales of Soviet-American relations. The matter of economic loans was on at least one agenda, but aside from a suggestion by Roosevelt that part of the American-British merchant fleet could be transferred to Russia after the war and Stalin's response that a plentiful supply of raw materials could be made available to the United States in exchange for equipment sent, the question of postwar aid was not discussed.[29] At the end of the conference, FDR wrote to Harriman: "I am sorry I did not get time to talk with the Russians about the whole question of reconstruction in Russia. I wish you would find out what the Russians think their requirements will be and what ideas they have in regard to it. I should like very much to have your recommendations regarding this matter."[30]

Meanwhile, in Washington a difference of opinion was

developing on the question of the possibility of large postwar trade with Russia and hence the viability of extending credits and by implication the importance of such credits in overall Soviet-American relations. On the one hand, strong proponents of assistance to Russia were predicting a greatly expanded postwar trade. Deputy FEA Administrator Lauchlin Currie wrote to Harry Hopkins on the last day of 1943 that "If a system of security removes mistrust and fear, the United States should be able to send a billion dollars worth of exports yearly to the USSR in the first five years of peace."[31] Hopkins himself was only a little less optimistic. "From what the [Russian representatives in the United States] told me," he wrote in the January 1944 issue of *American Magazine*, "I estimate that in the first year they will want to buy as much as $750,000,000 worth of goods from us. . . . They will have need to buy almost as much from us every year for the next ten years, perhaps longer."[32]

But there were others who were far less sanguine about the prospects for a big postwar business with Russia. One such skeptic was Elbridge Durbrow of the Division of European Affairs of the State Department. Durbrow was not optimistic about future Soviet-American relations and he grew even less so as victory in Europe drew nearer. At the end of November 1943, Durbrow wrote a memorandum that acknowledged that the interest of the United States would be served politically and economically by assisting Soviet reconstruction but also pointed out that it would be most difficult to increase trade with the Soviet Union because there were so few goods produced in Russia that the United States could buy in order to give the Soviet Union the necessary purchasing power to acquire large quantities of American products. He pointed out further that the Interdepartmental Committee on Commercial Relations with the Soviet Union had concluded that the United States could not increase its purchases from the USSR by more than six or seven times the average annual prewar amount of $25 million, and that the amount of reconstruction credits the Soviet Union could repay in a reasonable time (ten to twenty years) could not exceed $200 million. Durbrow concluded: "It will be seen therefore that extreme caution must be taken in order to avoid false impressions being created regarding the possibilities of postwar trade with the Soviet Union.''[33]

But in Moscow there was no mood of extreme caution as Harriman plunged vigorously into the task of fulfilling FDR's request to discover the Russians' requirements for reconstruction. In early January of 1944 he telegraphed to Harry Hopkins a report of a conversation he had just held with Foreign Commissar Molotov during which—at the latter's request— Harriman had discoursed at length on the question of U.S. participation in Soviet reconstruction. Molotov, he reported, had shown "the keenest interest" in the possibility of the extension of a credit for the purchase of equipment and supplies. Harriman saw this as an approach that would enable the United States to get its "proper share of Soviet postwar business" and also ease unemployment dislocation during the cutting back of war production. He asked Hopkins to advise him specifically whether this approach had Washington's approval and about the size and general terms of a credit and the agency that could extend it. A few days later, in two shorter messages to the State Department, Harriman repeated the points he had made to Hopkins, suggested terms for an initial credit of $500 million, and added, "As the Soviet government places the utmost importance on our cooperation in this field, it is a factor which should be integrated into the fabric of our overall relations rather than dealt with independently in its purely commercial and economic aspects." He concluded by urging prompt action and requesting authorization to negotiate the matter himself in Moscow.[34]

However, Washington was not moved by the same urgency and determination that fired Harriman. Hopkins was confined to a hospital bed, seriously ill and absent from deliberations on high policy. In the Foreign Economic Administration Oscar Cox was busily promoting his plan to use Section 3-c of the Lend-Lease Act to give the Russians a head start on reconstruction by enabling them to order lend-lease equipment with a postwar use. In the State Department uncertainty prevailed. Policy on loans, reconstruction, Russia, and the future of lend-lease for the postwar period was largely unformed, and the mood was one of hesitancy and caution.

Secretary Hull replied five days after Harriman's last message that the department was in substantial agreement with the considerations he had raised, but that the subject had to be "carefully and thoroughly studied by many officials of the Government" before he could be issued any definite instructions.[35] In the following weeks Harriman was informed of the 3-c Agreement proposal being prepared for the Russians, advised to delay any attempts to reach understanding with the USSR regarding reconstruction credits alone, and, in a message specifically approved by Roosevelt, told to make clear to the Russians that the United States was desirous of assisting them but could not at the time "indicate either the amount or the exact nature" of any long-term financial arrangements.[36]

To these messages Harriman responded quickly and vigorously. In a cable to Hopkins early in February he urged reconsideration of several points with which he was not in full agreement. In particular, he asserted his belief that it was in the interest of the United States to begin to work "at once" with the Russians on their reconstruction program as a whole, and he again rehearsed his arguments concerning the importance of this program for American business during the period of postwar reconversion. Four days later he cabled Hopkins again, and in the strongest language he had used to date he reargued the political merits of aiding the USSR. "If aid for Russian reconstruction," Harriman wrote, "is to be of real value in our overall relations with the Soviet Government as a benefit which they can obtain from us if they play the international game with us in accordance with our standards we must have a well forged instrument to offer them." Harriman set forth the hypothesis that Stalin had to offer his people quick reconstruction to retain supreme leadership, reminded Hopkins again of the importance of Russian business to U.S. manufacturers, and urged that "the subject be energetically pursued in the hope of finding a solution permitting prompt action." A day later he cabled essentially the same message to the State Department.[37]

Shortly after Harriman wrote, the matter was moved off dead center when, as previously discussed, the decision was made to seek legislation repealing the default provisions of the Johnson

Act and increasing the lending power of the Export-Import Bank. Early in March 1944 Harriman was duly informed of this development and of Roosevelt's approval of the offer of a supplementary 3-c Agreement to the Russians.[38] In talks with Soviet Foreign Trade Commissar Anastas Mikoyan in March and April, Harriman discussed these matters further and added his own personal hope that authority would soon be obtained for the bank to negotiate with the Soviet Union on postwar credits "in order that there be no inactive interval after the termination of the war."[39] At this point, pending development of the necessary legislation, further discussion of postwar reconstruction was suspended and attention focused on the 3-c Agreement negotiations being conducted in Washington.

Postwar Aid as Leverage

While Harriman had been exchanging views with Mikoyan and Molotov in Moscow in early 1944 and communicating with Washington, growing interest was being expressed in the U.S. capital about the possibility of using America's economic power for political leverage vis-à-vis the Soviet Union. As far back as 1933, when the United States was contemplating recognition of the USSR, Secretary Hull had expressed the opinion to Roosevelt that credits were "one of our most effective weapons . . . possibly the most effective" in dealing with the Soviet Union.[40] That Roosevelt and Hull were not averse to using economic pressures to achieve objectives in non-enemy states was further seen by their use of such means in relations with Vichy France and Spain in 1940. Later, as previously mentioned, Roosevelt had approved of the use of similar pressure against Portugal. In addition, Hull continued throughout his tenure as secretary to rest his hopes of obtaining acquiescence to his plans for freer world trade on U.S. promises of generous postwar assistance. Others in the State Department strongly believed in the leverage of American aid, a view to which Harriman gave his enthusiastic endorsement.

To suggest the possibility of using economic leverage was only part of the matter, however; it was also necessary to determine how much assistance Russia would need and how much the United States would provide. If postwar business with Russia turned out to be small then there would be little leverage. In the spring of 1944 the tempo of discussion on these matters picked up. In a book published early in that year the recently resigned undersecretary of state, Sumner Wells, wrote: "The needs of Russia in the immediate postwar period for credits, for expert services, and for machinery and equipment of many kinds will be great. At the same time, the commercial opportunities which such a situation will offer to American enterprise and to American export trade are almost unlimited."[41] Similar prophecies of "vast new markets" in Russia were also made by Foreign Economic Administrator Crowley in February, and by April several large U.S. firms, including Dupont, Westinghouse, and General Electric, were in various stages of contract negotiations with the Soviet trading agency, Amtorg.[42]

The volume of postwar business being discussed by these firms was small, nothing near the total of $1 billion annually that Currie had mentioned to Hopkins and that appeared from time to time in news stories. In Washington the one committee that had most to do with estimating the future growth of this trade, the Interdepartmental Subcommittee on the Soviet Union of the Committee on Trade Agreements, saw little prospect that it would become a great deal larger. In April 1944, it issued a report entitled "Aspects of Post-War Soviet Trade" in which it estimated possible U.S. exports to the USSR during the postwar decade. Based on studies of the postwar export potential of the USSR, and U.S. postwar commodity imports, the subcommittee concluded that the annual average of American imports from the USSR during the postwar decade would range from $30 to $70 million depending on the national income of the United States. Soviet imports from the United States would range from $100 to $200 million, the balance over its exports being covered by multilateral payments. If the United States were to grant large credits, the subcommittee concluded, these would have to be offset by amortization and interest requirements in later years and might thus impose a heavy burden on the Soviet balance of payments at that time.[43]

With such a variety of hopes, estimates, and uncertainties

swirling about, it was obviously difficult to develop policy, advise Ambassador Harriman, and plan for negotiations with the Soviet Union on assistance for postwar reconstruction. At the end of May, in an effort to obtain additional expert opinion to guide the State Department in these matters, Assistant Secretary Dean Acheson wrote to Dr. William L. Langer, chief of the Research and Analysis Branch of the Office of Strategic Services (OSS), requesting a study of Russian reconstruction and postwar developments. Specifically, Acheson asked for the OSS's opinion of Russia's capacity to use and service foreign loans, the character and volume of Soviet postwar trade, and the types of goods that the USSR might seek as reparations from Germany.[44]

Status of Postwar Aid at the End of 1944

On a visit to Washington during May, and in several messages from Moscow during the following months, Harriman continued to urge speedy action to increase the lending power of the Export-Import Bank and repeal the default provisions of the Johnson Act. However, no action was taken on these matters and, as the warm summer of 1944 gave way to fall, a distinct chill crept into Soviet-American relations. The 3-c Agreement negotiations had dragged on inconclusively and by mid-September had reached an impasse; the hopeful "shuttle bombing" operation—involving for the first time the stationing of American bomber crews on Soviet soil—was collapsing in a crossfire of countercharges and recriminations; and on the east bank of the Vistula River the Red Army had halted for sixty days while a brave but futile uprising of the Polish underground ignited, sputtered, and was snuffed out in the rubble of Warsaw. These and other events, some minor and others potentially more ominous, made the spirit of Moscow and Tehran of a year before a fast fading memory in the minds of many. From Moscow in early September Harriman wrote of the "more than unusually uncooperative" attitude of the Soviet government, and in long messages to Hopkins and Hull in the next two weeks he spelled out his growing apprehension concerning Soviet policy. To Hopkins he cabled, "Our relations with the Soviets have taken a startling turn evident during the last two months. They have held up our requests with complete indifference to our interests and have shown an unwillingness even to discuss pressing problems." For the time being Harriman proposed no "drastic action," only "a firm but friendly quid pro quo attitude," but he did request urgently to report these developments and his recommendations personally to the president. Ten days later, in response to a request from Secretary Hull, Harriman presented an even more detailed assessment. He enumerated a number of problems, especially regarding Soviet action in Eastern Europe, explained what he thought was the source of recent Soviet policy moves, and advised that "when it comes to matters of greater importance, we should make it plain that their failure to conform to our concepts will affect our willingness to cooperate with them, for example, in material assistance for reconstruction."[45] Strongly supporting the general thrust of Harriman's position—though with important differences on certain specific points—was the newly arrived counselor of embassy, George F. Kennan.

In the midst of this growing concern over the future direction of Soviet policy, the Research and Analysis Branch of the OSS gave to the State Department its long-awaited classified study on "Russian Reconstruction and Postwar Foreign Trade Developments." This report, dated September 9, estimated that as a result of the war Russia had lost $16 billion or 25 percent of its fixed capital (based on pre-1939 borders) and perhaps an additional $4 billion in inventory losses. It further reckoned that without foreign loans or reparations Russia should be able to reconstruct its economy in about three years after the cessation of hostilities, and that with $1.5 billion in foreign credits annually for three years, or with an equivalent amount of foreign reparations, it could accelerate that reconstruction by only a few months. Ultimately, however, the OSS study stated, the pace of reconstruction would depend on the level of military preparedness maintained—a high-level slowing down of the total reconstruction effort. Two "political implications" emerged from the analysis, concluded its authors: (1) economic credits offered a bargaining tool of only limited value since "success of Russian reconstruction will depend only to a very limited extent on foreign loans," and (2) in Russia's economic plans military expenditures constituted the largest and most important flexible element. A reduction in the size of the armed forces would speed reconstruction, the maintenance of a large number of men under arms would retard it.[46]

Although Ambassador Harriman earlier had been assigned the responsibility for discussing credits for purely reconstruction purposes, he was not informed of the conclusions of the OSS study until three and a half months later, at the end of January 1945. In Washington, however, word of the study circulated among those concerned with lend-lease and postwar reconstruction and provoked considerable discussion. Some disagreed with the study's findings; others felt that the study's analysis was consistent with theirs, but that the OSS had drawn the wrong conclusions from it. It was pointed out, for example, that it did follow from the study's analysis that under certain conditions it would be possible for the Soviet government to repay loans approximating $4.5 billion over a period of fifteen years at 2 percent interest.[47] The question, of course, was whether the USSR would estimate that on balance such loans were necessary and were in its best interest. No one knew for sure, but at the end of October 1944, Soviet Ambassador Andrei Gromyko gave an indication of continuing Soviet interest when he concluded a note to the secretary of state dealing mainly with the Fourth Lend-Lease Protocol by stating that the Soviet government had the intention of offering in the near future its own proposal on the question of long-term credits.[48]

Gromyko's note could have been considered indicative of a forthcoming initiative in the deadlocked 3-c Agreement negotiations, or of a proposal for reconstruction credits, or of both. While Washington waited, intensely preoccupied with FDR's bid for a fourth term, the armies of the Allies pushed across Europe hastening a day of decision devoutly wished for by all but adequately prepared for by few. At the end of December the State Department's weekly "Digest of Problems Before the Department" carried, as it had for weeks before, the item, "Soviet Union: Lend-Lease and Postwar Financing—Fourth Lend-Lease Protocol and the question of postwar financing of assistance to the Soviet Union remain unsettled."[49]

5

Cutback and Termination
of Lend-Lease to Russia

Policy for the ending of lend-lease was formed and carried out during that "melancholy void" when, as Churchill later described it, "one president could not act and the other could not know." Preoccupied as he was with concluding the war and attending to the increasingly contentious problems of the postwar settlement, Roosevelt paid less and less attention to his unique aid program and provided only vague direction for its administration. Truman was equally preoccupied, not only with the problems that had concerned his predecessor, but also with the overwhelming task of taking over an office for which he had no preparation and little experience at a time when the burdens on that office were probably as great as they had ever been in the history of the nation. Thus, it fell more and more to his subordinates to exercise initiative in the formation and implementation of public policy. This they did, guided by their own experiences and preferences but attentive also to whatever signals might come from their new chief; and some did come, for although Truman lacked the information and experience that had guided FDR, he was a man with distinct opinions of his own on both the substance and handling of public policy. This amalgam of presidential inexperience and opinion, and subordinate initiative and reaction, provided a perspective on Soviet-American relations quite different from that which had prevailed in the Roosevelt presidency and set a distinctive context for the execution of policy concerning the cutback and termination of lend-lease.

The Changing Context of Soviet-American Relations

The legacy of policy toward the USSR left to his successor by FDR on April 12, 1945, was a patchwork pattern of commitments, half-commitments, and postponed decisions whose final design had never been indicated by its creator. At times FDR was anxious to meet Soviet desires—at least half-way—for he believed this was necessary not only to preserve the wartime coalition but also to maintain the big power unity he considered so essential for keeping the peace. But he also realized that some commitments would create dissension and could fracture the tenuous wartime alliance, and these he either made in ambiguous terms or simply postponed. Furthermore, he was keenly aware of the domestic political constraints that inhibited him in such endeavors. The Congress, ever watchful of its prerogatives to approve treaties and appropriate monies, would hardly take kindly to any deals made secretly, or even openly, by the executive; the military, who might be required by postwar commitments to garrison indefinitely certain territories, would resist such plans; and the public, long sensitized by rhetoric oppugning power politics, and a force in any event to be treated carefully—especially in the months preceding the 1944 election—would react hostilely to either wartime bargains or new obligations. In addition, one of the strongest themes of the Wilsonian internationalists was the postponement of disputes pending the establishment of the world organization that would be called upon to settle them; it was convenient then, when other alternatives proved too difficult to pursue, to fall back on postponement. Finally, Roosevelt was haunted by the spectre of the secret deals of World War I. Wilson had enveighed against them, only to be later entangled by them, and Roosevelt strove mightily to avoid the same fate.

During the war FDR had no master plan, no precise blueprint for the future. As always, he was essentially an improviser. Confident in his personal charm and his ability as a negotiator, he proceeded step by step, crossing each bridge as he came to it, sustained to the end by the simple faith that the direction of his travel was toward the goals he sought. Nowhere is this confidence and faith better seen than in Roosevelt's last diplomatic message, closing yet another troubling incident in what had become a spring of increasingly troubled Soviet-American relations. In March 1945, in the midst of growing difficulties over the future regimes of Eastern Europe, the formation of a Polish government, and the treatment of liberated American prisoners of war, the clumsy handling of a German offer made in Berne, Switzerland, for surrender in northern Italy gave new offense to fragile Russian sensibilities. Charges and countercharges were exchanged until finally the matter became a subject of communication between Roosevelt and Stalin.

In a message sent on March 24 FDR explained the entire matter in detail and assured the Soviet leader that in any purely military surrender there would be "no political implications whatever and no violation of our agreed principle of unconditional surrender." Stalin, however, was neither convinced nor reassured, and in ensuing messages between the two leaders charges of bad faith escalated to the point of Stalin's accusation, in a message of April 3, that an agreement had already been signed with the Germans and that as a result war had ceased on the Western front while it was continuing against Russia. In a very sharp reply Roosevelt stated his "astonishment" over Stalin's accusation, explained why Allied forces on the Western front had been able to move so rapidly and concluded by expressing "a feeling of bitter resentment" toward Stalin's informers for their "vile misrepresentations" of his actions and those of his subordinates. Stalin's reply four days later, while not apologetic, was restrained and conciliatory in tone, and with the discontinuation of the contacts in Switzerland for the time being the dispute abated. On April 11, FDR thanked Stalin for his last message on the matter and stated that "There must not, in any event, be mutual distrust, and minor misunderstandings of this character should not arise in the future." In Moscow, Harriman delayed transmission of this message and suggested to Roosevelt that he drop the word "minor" as it seemed to him to be a misunderstanding of "major character." FDR's reply, his last cable—dispatched from the communication center at Warm Springs, Georgia, ten minutes before his fatal stroke—was pointedly clear: "I do not wish to delete the word 'minor' as it is my desire to consider the Berne misunderstanding a minor incident."[1]

For Roosevelt, in whom hope did spring eternal, periodically refreshed by the sunshine and close friendships of Warm Springs, it *was* a "minor" incident, one of a growing number in that difficult season before final victory, but one which the preservation of the alliance required to be managed and overcome. But for Harriman, sensitive to Russian needs but also sensitized by numerous rebuffs at the hands of his hosts, the Berne incident was a "major" misunderstanding and its gravity in the scales of Soviet-American relations should not have been weakened in Russian eyes. In retrospect, it seems hard to believe that even Roosevelt's enormous capacity to accommodate diversity, to orchestrate competition, and to mediate conflict could have forestalled the worst excesses of the Cold War. It is idle to speculate, yet it is clear that in the last hours of his life he had lost neither confidence nor hope. FDR was a realist and an idealist at the same time; with him there was always a gap between what he thought would happen and what he hoped would happen. That he always strove—and often succeeded—in bridging that gap was a measure of his greatness; that he failed at times to recognize that the gap was unbridgeable was a measure of his weakness.

Harry S. Truman was a very different man; but in the transition to his presidency there was continuity as well as change, and an understanding of both is necessary to comprehend the context of Soviet-American relations in the weeks preceding the fall of Germany. In 1934 Harry Truman had made strong support for Franklin D. Roosevelt the basic theme of his first campaign for the U.S. Senate, and for ten years in that body he loyally and strongly supported the foreign and domestic policies of the president. When he came into office as president himself he pledged publicly and privately to continue these policies, and for many months he retained and used his predecessor's most important advisers. Truman also shared FDR's faith that most men were men of reason, fairness, and good will, and like Roosevelt he believed that reasonable men could meet together and find accommodation on matters on which they differed.

But Truman's experience had been that of a judge and a legislator, not an executive, and though his chairmanship of the Special Senate Committee to Investigate the National Defense Program had acquainted him with many issues of national defense policy he was largely uninformed and inexperienced in matters involving interstate relations. In his acceptance speech as vice presidential nominee on August 31, 1944, he had presciently described the situation in which he was soon to find himself: "It is well recognized," Truman told the citizens of his birthplace, Lamar, Missouri, "that it takes a new president at least a year to learn the fundamentals of his job. We cannot expect any man wholly inexperienced in national and international affairs to readily learn the views, the objectives, and the inner thoughts of such divergent personalities as those dominant leaders who have guided the destinies of our courageous allies. There will be no time to learn, and mistakes once made cannot be unmade."[2] In this situation the new president counseled with Roosevelt's closest advisers and deferred to the experience of the cabinet officers FDR had appointed. The result was to increase their influence in policy making, a circumstance that was reinforced by Truman's initially strong feeling—unlike the man he replaced—that "the Cabinet was like a board of directors appointed by the president to help him carry out policies of the government; that in many instances the Cabinet could be of great help to the president by offering advice, whether he liked it or not."[3] Finally, Truman had a style of operation that was all his own. He felt that controversy should be aired in the open with the advocates of all positions present to defend their views and hear those of their adversaries; when the final decision was his he believed in clearly making it, not letting it be made for him by default or delay; and in the decisions he made he felt he should be guided by what he once called the "most precious heritage" of the average American, "common sense of the Missouri 'show me' brand."[4]

When applied to problems of foreign policy, and in particular to relations with Russia, this pattern of continuity and change led Harry Truman to rely heavily on the advice of men Roosevelt had chosen but only selectively listened to; and it inclined him to interpret to the letter all the agreements of his predecessor—those that were quite precise as well as those that necessity left open to ambiguous interpretation. The result at first was neither a continuation of Roosevelt's policies toward Russia nor an abrupt reversal of them. It was instead a change of direction. The combination of the absence of Roosevelt's longer experience and larger perspective, plus the advice of those who had felt most sorely tried in their dealings with the Russians, led to a distinct shift in the presidential view of postwar Soviet-American relations. Roosevelt had believed to the last hour of his life that Soviet cooperation would be vital to the maintenance of peace in the postwar world and he had bent every effort to see that nothing disturbed this prospect. Truman was persuaded of a different view. Soviet cooperation was still regarded as important, but if that cooperation could not be obtained largely on American terms then the United States would go it alone. Thus, in the transition from Roosevelt to Truman the presidential opinion that "we need the Russians" became "the Russians need us more than we need them." With this shift the fragile and already weakened alliance began to fall apart.

This change of direction was clearly seen in Truman's meeting with Soviet Foreign Commissar Molotov only ten days after Roosevelt's death. At Stalin's urging Molotov had come to Washington to call on the new president and attend the opening sessions of the San Francisco Conference. Truman's first session with the foreign commissar, on April 22, was brief and cordial, consisting mainly of an exchange of amenities and mutual pledges of support for the Yalta Agreements. Then, the next day—following a long meeting in which most of his aides supported and encouraged his determination to get tough with Molotov—Truman took the offensive. He began the meeting by expressing his regret that no progress had been made on the Polish question. He reiterated the U.S. position that the new Polish government should be representative of all democratic elements and expressed bluntly his disappointment that the

Russians had consulted only with representatives of the Soviet-backed Warsaw regime. Truman then told Molotov that the United States intended to go ahead with plans for the new world organization "no matter what difficulties or differences may arise with regard to other matters" and he tied future economic assistance to Soviet cooperation by pointing out that foreign economic measures required congressional and public support and by implying that such support would not be forthcoming in the face of Russian rejection of British and American proposals on Poland. Molotov replied that his government stood by the decisions made at Yalta and that he personally could not see why the formula that had been agreed to concerning the composition of the Yugoslav government (which gave Tito's supporters almost complete control) could not also be applied to Poland. Truman continued, in language Admiral Leahy later described as "not at all diplomatic," that agreement had already been reached regarding Poland and the only thing to do was for Marshal Stalin to carry it out "in accordance with his word." To Molotov's protest that he had never been talked to like that in his life, the president replied: "Carry out your agreements and you won't get talked to like that."[5]

In the days that followed, the president's appraisal of Soviet-American relations undoubtedly reinforced in his mind the strong stand he had taken with Molotov, for that appraisal included: acrimonious controversies with the Russians at the San Francisco United Nations Conference concerning chairmanship of the meeting and the admission of Poland and Argentina; renewal in Washington of the dispute with the USSR concerning repatriation of Allied prisoners of war; and in Moscow widening differences with the Soviet government on reparations, future cooperation in the Far East against Japan, and a host of minor issues. More ominous than any of these matters, however, was the rapidly developing situation in Eastern Europe. Throughout the area the Russians were seeking so vigorously to advance their interests and those of their supporters in the closing days of the war that on May 6 Churchill advised Truman that their armies "should hold firmly to the existing position obtained or being obtained" in those countries. In the same message the British prime minister recommended that when the V-E celebration was over, "we must most earnestly consider our attitude towards the Soviets and show them how much we have to offer or withhold."[6]

It is indeed ironic that at the very moment when the goal for which the Allies had joined—the defeat of Nazi Germany—was at hand, relations between the wartime partners had plunged to a new low. It is impossible to say how much of this was attributable to the shift from Roosevelt to Truman; probably very little, since most of the matters in dispute were already well established by the time the transition occurred. But it is clear that a new American attitude was influencing these issues and would affect their future development. Truman had made clear that henceforth he would be speaking to the Russians "in words of one syllable" and that if necessary the United States was prepared to act alone. "It was now or never," Bohlen recorded the president saying to his advisers before his second meeting with Molotov; "He intended to go on with the plans for San Francisco and if the Russians did not wish to join us they could go to hell."[7] This represented a vast change in approach from FDR. To Truman's advisers the message was clear: the time had come to be firm with the Russians and to press forcefully whatever advantages the United States possessed.

The Post–V-E Day Cutback of Lend-Lease

The most obvious advantage was America's vast economic power. Lend-lease was a visible manifestation of that power, and U.S. potential to aid postwar reconstruction was clearly another; yet when Germany surrendered on May 8, 1945, there was no officially approved policy for readjusting lend-lease, either in its entirety or to specific recipients, nor was there any policy for extending assistance for reconstruction.

Concerning lend-lease, Roosevelt's letter of the previous September had halted all formal planning for its post–V-E Day readjustment; but in the early spring of 1945 that planning had tentatively resumed when the War Department had sought authorization from the president to plan for lend-lease supply for the period following Germany's defeat. The response to this request was made after Roosevelt's death by President Truman, who merely directed that the War Department take up with Director of War Mobilization and Reconversion Fred M. Vinson any problems that arose in its planning. This it eventually did, but not until a week after the war in Europe had ended.

It was in this absence of high-level planning that the chief of the USSR Branch of the FEA, General Wesson, had begun developing his own plans for the readjustment of Russian lend-lease, plans that brought the sharp dissent of the executive of the President's Soviet Protocol Committee, General York. In his opposition, York found himself without the support that previously had carried him successfully through such contests. Roosevelt was dead, and Harry Hopkins—to whom York vigorously appealed—was hospitalized in Minnesota, too ill to render any assistance. In addition, Ambassador Harriman was in town preaching to all who would listen a gospel of "firmness" toward Russia, advocating an end to the "generous" policy that thus far had been applied to material aid to the USSR; and to many, the recent actions of the Soviet Union in Eastern Europe gave decisive weight to his counsel. In these circumstances it became clear to the members of the USSR Branch that important changes were in the offing. On the eve of the German surrender John Hazard wrote in one of his regular letters to General Spalding in Moscow that "no final conclusion has been reached although the outlines are now taking form." He went on to explain that the post–V-E Day program would probably be limited to what was necessary for military operations and would exclude most types of industrial equipment and some raw materials. There was also a question, Hazard wrote, of whether or not the program would continue on the basis of a formal protocol. "I do not know how this question will be settled," he concluded, "but we expect something from the White House on it."[8]

In his memoirs Harry Truman has recorded that the White House did indeed issue something on this matter the very next day. Truman has written that "after the Cabinet meeting on May 8" FEA Administrator Crowley and Acting Secretary of

State Grew came into his office with "an order authorizing the FEA and the State Department to take joint action to cut back the volume of lend-lease supplies when Germany surrendered." Truman states that he signed it, that because of the precipitous manner in which it was carried out, "a storm broke almost at once" and that as a result he subsequently "rescinded" the order. He also pointed out that this incident taught him early in his administration the important lesson that he had to be sure he knew what was in the documents he was signing. "If I had read the order," Truman reflected, "the incident would not have occurred."[9] This account, which most historians have accepted as accurate—some even pointing to the "symbolic" significance of Truman taking action on V-E Day itself—is incorrect and evidently based on faulty recollection.[10] As the following discussion will show, Truman signed an order concerning lend-lease on May 11 (not May 8), it dealt exclusively with Russia, and it was never rescinded. Furthermore, there was no cabinet meeting on May 8 (only a brief gathering at the White House of department heads and congressional and military leaders for the surrender announcement), and there is ample evidence that Truman had been well informed of the plans his subordinates were making for adjustments in the lend-lease program to Russia before he signed their order on May 11.

Preparation of the Directive for the USSR

The most important questions about adjustments in lend-lease following the termination of hostilities in Europe concerned the status of the two major recipients, Britain and the Soviet Union. In the light of the Phase II agreement dating from the previous fall, the British felt fairly sure of an uninterrupted flow of material following V-E Day in accordance with the terms of the agreement. But this agreement was not regarded as binding by the United States. In addition, by the end of April there was a growing feeling in some quarters of the American administration, particularly in the War Department, that the British were taking advantage of lend-lease to improve their own financial position at the expense of the United States.[11] Thus, when the European war ended, American military leaders ignored the provisions of the Phase

II agreement and on May 10 (the day before Truman signed the order concerning Russian lend-lease) they repossessed most of the material awaiting shipment to Britain that was not clearly destined for use in the war against Japan. British representatives in Washington protested bitterly and at the end of the month Churchill sent Truman an urgent cable requesting fulfillment of the Phase II plans. A compromise was finally reached (strongly favoring the American position) that permitted a diminished flow of lend-lease to continue to the United Kingdom until the end of the Pacific war.[12]

The problem with regard to the USSR was more complex. First, lend-lease to Russia operated under the protocol system, an arrangement that was much more binding than that covering aid to Britain. Second, the Soviet Union—not yet at war with Japan—was no longer a cobelligerent of the United States following V-E Day, though it had promised to commence hostilities in the Pacific three months after the defeat of Germany. Finally, there was the growing feeling that the time had come to adopt a much more restrictive policy regarding aid to the USSR. Complementing this was increasing apprehension over Soviet foreign policy and the widespread view that the United States could use its economic power to influence that policy. It was in this context that the German surrender suddenly made Russia's lend-lease status an urgent matter. If a change was to be made—for whatever reasons—it would have maximum impact if it were made quickly and implemented decisively. Discussion began on May 9, not in Washington, but 3,000 miles away, on the Pacific Coast.

In San Francisco the United Nations Conference on International Organization had been under way since April 25. The United States delegation was headed by Secretary of State Edward Stettinius and included in its entourage for the first two weeks of the conference Ambassador to Moscow Averell Harriman. During this period Harriman had spent much of his time in meetings with Eden and Molotov, trying to overcome the impasse they had reached on the question of the reorganization of the Polish government. On May 8, with the deadlock on this and certain matters relating to the UN Charter still unbroken, Molotov left for Moscow. The following morning Harriman met with Stettinius and his advisers, announced he would leave for Washington that day to talk with Truman, and inquired about the department's view of the extent to which it felt the Polish question was a real issue affecting general U.S. relations with the Soviet Union. It was important to know this, Harriman added, because it brought in such questions as lend-lease and postwar credits to Russia.

After some discussion it was decided that the United States should impress on Stalin the gravity of the Polish question for future Soviet-American relations, but that "no specific acts of pressure or retaliation should be suggested or considered until the end of the San Francisco conference." It was also agreed that lend-lease shipments to Russia should be curtailed on a purely supply basis, "but without any hint of relationship with the Polish or other political problems with the Soviet Union," and "that the list of supplies for Russia involving the Pacific war should be treated separately and carried out to the full—or in complete agreement that the needs of Western Allies should come first even at the expense of the Soviet Union."[13] These conclusions were then telegraphed to Acting Secretary of State Grew in Washington with instructions that he bring them to the attention of the president.[14]

On May 10 Harriman arrived in Washington for a round of high-level talks and meetings. In the morning he met with Truman and explained the new lend-lease policy for Russia that had been agreed on in San Francisco. To this the president gave his approval.[15] Later that afternoon Harriman met in the office of Assistant Secretary of State William Clayton to discuss with representatives of the various involved agencies a policy statement on Russian lend-lease that would accord with the conclusions reached the previous day in San Francisco and approved that morning by the president.

Although evidently no minutes of this meeting were kept, several memoranda made by the War Department's representative, Brig. Gen. George A. Lincoln, indicate the tenor of the discussion and the decisions taken. The purpose of the meeting, Lincoln reported, was to obtain concurrence in principle to a draft memorandum to the president containing an aide-memoire from the State Department to the Russians informing them that the current lend-lease program to the USSR would be immediately adjusted to take into account the end of hostilities in Europe, that the United States intended to fulfill the terms of Annex III (the MILEPOST program for the Pacific) in the Fourth Protocol, and that future military requirements would be met without the conclusion of a Fifth Protocol. In addition, no mention was to be made in the aide-memoire of a 3-c agreement and the Soviet Union was specifically asked to provide information justifying both the further delivery of goods then on hand and future requests for equipment.[16] Thus, with the exception of those changes necessitated by the ending of the war in Europe, the provisions suggested for these documents followed closely those drafted by General Wesson the preceding month and strongly resisted at that time by General York.

The outcome of the meeting in Clayton's office was approval by all present of the general wording of the memorandum and aide-memoire in accordance with the provisions set forth above. General Lincoln and his colleague from the Navy Department, Admiral Reeves, were careful, however, in giving their approval, to state that these provisions referred only to the necessity "to adjust" lend-lease and that there was no mention of "cutting off" aid to Russia. In this connection Lincoln noted that he "pointed out to Mr. Harriman in private conversation that probably our previous commitment to Russia would necessitate in all fairness continuance of a flow of spare parts, such as spark plugs for American equipment, and that appropriate administrative arrangements would have to be made."[17] Still, Lincoln remained apprehensive of the interpretation that would be given to what had been decided; the comments of some at the meeting indicated to him that their desire was to do more than just make adjustments necessitated by the changed military situation. He wrote to Army Chief of Staff General Marshall the following day: "There was an indication in the discussion by State Department members present that they were considering using lend-lease as a political weapon in connection with our difficulties with the Russians in central Europe."[18]

Although Lincoln mentioned no names, one State Department representative whose previous statements indicated strongly that he favored such action was the one who was assigned to the task of putting the documents into final form. This was Elbridge Durbrow, chief of the Division of Eastern European Affairs of the State Department. Since at least February of 1944 Durbrow had been urging "firmness" with the Russians and had been a staunch advocate of using economic aid as the "best lever" to convince them to drop their "Comintern foreign policy."[19] Just three weeks before the May 10 meeting Durbrow had returned from a seven-week assignment in the embassy in Moscow. This assignment, at a time of growing tension in Soviet-American relations and in the company of men like Harriman and Deane who held strong opinions about these relations, had undoubtedly reinforced Durbrow's views of the necessity of a tough policy toward Russia. Such attitudes evidently influenced him in drawing up the final version of the documents that had been agreed upon at the meeting in Clayton's office. The result was that the memorandum to the president was considerably strengthened, notably by the inclusion of the words "should be cut off immediately as far as physically practicable" in a key passage dealing with supplies programmed for the USSR.[20]

Since the basic memorandum to the president was to be signed by the FEA and the acting secretary of state, the two draft documents went next to these departments for further discussion and eventual presentation to their chiefs. In the FEA this responsibility was undertaken by General Wesson, head of its USSR Branch. Wesson's views regarding the lend-lease program for Russia already have been discussed. In sum, he was a strong opponent of the policy of unconditional aid to Russia and an advocate since August of the preceding year of plans to cut back sharply on supplies to the USSR following Germany's defeat. Early the following morning, May 11, Wesson presented the draft memoranda to John Hazard and other members of the USSR Branch. He explained that a final draft was being prepared for the president's signature but that it appeared on the basis of the decisions already reached that only those aid programs relating to the Far East would continue.[21] However,

Wesson decided to begin the process of cutting back without waiting for Truman's signature. He thereupon called Clifton E. Mack, director of procurement of the Treasury Department and told him not to proceed with any Russian contracts that he had on hand and not to make any new ones. Mack immediately relayed this news to his chief, Henry Morgenthau, and the Treasury secretary—who was anxious to curtail the entire lend-lease program but sensitive to anything directed exclusively against Russia—asked his assistant Daniel Bell to call Leo Crowley and find out why this decision had been made.[22]

Leo Crowley had his own reasons for wanting to cut back the lend-lease program to Russia. As a businessman from Madison, Wisconsin, with a lifelong involvement in banking, Crowley had no well-developed interests in foreign relations. He could probably best be characterized as nationalistic, neo-isolationist, and in general skeptical of international movements, whether of the political, economic, or ideological kind. Regarding Russia he had made no strong pronouncements, but Truman related to one of his biographers that "Crowley was as anti-Russian as Wallace was pro-Russian," and years later the former FEA administrator recalled that he had felt that the best way to deal with the Russians was to be "firm" with them.[23] Crowley's attitude toward post–V-E Day adjustments in the lend-lease program was rooted instead in the opinions he had formed and expressed about the nature and purpose of the program. He saw his role of over-all administrator of lend-lease as that of an executive who held in trust public funds to be used very carefully for clearly delineated purposes. This mentality, undoubtedly the product of his years in banking, not only attracted him to Roosevelt and earned him his earlier post of chairman of the Federal Deposit Insurance Corporation, but it also endeared him to congressmen habituated to holding taut the nation's purse strings. Crowley reciprocated congressional approval of his stewardship by declaring with increasing vigor in committee hearings his intention not to spend lend-lease funds for purposes for which they were not intended and not to spend them beyond the termination of hostilities.

For Crowley the cutback of lend-lease to Russia, a nation no longer engaged with the United States in hostilities against a common enemy, was thus simply a matter of following the letter of the law and redeeming his oft-repeated promises to the Congress. But he also recognized that this decision, singling out Russia for special treatment, had important political implications and he responded cautiously on May 11 to Daniel Bell's request for information. In a memorandum to Morgenthau, Bell reported that Crowley had told him that the order to cancel lend-lease contracts involving the delivery of material to Russia was the result of "a high political decision made by the president and the State Department" and was "highly confidential."[24]

While these exchanges were occurring in and between the FEA and the Treasury Department the two draft documents were also being discussed in the State Department. On the same May 11 morning the Secretary's Staff Committee met to hear as an item of "urgent business" the question of lend-lease to the Soviet Union. In the chair as acting secretary, in the absence of Stettinius, who was still at the San Francisco conference, was Under Secretary Joseph C. Grew. Grew, who had been in the Foreign Service over forty years and was a diplomat of the old school, with a pronounced distaste for the manners and practices of Bolshevik diplomacy, had been in charge of the department since April 19. During that time he had become one of the strongest advocates of a "tough" policy toward the Soviet Union and a strong believer in the use of American economic power as leverage to influence Soviet policy. Like Harriman and Stettinius he was aware of the importance of keeping Russia as an active participant in the United Nations Conference, but he also felt Russia's interests would dictate its continuation in the organization no matter what the United States did. On the eve of the San Francisco conference he wrote to Stettinius, "If the Soviets try to wreck the Conference through intransigence, we must go on without them; *they cannot afford isolation and they know it* [emphasis added]."[25] During the last week in April and the first week in May Grew's comments at meetings and in memoranda revealed a mounting impatience with Soviet activities in a number of areas and a growing desire to arrest them in some way. On April 30 Grew counseled Truman to "consider seriously" keeping U.S. forces at their forward positions in eastern Europe (advice Churchill had given also); on May 5 he urged "hard bargaining" to counter "unilateral acts on the part of the Soviet Union" in Austria and Czechoslovakia; on May 9 he wondered aloud "whether the time had not come to discuss with the President the question of making public the full facts regarding current issues in relations with the Soviet Union"; and on May 10, when Truman reversed his previous position regarding Tito's Soviet-backed occupation of Venezia Giulia and opted to "throw them out," Grew expressed his "relief and satisfaction."[26]

It was with the background of these events and feelings that Grew opened the May 11 staff committee meeting by having Assistant Secretary William Clayton discuss the documents that had been drawn up in accordance with the decisions made the previous day in his office. In making his presentation Clayton said that all the agencies had agreed that the lend-lease program to Russia "should be so flexible that it could be cut off at any time." He also stated that the new policy would have a further advantage in that it would require the Soviets to provide proof of essential need for any further lend-lease goods to be furnished them, a requirement that heretofore had not existed. At this point Grew broke in to state that the determination of lend-lease policy ought not to be influenced by any consideration of how it might affect Russia's entry into the war against Japan. In his opinion, Grew went on, "the Soviet Union will enter the war against Japan in order to participate in the settlement regardless of any factor such as lend-lease assistance." Furthermore, the acting secretary argued, "lend-lease assistance is this government's only leverage against the Soviet Union." The United States, therefore, should make no commitment for the future and, he stated, with Clayton's concurrence, the documents under discussion made no such commitment. The implication was clearly that future commitments should only be made in exchange for a suitable quid pro quo from the USSR. The committee then approved the memorandum and aide-memoire and Clayton stated that when Grew and Crowley had signed the final copies they would be ready for presentation to the president.[27]

Later that afternoon Crowley called Grew to ask the time of his appointment with the president since he wanted to accompany him when he presented the Russian lend-lease documents to Truman. Crowley assured Grew that he agreed with him on the matter but, as the acting secretary recorded, "he wanted to be sure that the President thoroughly understands the situation and that he will back us up and will keep everyone else out of it. He stated that we would be having difficulty with the Russians and he did not want them to be running all over town looking for help."[28] Thus it was well understood that the proposed policy was directed exclusively against Russia and would probably provoke a strong reaction. This is further indicated by a comment Harriman made when he told Stettinius the following day of Truman's decision. "We would be getting a 'good tough slash-back' from the Russians," Stettinius recalled Harriman saying, "but that we have to face it."[29] In the light of this conversation and all the preparations that preceded it, Stettinius's observation later that "this order . . . caught the State Department completely by surprise" is a sad reflection on how little he understood of what was happening in his own department.[30]

In the early evening of May 11, Grew and Crowley, accompanied by Clayton and Charles Bohlen, brought their memorandum and aide-memoire to the White House. According to Grew's account, "Mr. Clayton presented our proposed lend-lease agreement with Soviet Russia, the highlights of which he and Mr. Crowley explained to the President. . . . The President approved and signed the agreement."[31] This was undoubtedly the document Truman later incorrectly recollected signing on May 8, the day of the German surrender. In his defense, it can be argued that he did not read it carefully and that he did not recognize the full import of the actions it appeared to mandate. But by the evening of May 11 Truman had discussed its subject matter and contents with Grew, Harriman, Stettinius and Stimson, and then finally its highlights with Crowley and Clayton. It should have been clear to him by then that he was signing a document that unilaterally inflicted a deep cutback on lend-lease supplies to Russia exclusively, an action that was sure to produce repercussions of some kind, desired or undesired.[32]

The memorandum Truman approved contained these points:

1. Immediate adjustment of deliveries of supplies to take account of the end of organized resistance in Europe.
2. Continuation of deliveries under Annex III of the Fourth Protocol.
3. Delivery of additional supplies on hand or on order to the extent they are necessary to support military operations in the Pacific theater.
4. Delivery of supplies needed to complete industrial plants already partially made available under previous commitments.
5. Immediate cutoff as far as physically practicable of other lend-lease supplies programmed for the USSR and their diversion to programs for Western Europe.
6. Development of current and future supply programs without the conclusion of a Fifth Protocol and on the basis of adequate information regarding the essentiality of Soviet military supply requirements.[33]

The accompanying aide-memoire informed the Soviet ambassador that deliveries of supplies under the current lend-lease program would be adjusted immediately, that the government intended to fulfill the Annex III program and "to deliver such other supplies now on hand or on order for the USSR as are justified on the basis of adequate information regarding the essentiality of Soviet military supply requirements and in the light of competing demands for such supplies in the changed military situation." The note further stated that future lend-lease programs would be designed to meet new military situations as they arose and that these should be arranged without the conclusion of a Fifth Protocol. It concluded by requesting the Soviet Embassy to furnish "with a minimum of delay, a statement of the military requirements of

the Union of Soviet Socialist Republics for all categories of
lend-lease supplies for the remainder of the calendar year 1945
and adequate information regarding the essentiality of these
requirements in the light of the new military situation."[34]

Implementation of the USSR Directive

Implementation of this new policy began the following day,
Saturday, May 12. Early that morning the members of the
Soviet Protocol Subcommittee on Shipping gathered in Room
111 of the Public Health Service Building to decide how to
carry out the president's orders. Present were General York of
the protocol committee, General Wesson of the USSR Branch
of the FEA, Generals Edgerton and Shingler of the War
Department, Captain Doyle of the Navy Department, and
representatives of the Army, the Air Force, the Munitions
Assignment Board, the War Shipping Administration, the
Transportation Control Committee, and the Office of Defense
Transportation. John Hazard, secretary of the protocol
committee, and Willis Armstrong, secretary of the Shipping
Subcommittee, kept the minutes of the meeting.[35]

General York opened the meeting by having Armstrong read
the memorandum approved by the president the night before.
He then explained that the protocol committee would meet the
following Tuesday to deal with the question of supplies, but
that the matter of shipping was urgent and had to be dealt with
immediately. General Wesson set the tone of the meeting by
declaring that he had worked on the statement of policy and
that he was certain "the Government meant business." The
former approach of "when in doubt, give" was to be replaced
by a new approach of "when in doubt, hold," he added.
General York, either won over finally to this view or convinced
that further opposition was fruitless, said he agreed with this
interpretation of the new policy.[36]

The committee then turned to specifics. The first question
was what to do with ships that had already sailed. After a
discussion that indicated it was feasible to bring them back and
unload them, General Wesson argued that if the committee did
not call back the ships it would have to explain why. Lt. Col.
William McChesney Martin, representing the Munitions

Assignment Board, agreed that the ships should be called back since that seemed to be what the memorandum required. At this point Captain Doyle of the Navy Department wondered if the policy was meant to be so broad as to prevent shipping anything not in Annex III. Wesson replied that this had been considered and that a proposal to include equipment necessary for liquidating the situation in Europe "had been specifically ruled out with a blue pencil." General Edgerton, with General Shingler's support, then stated that in his opinion ships that had sailed should continue. He argued that the Russians undoubtedly had made plans for the equipment on these vessels and that the custom was to let a ship continue that had already started its voyage. General York replied that he thought Edgerton's point was good but that he felt that the Congress would want the action taken that was being contemplated. Wesson argued in addition that the ships should be stopped because, unlike the United Kingdom, Russia was not yet at war with Japan. No one challenged him further and the decision to call back the ships stood.

With this first interpretation made, largely on the strength of Wesson's arguments and the authoritative position he was able to assume as a participant in the drafting of the memorandum, the committee next considered the details of stopping points for ships, convoys under way and in preparation, special cargoes, and supplies enroute to ports. By this time, well caught up in the momentum of its own self-generated mood of cut-cancel-and-call-back, the committee decided that ship repairs be reduced to a minimum and that U.S. vessels needing such repairs be repossessed, that airplanes to Russia be cut off at Fairbanks, Alaska, and that War Department port agencies take back War Department–procured items. Only once, when John Hutchins of the War Shipping Administration asked if stopping the ships that had already left Britain would upset the Russians politically, did anyone consider the possible implications of the decisions they were making; but Hutchins quickly answered his own question when he noted that "perhaps the memorandum takes this into consideration."

After the meeting the members of the committee dispersed to their offices and gave orders that resulted in the following

actions: future commitments of matériel to the Russians were
stopped;[37] all lend-lease purchases for the USSR were
suspended pending determination of a method for screening
future requests;[38] an embargo was placed on Russian freight to
all ports except those on the West Coast;[39] all vessels en route
with cargo for Russia, except those that had passed Istanbul,
were ordered to return to port to discharge all but those cargoes
that were part of the Annex III program; Russian-bound ships
were ordered withdrawn from Convoy JW-67, four vessels
intended for JW-68 were directed to return to New York, and
planning was stopped on vessels for JW-69; no new vessels were
berthed for Russian cargo, loading was stopped on those
berthed and those already loaded were ordered to discharge
their cargo; and, finally, on the West Coast, cargo not part of
Annex III was ordered segregated out of Russian shipments, to
be retained for further disposition.[40]

At 1:30 in the afternoon, while these actions were being
taken, John Hazard and John Howard of the USSR Branch of
the FEA decided to check with Emilio Collado, chief of the
Division of Financial and Monetary Affairs of the State
Department, to be certain that the recall of ships on the high
seas was in accord with the department's wishes. Reached at
lunch, Collado replied that he thought this was a misinter-
pretation of the president's directive and that he would call
Harriman to check further. When Harriman learned what had
been done, he was "shocked by the action" and said he would
take steps to change it. Assistant Secretary Clayton, lunching at
the French Embassy, was also called by Collado and he, too,
stated that the ships should not be recalled and that Wesson
should be told to change his orders. Wesson, in the meantime,
had already been reached by Harriman and by mid-afternoon
was in the process of revising the committee's actions. Ships
that had already sailed from the United States via the Atlantic
were allowed to proceed to the USSR and ships that had been
on loading berth in Atlantic or Gulf ports on the morning of
May 12 were allowed to load the cargo that had been allocated
to them as of that morning.[41]

By this time, however, activity occasioned by the morning's
decisions was rapidly becoming known in Washington, and

among the first to learn of it were the Russians. In the afternoon Acting Secretary Grew was called by the Soviet chargé d'affaires, Nikolai V. Novikov, who said that he had received word that the loading of lend-lease on Soviet ships had been ordered discontinued and that he wanted further information on the matter. Grew then called Clayton, who evidently told him of the interpretation that had been given to the president's directive and the subsequent change that had just been made. With this information Grew called back Novikov and told him that he had "looked into the matter and found that there was absolutely no truth in the rumor—we are not stopping the loading of Soviet ships." This was accurate at the moment Grew called, but it was hardly a truthful accounting of what had already occurred that day. Grew then added that he had sent a note (the approved aide-memoire) that afternoon "which would explain everything."[42]

In addition to the Russians, the press also learned of the sudden lend-lease stoppage. The Associated Press news service picked up the story—evidently when activity on the docks indicated what had happened—and papers on both coasts were soon running it.[43] In these circumstances Crowley and Grew began working on a statement for public release to cover what had happened. The problem, they both realized, was to say something that would make it appear that the change in policy was not directed solely against the Soviet Union. Grew made this clear later in the afternoon when he commented to Crowley over the phone about a suggested text. "I said," the acting secretary later recorded, "the statement did not seem to bring the Russians in directly and I thought it was good. I said we wanted to be sure of it since this whole thing is full of dynamite."[44] Later that evening Crowley issued the statement they had discussed. It referred to his frequent testimony before Congress that lend-lease was "purely an instrument for winning the war" and stated that with the end of hostilities in Europe it was necessary to review the lend-lease program. Pending the completion of this review, the statement concluded, "new shipments to Europe are being held up except those destined to countries through which redeployment of our troops now in Europe will be facilitated thereby."[45]

Following the confusion created on Saturday, May 12, by the orders that were given and then cancelled concerning the Soviet aid program, it was necessary to make an authoritative interpretation of the May 11 cutback directive approved by President Truman. This was done at two meetings on Monday and Tuesday of the following week. The first of these meetings brought together in Clayton's State Department office on May 14 most of those who had been involved in the directives and decisions of the past few days, including Harriman, Bohlen, Collado, Durbrow, and Generals York, Wesson, and Lincoln. Harriman apparently was deeply concerned about the possible repercussions of the actions taken by the Shipping Subcommittee the previous Saturday and he proceeded to argue for a rather liberal interpretation of the cutback directive. According to General Lincoln, Harriman had "cooled off considerably . . . and seemed to be supporting a reasonable approach to the adjustments in the instance of tapering off the flow to Russia."[46] After a brief discussion of what went wrong the previous Saturday the following interpretation of the directive was agreed upon:

1. Supplies in Annex III, and other supplies on hand or on order that were necessary to support Soviet military operations in the Far East, would go forward.
2. Ships at sea and ships already loaded would be allowed to go forward.
3. Deliveries of additional supplies on order would be withheld so far as physically practical and diverted to appropriate programs in Western Europe.
4. Information from the Russians justifying their future requirements would not be expected to be as detailed and satisfactory as that received from the British concerning their requirements.[47]

The following day a meeting of the full protocol committee was held to acquaint all departments with this interpretation and to make specific decisions in accordance with its recommendations. In addition to the usual departmental representatives, the meeting was attended by FEA Director

Crowley and Ambassador Harriman, and it soon developed
that the two differed in their interpretation of the cutback,
Harriman advocating a more liberal reading of the directive
while Crowley held out for a stricter interpretation that would
have limited future shipments almost exclusively to programs
supporting the Pacific war effort.[48]

Despite these differences between Harriman and Crowley,
which were to be of increasing importance in the remaining
months of the program, an agreed interpretation was finally
reached on most aspects of post–V-E Day lend-lease policy for
Russia. In sum, the new policy that was transmitted to all
departments and agencies provided that shipments under the
Fourth Protocol would be terminated (except for Annex III and
programs related to it), that there would be no Fifth Protocol,
and that future requirements of the USSR were to be presented
like those of other lend-lease nations and screened—in
consultation with the Military Mission in Moscow by cables
sent through the protocol committee—as requirements essential to war or preparation for war against Japan.[49]

The Influence of the Implementation Phase
of the USSR Cutback

The sudden cutback of lend-lease to Russia and the manner
in which it was initially carried out considerably heightened
Soviet suspicion of American behavior and did so at one of the
most critical moments for the wartime alliance. In the spring of
1945 the United States and Russia found themselves—
somewhat unexpectedly for both—in a bitter contest over the
future of Eastern Europe. Earlier in the year at Yalta there had
been high hopes; then, when the fruits of that conference
soured pessimism set in. With the Berne surrender incident,
and a host of minor disputes, the pessimism increased. The
long-sought surrender of Germany provided a moment of
shining triumph which all shared, but for the Russians it was
soon clouded by the abrupt cutback of the program that had
epitomized the common will that had brought victory. Under
the circumstances they could only account for this act as an
effort by the United States to use its economic power to force
concessions on matters in dispute between the two nations, and

this is how they read it. When Harry Hopkins visited Stalin at the end of May this was precisely the charge the Soviet leader made. At Potsdam two months later, as Harry Truman recalled to Arthur Krock in 1950, "all Stalin wanted to talk about was the abrupt cessation of lend lease." Four years afterward Deputy Foreign Minister Andrei Gromyko related that Stalin had been shocked by the abrupt cutback of lend-lease and that the incident had changed his pro-American sympathies.[50]

The question of whether or not the cutback of lend-lease to Russia was a deliberate effort to exert pressure on the Soviet Union can best be answered by examining the formation and implementation of the decision that was made. It is clear that the decision was taken unilaterally by the United States, without consultation with the other protocol signatories.[51] It is also clear that it was intended to apply exclusively to the USSR. Beyond this, the major participants in its formation and drafting—notably Harriman, Grew, Durbrow, and Wesson— and in its implementation—again Wesson—were on record favoring a tougher policy toward Russia, including an end to unconditional lend-lease, and believing that the United States should use its economic power to achieve its objectives vis-à-vis the USSR. In addition, they apparently succeeded with Truman—where they failed with Roosevelt—in acquiring as an ally to their cause the most important decision maker of all, the president of the United States. There is no doubting then that in making this decision these men were trying to convey to the Soviet leaders a message that would affect the future course of Russian-American relations.

Yet the decision to cut back lend-lease and the manner in which it was carried out cannot be attributed solely to the desire to influence Soviet behavior. The Lend-Lease Act, because it was passed before the United States was at war, and the subsequent lend-lease agreement and protocols with Russia, because they were meant to cover unforeseen contingencies, were all written broadly and were subject to a number of interpretations. However, the Congress, in its debates and subsequent renewals of the act and appropriations for it, made increasingly clear its particular interpretation of lend-lease. This was that the program was limited, that it was exclusively a wartime measure, that it was to end with the termination of hostilities, and that it was not to be used for relief, rehabilitation, or reconstruction. Its view was a reflection of what it perceived was the public's opinion of the program. The attitude of the public—to the extent it can be read from polls that were taken during the war—was in part ignorance of the nature and goals of the program and in part anxiety lest the United States be taken advantage of and not get full return for this unprecedented outpouring of its productive wealth. No one understood better the feelings of the Congress and the attitude of the public that lay behind them than the administrator of lend-lease, FEA Director Leo Crowley. Crowley basked in the glow of the satisfaction expressed by the Congress for his work in handling the nation's foreign economic affairs. This was his personal reward for public service rendered and he was anxious to continue to earn it by carefully adhering in his public statements and actions to what he perceived to be the express interest of that body. Thus, in May 1945, Crowley was determined to cut back lend-lease to Russia, not so much because it was Russia that was affected (it conceivably could have been any country), but because it seemed to him that the letter of the law required such action. Crowley was reinforced in his opinion by two important facts: the Soviet Union was no longer engaged with the United States in hostilities against a common enemy, and it had not signed a 3-c Agreement, which would have made possible an uninterrupted flow of supplies after the termination of the European war.

Truman had also been influenced by congressional opinion and action. Just one month earlier he had presided over the Senate debate on the final extension of lend-lease and he had seen strong sentiment in that body come very close to severely restricting presidential options in the terminal phase of lend-lease. He also knew that in the month ahead he would be seeking congressional support for a whole program of demobilization and reconversion legislation, and he probably suspected—as a former member of the Congress—that that body would be anxious in the postwar period to reassert the power and authority it had necessarily relinquished to the executive branch during the period of hostilities.

In addition to congressional sentiment, public feeling, and Crowley's reading of both, the cutback was also affected by the unique status of the Soviet lend-lease program. It was controlled by a series of protocols—international agreements with the force of law that seemingly bound the United States to the fulfillment of their provisions. It operated through its own organization, the President's Soviet Protocol Committee, which, with its direct link to the White House, was largely insulated from the competitive political process that affected the rest of the lend-lease organization. And from the very beginning of the program, the Russians, unlike all other lend-lease recipients, were not required to provide information justifying their supply requests. This unique status seemed vital at the beginning of the war—for no other reason than the necessity of keeping Russia in the conflict—but by the end of the war it was for many in the program an invidious anomaly. They saw little reason for continuing Russia's preferred position and many reasons for ending it, not least among these the drain on equipment that could be used by American forces fully engaged in both theaters of war.[52] When the opportunity came on May 12 to redress this situation lower-level officials moved with alacrity, and their attitude largely explains why Truman's directive—with wording strengthened by others with different motives—was interpreted so severely. In one sense these factors, which lay outside considerations of Soviet behavior, made it possible to make the decision that was made; in another sense they went a long way toward insuring that it would be made.

Finally, the principal architect of the decision to cut back lend-lease to Russia, Ambassador Harriman, was anxious to show the Russians that things were no longer to be as they had been, that a new game had begun in which the United States would look strictly after its own interests and would dispense its largesse only for well-justified needs and a suitable quid pro quo. But as his meeting with Stettinius in San Francisco on May 9 revealed, Harriman did not intend to use the lend-lease cutback to force Soviet concessions on Poland or any other matter. In the first place, the sensitive diplomatic atmosphere would have been upset by the tempest such bludgeoning tactics would have caused. Second, Harriman undoubtedly understood that the United States could hardly hope to gain something by taking away something. However, this subtle distinction between signalling a change in attitude and forcing a concession was not fully appreciated by those in Washington who implemented the policy initially formed in San Francisco. They had been sensitized by a long train of what they perceived to be Soviet malfeasances; ironically, their perception had been significantly influenced by the grim messages Harriman himself had been sending from Moscow in increasing numbers. For them the lend-lease decision was more than a signal; it was a weapon to be used in some not fully thought-out strategy to undo past wrongs and prevent future misdeeds, and together with those who for other reasons sought to reduce Russian aid they carried out the cutback of May 12. The product of their combined efforts was not the point Harriman sought to convey, but rather the outcome he thought he had taken precautions to prevent. He simply failed to understand the strength of the forces set in motion, partly by him, and the inability of a large bureaucratic structure to make the subtle response he desired. As a result, the foundation for postwar great power unity was not strengthened, as he had hoped, but instead was weakened still further.

The Ending of Lend-Lease

President Truman's directive of May 11 had set forth the policy to be followed by those in charge of Soviet aid, but it had not resolved problems of interpretation nor did it settle difficulties that continued to arise because of the lack of overall direction that plagued the entire lend-lease program. The initial result of the meetings held immediately following the president's directive had been a clarification that permitted lend-lease to go forward to the Soviet Union primarily from the West Coast in support of programs strengthening Russian forces for their eventual participation in the war against Japan. These programs included: Annex III (the MILEPOST list approved the previous November); a program to support the

northern air route from Alaska through eastern Russia and
Siberia; the annual summer program for the Soviet Arctic; and
the maintenance of other items of equipment previously
shipped. Any Soviet needs beyond these programs were to be
considered in two categories. The first consisted of military
requirements (exclusively for the Pacific war) for lend-lease
supplies after July 1, 1945. The Russians had been told in
Grew's note of May 12 to Chargé Novikov to submit a statement
of such requirements as soon as possible and to furnish along
with it adequate information justifying their need. The second
category consisted of industrial plants on which only
"proportionally small deliveries" had been made and other
equipment and supplies that had been ordered but could not be
delivered under the principles set forth in the president's May
11 directive. The Russians had been informed earlier that these
items could be purchased on a cash payment basis for their
contract price plus 15 percent to cover transportation, storage,
and accessorial charges.[53]

It was while the Russians were considering their response to
these newly announced policies that Harry Hopkins was in
Moscow at the request of President Truman to try to break the
impasse that had developed over the question of the formation
of the Polish government as well as to discuss with Soviet
leaders several other matters troubling Russian-American
relations; and it was on that occasion that he had faced Stalin's
vigorous criticism of the "scornful and abrupt manner" in
which lend-lease to Russia had been curtailed. Hopkins had
replied to the Soviet leader that the precipitous manner in
which lend-lease to Russia had been cut back was the result of a
"technical misunderstanding" that had been promptly recti-
fied. Nevertheless, he had explained, the end of the war with
Germany necessitated a reconsideration of the lend-lease
program, and he assumed that this had been clear to the
Russians. Hopkins then sought to reassure the Soviet leader
that the curtailment of lend-lease was strictly a legal action that
"did not have any fundamental policy significance" and that it
was not intended as a "pressure weapon," and, as added
assurance of America's intention to assist the Soviet Union, he
pointed out that the United States had accepted in full a

commitment to deliver supplies for use in the Far East and that it was in the process of carrying out this obligation.[54]

To fulfill this commitment Ambassador Harriman then met with Molotov and Mikoyan and received from them a program of military requirements for supplies for the period July 1 to December 31, 1945. This program (which subsequently became known as the May 28 list) was in response to the request made in the note delivered to Novikov in Washington on May 12. It consisted mainly of materials that had not yet been delivered under the Fourth Protocol and additional supplies that Soviet negotiators had wanted to include in the Fifth Protocol. All of its items were said by the Russians to be necessary for use in the Far East and for support for those programs that were allowed to continue after V-E Day. In reporting this list to Washington, Harriman and Deane stated that in accordance with the new policy they would seek justification from the Russians of the need for these supplies and then would make their own recommendations as soon as possible.[55] However, as they undoubtedly must have expected, such justification was not quickly forthcoming. At the end of the first week of June, Deane reported that since receipt of the May 28 list they had "maintained continuous pressure" on the Soviets for justification of their requests. The response, however, had been minimal, limited mainly to assertions that there should be no doubt that the requested materials were fully for the Far East and related programs. Nevertheless, Deane and Harriman felt that there was ample reason for supporting many of the items on the May 28 list and that to avoid delay they should be supplied even in the absence of adequate justification by the Russians.[56]

To both civilian and military officials in Washington, however, specific justification was considered much more important. Following V-E Day the feeling of many of those concerned with the Soviet lend-lease program was that supplies should be provided only for substantial military reasons or upon the receipt of some important concession in return. In mid-May, Secretary of War Stimson had asked the State Department to provide protection for the properties of the Singer Sewing Machine Company in the Soviet-occupied zone of Germany. The memorandum sent by his department argued that "perhaps the time has arrived when the claims of American citizens against the Soviet government may be asserted, particularly if any future aid in the nature of lend-lease or loans to Russia is in contemplation." The State Department, which in the past had consistently refused to tie claims of private citizens to delivery of supplies, replied two days later: "We shall try not to overlook anything possible we might do to protect this legitimate interest."[57]

Renewed firmness in the State Department was also evident in other matters connected with the Russian lend-lease program. On May 19 the Coordinating Committee of the department, chaired by the under secretary of state, considered a document concerning lend-lease transfers to third countries which proposed to penalize Russia by cutting off future shipments of items transferred without authorization. In discussing this document, Emilio Collado of the Office of Financial and Development Policy stated that it had little strength since the goods being shipped were those that it was in the U.S. interest for Russia to have. Nevertheless, others on the committee, led by Elbridge Durbrow, argued that a strong stand would be taken and that "The Russians . . . should now be told not asked." According to the minutes of the meeting, Durbrow's opinion was that "the recent reaction of the USSR representatives to the threatened curtailment of lend-lease—a reaction which indicated some alarm—might be indicative of the extent of the power we still held. He favored going ahead and using those sanctions, however limited, which we had." These sentiments prevailed, and in the final draft of the document the word "requesting" in the paragraph concerning acceptance by the USSR of the principle of no transfer to third countries was replaced by "demanding" and the phrase "reasonable time" regarding receipt of assurances from Russia was removed in favor of "promptly."[58]

Others in the administration held similar views. Admiral Leahy was critical of Harriman's and Deane's generous attitude, and FEA Administrator Crowley urged that the USSR should pay for supplies sent after V-E Day. Crowley was particularly vehement in his belief that the USSR should pay for all industrial equipment it received, because, in his opinion, such equipment was not essential to Soviet military requirements and would serve only for rehabilitation of Soviet industry, a purpose he considered contrary to both the Lend-Lease Act and his promises to Congress.[59] The divergence of views between Crowley and Harriman, which had first surfaced in the aftermath of the V-E Day cutback, was considerable. Under Harriman's and Deane's more generous interpretation, prompted by their concern over the damage done by the precipitous May cutback, shipment to Russia of approximately 1,500,000 tons was recommended for the last six months of 1945. Crowley's stricter definition, which was already causing cancellations of orders and diversions of FEA-controlled nonmilitary supplies, would have permitted only about 500,000 tons to go to the USSR during this period. As long as such differences existed there was uncertainty in the United States about what was to be shipped and uncertainty in Russia about what would be supplied under lend-lease and what would have to be purchased.

By the beginning of August, with General York on convalescent leave and Harry Hopkins out of the government, the nonmilitary Soviet aid program was under the almost complete control of Crowley and USSR Branch Director General Wesson, each of whom for his own reasons wished to keep it as small as possible. Wesson's attitude at the time was expressed in a long memorandum he wrote to Crowley on August 2 entitled "Settlement of Current Problems with Russia." Wesson pointed out to his chief that Russia wanted credits and technological help from the United States, as well as minimum terms for the lend-lease aid that had been rendered. The United States wanted from Russia a trade agreement and also, he added, "a distinct change in the set-up she has created in the eastern European states—Hungary, Rumania, Bulgaria—which is such as to exclude American trade with those countries except under such terms as Russia may prescribe." Wesson stated that the extent to which Russia went in meeting what the United States wanted should affect the extent the United States should go in meeting Soviet requests and that, in particular, no credits should be extended to the USSR until an understanding had been reached "on questions of paramount interest to the U.S." Two days later Wesson went on vacation, leaving word that no industrial equipment was to be given to the USSR without the consent of Crowley.[60]

With its hopes for expanded lend-lease proving unwarranted and—as will be seen—its expectation of large-scale credits for reconstruction falling afoul of the uncertain course of American policy, the USSR turned to the United Nations Relief and Rehabilitation Administration (UNRRA). Although it had been an active participant in the establishment of UNRRA, the Soviet Union had never made a formal request for assistance from the organization and, until the summer of 1945, it had given no indication that it intended to. But in July, just before the third session of the UNRRA Council in London, the Soviet Union presented the organization with a request for $700 million in relief and rehabilitation supplies. This request caused considerable anxiety for Assistant Secretary Clayton in London, who in turn passed it on to the State Department, where it was made an item of urgent business for the Secretary's Staff Committee meeting of August 8. At that meeting Assistant Secretary Acheson reported that he had telegraphed Clayton the previous day that the request should be withdrawn or else the entire UNRRA program would be jeopardized. Acheson argued that UNRRA was already unpopular among members of Congress and that adding the Soviet request would risk congressional disapproval of the whole program. He also questioned Russia's eligibility for UNRRA aid in view of its capacity to pay for supplies (through gold holdings and foreign exchange), its future acquisition of German reparations, and its probable receipt of long-term credits. Although others at the meeting pointed out that Russia could tellingly argue that its enormous sacrifices and suffering warranted it special consideration, Acheson's view prevailed and for the time being his instructions to Clayton stood.[61]

It was on the very date of this meeting that the Soviet Union became a full-fledged partner in the struggle against Japan by keeping to the day its promise to enter the Pacific war three months after the fall of Germany. For the Japanese, who two days before had suffered history's first atomic attack, the Russian declaration set in motion the final process of surrender. Thus, once again, the Allied coalition had prevailed; but once again it was cracked and splintered with dissension. In the months since Germany's surrender hope had alternated with suspicion in Soviet-American relations, one fed by the lofty realization that future peace required present cooperation, the other by the baser fear that each would seek to gain at the advantage of the other. At the moment of Germany's surrender the United States and the USSR had been split on a wide range of issues fundamental to the future of the continent they had just liberated. A heroic final effort by the dying Hopkins, last symbol of the New Deal world FDR had hoped to create, had for a time seemed to close the breach. But the all but irreconcilable positions of the two sides, their mutual misperceptions of each other's intentions, and the uncertainties and inconsistencies of new, untried American leadership had contrived to reopen the split. The Potsdam Conference, in late July and early August, had at first given the appearance of Allied unity in victory, but only because its participants had chosen to postpone rather than face the differences they knew would belie the unified appearance they had created. Potsdam had been long on words but short on deeds, and within days of its termination East and West were sharply divided in both Europe and Asia. Truman had hoped that he could play the trump card of atomic power to advance U.S. plans for the postwar settlement, but he made no effort to do so for there was in fact no clear way he could. In his hand he held also the formidable economic power of the United States. The end of hostilities with Japan appeared to provide an opportunity to use this power, for it required a decision on the future of the massive lend-lease program. Since Russia's status under lend-lease was ill-defined (no longer governed by protocol, but without a 3-c termination agreement) some reasoned that a decision on the future of the program for Russia could be used to signal the USSR that its continued intransigence on matters of importance to the United States could prove costly to its hopes to benefit from America's vast economic power.

Termination Procedures for the Entire Program

This was not the central concern of FEA Administrator Crowley, yet it did complement nicely his intention—and his repeated promises to Congress—that lend-lease would end with the war. But the sudden end of the war took everyone, including Crowley, by surprise. As the month of August 1945 began, the final shot of the war appeared to be still many months away and termination questions concerning the disposition of requisitions, goods in production, and supplies in transit seemed largely academic. The explosion over Hiroshima on August 6, with its promise of a rapid end to hostilities, quickly changed all this and spurred planning for an equally abrupt end to lend-lease. On August 7 Crowley directed that a committee be set up "to study the discontinuance of lend-lease in case the Japanese war should be over shortly and also to study the cancellation of contracts . . ."[62] Meanwhile, some thinking had already been done on the matter in the British Empire and Middle East Branch of the FEA, and on August 9 the acting director of this branch, Ambrose C. Cramer, submitted to the FEA Executive Policy Committee a memorandum setting forth certain principles for termination, several of which were later incorporated in the general directive ending lend-lease.

Cramer assumed that the president would set a specific date for cutting off lend-lease, though he anticipated that there might be exceptions for the redeployment of troops and other purposes. He proposed that no requisitions be approved after the termination date and that contracts under previously approved requisitions be cancelled unless either the United States found it in its interest to continue them or the British took them over. As for completed goods not yet transferred to the British by the termination date, Cramer proposed that these "be disposed of on such terms as may be satisfactory to the U.S. government."[63] But even before this memorandum was discussed by the Executive Policy Committee, Crowley was taking the first steps to end lend-lease. On the morning of August 10 he directed that each branch of the FEA begin a review of its requisitions in preparation for cancellation after

V-J Day. Later in the day he decided on the cancellation of orders for raw materials and some industrial equipment in the event of V-J Day.[64] At the same time, War and Navy Department officials in charge of military lend-lease apparently decided on the immediate suspension of all sailings of U.S. ammunition ships. News of these activities soon began to leak and for the officials of the Supply Mission of Great Britain—the nation with the greatest stake in lend-lease—they were a source of considerable consternation.[65]

On Monday, August 13, Leo Crowley met with Admiral Leahy to discuss consulting President Truman on immediate action to be taken in regard to lend-lease after the ending of hostilities with Japan. Both agreed that future assistance should be restricted to areas where it would be needed for military purposes and that this probably would be only in China for the transportation of troops.[66] The following day— the day of the announcement of the surrender of Japan— Truman gave Crowley informal instructions to begin immediate steps to terminate lend-lease.[67] To others the president made known during the next two days his intention to curtail all lend-lease very promptly and his reluctance to allow even assistance for troop redeployment to continue for fear this would be misconstrued as rehabilitation. Crowley himself predicted in a press conference of August 15 that lend-lease would soon end.[68]

In the meantime, both the Joint Chiefs of Staff (who had authority over the transfer of military lend-lease) and the agencies controlling nonmilitary lend-lease were busy drawing up directives covering the termination of their phases of the program. The directive approved by the Joint Chiefs of Staff on August 11 proposed the cessation of Army-Navy lend-lease goods and services with the exception of mopping-up operations and certain cases where termination would cause undue hardships. It precluded in any case the issue of arms and ammunition and it limited supply to items such as rations, fuel, transportation services, and medical supplies where these could not be reasonably furnished by the foreign government receiving them. The substance of this directive—which went into effect on August 17—was eventually approved by

President Truman on September 5, 1945, as the established policy for all military-controlled lend-lease.[69]

The directive on nonmilitary lend-lease, of greater importance in the post-hostilities period—particularly to Britain and Russia—was in draft form by at least August 13. Basically, it was an expansion of the principles originally set forth by Ambrose Cramer in his proposal of August 9. It began by noting that although the Lend-Lease Act permitted the president to deliver supplies and furnish services as long as he determined such action was in the interest of the defense of the United States, nevertheless the administration had stated numerous times to the Congress that lend-lease would be discontinued at the end of the war. "In order that the best faith may be observed toward Congress," the draft directive went on, "and the administration protect itself against any charge of misuse of congressional authorization," certain steps were recommended "immediately upon the cessation of hostilities with Japan." These were:

    a. No new contracts will be entered into for goods to be furnished under lend-lease except for such items as the Joint Chiefs of Staff may approve for payment out of military appropriations.
    b. Countries with which 3-c agreements are in effect will take and pay for goods involved in contracts yet to be completed, goods awaiting shipment, those in transit, and inventories abroad.
    c. Countries which have not entered into 3-c agreements may obtain goods now in process of manufacture, in storage, awaiting shipment, being shipped or in inventory abroad, upon their agreement to pay for them on such terms as may be determined by this Government.
    d. All uncompleted contracts for goods not to be delivered under (b) and (c) above shall be immediately reviewed to determine whether their completion would be in the best interest of the Government and, unless so determined, such contracts will be cancelled.[70]

An accompanying "Memorandum for the President" explained that presidential reports to the Congress had emphasized several times that lend-lease would be discontinued at the end of the war. It further added that the FEA administrator had stated repeatedly that lend-lease would be used only for the war and not as a means for financing postwar relief and rehabilitation. The memorandum argued that the proposed directive would be "completely consistent" with these statements; then it went on to detail the effect of its provisions for the several major lend-lease recipients.

August 15 and 16 were declared holidays in celebration of the end of the war and very little important government business was conducted during those two days. On Friday, August 17, at 10:30 A.M., Truman met with Secretary of State Byrnes, Treasury Secretary Fred Vinson, War Mobilization and Reconstruction Director John Snyder, Crowley, and Admiral Leahy for the express purpose of talking about the cancellation of lend-lease. The discussion centered on the draft directive quoted above. Crowley, with the strong support of Snyder, vigorously supported the directive and advocated the immediate stoppage of lend-lease aid. Vinson just as strongly advocated its continuation. According to Leahy, the treasury secretary felt continuation was necessary "in order to preserve order in Western Europe and to prevent the spread of communism in the area." Vinson was alone, however, in this view, and after making his case he left the meeting. The group made no immediate decision, but the preponderance of opinion was clearly for prompt termination, and within two hours Truman informed Crowley that he had decided to approve the draft directive and that its provisions should be promptly carried out.[71]

That afternoon Crowley sent a memorandum to all FEA executive directors and branch heads informing them of the president's action but directing that no information about it be released pending notification of the governments involved. Truman had felt that immediate public announcement of the termination of lend-lease would be met with strong domestic approval, but Crowley prevailed upon him to wait at least until notice had been given to the recipient nations. He then directed on the following day, August 18, that letters be prepared notifyng each government of the change of policy. Six different

letters were prepared, designated "Type A" through "Type F."
In general they stated that no new requisitions would be
accepted and no new contracts made and that supplies then in
process could be purchased; but there was also considerable
variation among the letters depending on whether the nations
involved had signed a 3-c agreement as well as just how strictly
the United States wanted to enforce the termination of
particular assistance programs (as will be seen, the Soviet
Union was one of those marked out for special treatment and its
own "type" letter). On the same date an additional group of
letters was sent out by the FEA setting forth the new policy to
the various departments and agencies that procured lend-lease
materials. The letters described the actions to be taken
regarding requisitions, contracts, and supplies on hand and
stated that the transfer of goods should continue under existing
delivery schedules until 12:01 A.M. of the date to be proclaimed
as V-J Day (later set as September 2). There were two major
exceptions, however. One concerned Italy, where the army was
to continue shipments under special arrangements made with
that country. The other concerned the Soviet Union. (Later, the
decision to continue lend-lease to China constituted a third
major exception.) For the Russians the relevant passage
stated: "The action to be taken pursuant to this letter . . . will
not apply to procurement or transfer of lend-lease goods or
services for the USSR which has been covered in separate
instructions."[72]

Termination Procedures Specifically for the USSR

The "separate instructions" for the USSR were signed by the
acting director of the President's Soviet Protocol Committee,
Col. William McChesney Martin, on August 11, 1945, three
days before the Japanese surrender and six days before the
decision to terminate the entire lend-lease program. Action in
anticipation of these instructions had begun even earlier, in the
first days of August, and had accelerated following the
explosion of the two atomic bombs on Japan. On August 2 and
3, members of the USSR Branch of the FEA held meetings on
the future of the Russian shipping program and the possibility
of cancelling contracts for equipment and machinery for the

Soviet Union. Similar meetings were held on August 7 and 8, and on August 9 Colonel Martin and Lieutenant Colonel Hicklin of the Army Service Forces agreed in a telephone conversation that "any material [for Russia] already shipped from depot or facility will be allowed to go forward but that any quantities of material not yet shipped from depot or facility would be withheld and not made available to the USSR until further notice.[73] The following day Martin called John Hazard of the USSR Branch and discussed shipping policy in the event of V-J Day. It was agreed that loading on all ships should be stopped and that they should be held pending a decision on unloading them. On the same day Gen. Sidney Spalding, just returned to the United States from his post in Moscow, called Hazard to express his hope that "it would be possible to act less vigorously than on V-E Day, since that action had caused a great stir in Moscow." This was but a single vote for less haste, however, and in the rush of events its advice was soon forgotten.[74]

Colonel Martin's instructions of August 11, subsequently approved by Leo Crowley, stated that "immediately upon official announcement of termination of hostilities" appropriate steps should be taken by each agency responsible for Russian shipments to insure the application of certain prescribed principles. These included: cessation of loading of Soviet-flag steamers in U.S. ports; cessation of loading and discharge of cargo of U.S.-flag steamers bound for the USSR; permission for loaded and cleared ships to sail to the USSR; the prohibition of further berthing of ships to load lend-lease cargo; the cessation of lend-lease assistance in stores, supplies, bunkers, and other port charges incurred by Soviet-flag steamers; the stopping of repairs to Soviet vessels undertaken on a lend-lease basis; and the halting of lend-lease cargo moving to port from interior points of production or storage.[75] These instructions were not immediately transmitted to the Russians, but their substance was conveyed to U.S. agencies involved in lend-lease procurement and shipping. On August 11 General Wesson wrote to the Procurement Division of the Treasury Department requesting it to cancel Russian lend-lease requisitions and contracts upon the official announce-

ment of V-J Day. Other agencies were asked to do what was
necessary to assist in this cancellation, and on the same day the
War Shipping Administration instructed its port officers
concerning the cessation of cargo loading and related activities
in the event of V-J Day.[76] Two days later General Wesson went
even further.. Apparently sensing the imminence of the
Japanese capitulation and anxious to terminate the Russian
program as soon as possible, he directed his branch on August
13 to suspend the processing of all requisitions and requested
Treasury Procurement to hold up the awarding of any more
contracts.[77]

At seven o'clock on the evening of August 14 President
Truman announced Japan's acceptance of unconditional
surrender, but he did not at that time officially proclaim V-J
Day since the formal Japanese surrender had not yet been
arranged. On August 16 Colonel Martin, with the approval of
Leo Crowley, transmitted to General Rudenko of the Soviet
Purchasing Commission a copy of the special instructions of
August 11 summarized above. In his covering letter Martin
stated that the instructions were being sent because "V-J Day is
upon us." He added that items "now unshipped or under
procurement" could be purchased for cash or through credit
from the Export-Import Bank and he advised Rudenko to
apply directly to the bank's Washington address.[78] Copies of
this covering letter and the enclosed instructions were then sent
for action and information to all members of the protocol
committee and to the Military Mission in Moscow. Early the
following morning, and *before* the decision made at the White
House to terminate lend-lease, Martin instructed the War
Shipping Administration to stop all shipping to Russia. Later
in the morning, but still before the White House meeting,
Martin informed the USSR Branch that Crowley wished to
continue loading vessels to the USSR and that orders had been
changed accordingly. Finally, at 1:20 P.M., Martin called the
USSR Branch again and, according to Hazard's journal, "said
that Mr. Crowley had reported to him that the policy to stop
shipments had been approved by the president to become
effective immediately, but with a minimum of disturbance. No
more cargo is to be loaded or moved to port except to round out
the ships."[79]

This confused and precipitous cutoff of lend-lease to Russia was thus almost a mirror image of the cutback made on May 12 following V-E Day. Policy was changed several times, orders were issued only to be shortly cancelled, and lower echelon personnel were left uncertain for several days as to just what procedures to follow. The records of August 17 of the agencies involved show a confusing collection of letters and telegrams issuing and rescinding orders, many of them received out of the sequence in which they were sent. John Hutchins of the War Shipping Administration, who had suffered and lamented the confusion of the May cutback, summed up his frustration over the situation when he telegraphed his San Francisco representative at the end of the day: "Policy still highly confused at top levels. Orders to cancel have been on and off several times yesterday and today. Suggest no action your end pending instructions."[80]

Even more significant than the confusion of August 17 was the fact that lend-lease to Russia was cut off immediately and not allowed to continue until the officially declared V-J Day, as was the case with every other recipient nation. This was implicit in the letters of August 18 to department and agency heads mentioning the "separate instructions" covering lend-lease for the USSR. It was explicit in a number of other written and verbal communications noting that a very different policy was being applied to the Soviet Union. An example of this was a note, added during the morning of August 17 to an earlier letter regarding procedures for future Russian lend-lease cancellations, which stated: "Notified WPB [War Production Board] and Treasury that it had been decided to institute cancellations immediately without awaiting official announcement of V-J Day." A further illustration is found in a memorandum written by the assistant chief of the State Department's Division of Lend Lease and Surplus War Property, which noted that lend-lease transfers to other countries were continuing until V-J Day and then added, "the outcome is, therefore, that the USSR is being treated on a different basis from other countries."[81]

The Russians were not specifically informed of their unique cancellation status, but it was not long before they learned of it. The letter (designated "Type F") that notified them of the end of the program was dated August 18 and delivered at noon on the twentieth. It mentioned no precise termination date, but it expressed the FEA's desire to enter into negotiations "immediately . . . relating to the discontinuance of its lend-lease aid." As general principles to guide these negotiations it mentioned the prohibition of any new contracts on lend-lease terms and the possibility of the USSR obtaining for payment supplies then in the process of manufacture, in stowage, or awaiting shipment.[82] By at least the next day the Russians were aware from reports and shipping activity that cancellation procedures for them were different from those for other lend-lease recipients. On that date they raised this matter with officials of the Army Service Forces and at the same time cancelled or diverted calls of Soviet cargo vessels at U.S. ports.[83]

For the next four days the status of lend-lease to the USSR remained unchanged; then quite suddenly, on Saturday morning, August 25, Crowley informed General Wesson that necessary changes were required in lend-lease shipping policy to provide the same treatment for the USSR as that being received by other countries. After a conference with Wesson and Colonel Martin, Willis Armstrong, acting deputy director of the USSR Branch, issued new instructions superseding all previous orders regarding Russian lend-lease. These new instructions directed that all lend-lease cargo on approved USSR programs could be loaded on available Soviet flag-ships, that additional Soviet flag-ships could be berthed to load such cargo, that Soviet-flag vessels under repair on August 18 would be completed on a lend-lease basis, and that services and supplies would be furnished in the customary manner to all ships carrying Russian lend-lease cargo of any category. The statement concluded by stipulating that the foregoing principles would be maintained until 12:01 A.M. on the day designated as V-J Day.[84] The effect of these new instructions was to place the Soviet Union in the same lend-lease status as all other recipients in accordance with the directives of August 18 to department and agency heads; and until final termination (actually September 20, the date of the last sailing of a vessel for Russia with lend-lease cargo) the Soviet Union retained this status.

The Role of Implementation
of the USSR Termination

In the light of this discussion of the ending of lend-lease, two important questions need to be examined: First, why was the whole program ended so precipitously? Second, why was lend-lease to Russia terminated immediately, then a week later allowed to run until V-J Day in the manner applicable to other recipients?

The precipitous ending of the entire lend-lease program has been strongly criticized, especially by those who were most closely involved. Two months after the event Truman's press secretary, Charles Ross, referred to it as the one instance he could recall of harm having been done "from somebody's not having taken time to think." In an article in *Collier's* magazine two years later, former Treasury Secretary Morgenthau wrote that "the U.S. government, without warning, brutally terminated the operating of the Lend-Lease Act, cutting our Allies adrift at a time when they were still maimed and crippled by the war." In his memoirs, published in 1969, Dean Acheson called the decision "disastrous," complained that "it knocked the financial bottom out of the whole Allied military position," and recalled that even President Truman later came to think of it as a "grave mistake."[85] At the time there was also considerable dissatisfaction over the manner in which lend-lease was ended, though most of this was expressed by second-echelon officials and not at the level of department and agency heads. In the FEA, Crowley's deputy, Oscar Cox, made strenuous efforts to partially continue lend-lease beyond the end of hostilities, or at least to delay its termination and mitigate the effects of its cessation. He was able to do little more, however, than influence Crowley to orally inform the governments involved of the new policy before it was officially announced; and even this was largely thwarted by leaks and the absence of top embassy personnel, many of whom had taken leave of Washington during the first weekend of peace.[86] In the Treasury Department, Vinson's assistant, Edward F. Pritchard, Jr., informed the secretary on August 20 that the president was about to release a statement on lend-lease and warned that

"Unless something is done, Crowley will try to put over something pretty rough." To his suggestion that Vinson take the lead in proposing a program to Congress to ease the transition from lend-lease, the secretary—evidently chastened by the negative response his ideas on the subject had received at the White House on August 17—replied on the memo, "Think not, I do not care to initiate it."[87]

In London, just before the termination was announced, a visiting State Department delegation consisting of Assistant Secretary William Clayton and Director of Financial and Development Policy Emilio Collado had been listening sympathetically (and in the same manner advising the State Department) to Lord Keynes's hopes that there would be a lend-lease transition period following V-J Day and that in any event "no hasty decisions" would be taken. But their advice went unheeded and they were deeply disturbed when they learned from their British colleagues on Saturday, August 19 of the sudden cutoff. Clayton took to the trans-Atlantic telephone in high dudgeon the following day, but other than influencing a few minor adjustments (e.g., that terms of payments for goods in the pipeline be agreed upon mutually rather than set unilaterally) his efforts to alter the basic decision were of no avail.[88]

In Washington the FEA and the White House stuck by the policy made on August 17 but soon found themselves forced by widely circulating rumors to make a public announcement explaining the actions being taken in the wake of their decision. A presidential directive, released on Monday, August 21—before several recipient nations had received written notification of the end of the program—crisply announced the cancellation of all outstanding lend-lease contracts (except where Allied governments were willing to take them over or the United States to complete them) and instructed the FEA director to negotiate with recipient nations for possible procurement of inventories in stockpile or in process of delivery.[89] The reaction to this announcement in the Congress and from the public provides an important clue for the explanation of why the decision was made to end lend-lease so abruptly. In the Senate and House, members of both parties hailed the White House statement and generally indicated that it was precisely the course of action they had expected. Public response also favored the termination. The FEA received 67 letters on the subject, 58 of which approved the action taken. Of 208 letters received at the White House, 119 supported Truman's directive while 89 either disapproved or at least thought some aid similar to lend-lease should be continued to help those who had suffered from the ravages of the war. Four months later a *Fortune* poll showed that 67.8 percent of those questioned approved the cutoff of lend-lease while only 19 percent thought it should have continued for another year.[90]

Crowley had promised the Congress on numerous occasions that lend-lease would end with the war. He believed this was the view of the late President Roosevelt, and he apparently obtained complete acquiescence from his successor. Truman had been presiding in the Senate at the time of the final extension of lend-lease, and while he had opposed the very restrictive amendment offered by Senator Taft, he had later expressed the opinion that lend-lease was strictly a wartime measure. In addition, Truman had important programs of postwar demobilization and reconversion that would need Congress's approval and he was anxious to bank all the good will he could in that body. Both Crowley and the president, as well as many others in the lend-lease program, felt that the war-weary public would be in no mood to countenance additional expenditures for foreign nations (and possibly extended controls and rationing) that had little prospect of tangible return, and Truman especially felt that the American taxpayer would applaud the savings that a prompt termination of lend-lease would bring. (It was undoubtedly for this reason that his August 21 directive concluded by implying a savings of $3.5 billion in goods that would not have to be transferred.)

It seems clear from the foregoing that the abrupt end of lend-lease stemmed mainly from a desire to redeem past promises as quickly as possible so as to convey to Congress and the people an impression of both rectitude and economy. The termination was not preceded by any threat that it would be taken unless certain concessions were forthcoming from recipient nations, nor was it used as a lever to gain support for economic principles favored by the United States. Some, in fact, were critical that this was *not* attempted. The most lasting criticisms, however, dealt with the manner in which the cutoff was made. It was unilateral and it was abrupt; there was no transition period and there was no tapering off to allow already strained economies to adjust to the inevitable end. In part this was due simply to the abrupt end of the war; but even more it was due to a failure to understand the major role played by lend-lease in the economies of the countries it aided and hence the enormous impact of its sudden termination. That the failure was attributable less to deliberate design than to an insensitivity born of inexperience in foreign politics and nurtured by inordinate attention to domestic politics made little difference to the final consequence of the decision: it hurt rather than helped the construction of a base of international cooperation on which American leaders hoped to erect a more peaceful postwar world.

The manner in which lend-lease for the USSR was terminated is less easily explained. It is clear that the decision to cut off the Russians immediately, thus treating them differently from other recipients, was deliberate and not accidental. It also appears that this was done with the knowledge and acquiescence of the president. Circumstances at the time appear at first glance to support an explanation that depicts these events as an American effort to use economic pressure against the Soviet Union: the weeks following Potsdam had seen a rapid resurfacing of the underlying conflicts that the conference had only glossed, and in the third week of August several of these conflicts had become severe irritants in Soviet-American relations. In the Balkans the isolation of U.S. and British representatives in the Soviet-dominated Allied Control Commissions had become so pronounced that the State Department instructed Ambassador Harriman to lodge a protest with the Kremlin.[91] In the Far East a Soviet demand for a veto over the appointment of a supreme commander for Japan had been countered a few days later by an American demand for base rights on the Kurile Islands, where the Russians were taking over in accordance with the Yalta Agreements,[92] and in London the Russians remained intransigent in their request for $700 million worth of relief and rehabilitation supplies from UNRRA.[93]

This explanation is given support by the response on August 21 of John Hazard to the inquiry of James Maxwell, assistant chief of the State Department's Lend-Lease and Surplus Property Division, concerning the reason for the different lend-lease status of the USSR. According to Maxwell, Hazard replied "that the decision was taken deliberately and probably was part of a general squeeze now being put on the USSR."[94] In addition, the reinstatement of Soviet lend-lease deliveries to the same status as that of other recipients on August 25 coincided with a significant relaxation of Russian pressure on several of the matters that were disturbing Soviet-American relations. For example, in the Balkans the Bulgarian government announced on August 24 that it was postponing elections that had been set for two days later, prompting the fears of resident Allied representatives that a communist-dominated totalitarian government would be the outcome.[95] With regard to the occupation of Japan, an exchange of messages between Stalin and Truman commencing on August 25 suggested that misunderstandings had occurred and served to soothe ruffled feelings; and in London, beginning on August 22, the Soviets started backing off from their $700 million UNRRA request and eventually settled for a compromise plan of $250 million in aid to the Ukrainian and Byelorussian republics.[96]

However, such a view of the cutoff is based on circumstantial and coincidental evidence; it fits facts to an explanation that seems to account for them. However, it does so in the absence of any evidence of a causal link between motives expressed and actions taken, and in the presence of several points that visibly weaken the argument for a deliberate policy of pressure. In the published memoirs and private papers of the participants, and in the records of their departments and agencies, no evidence has been found to support the view that the United States cut off lend-lease to Russia on August 17 to deliberately apply pressure for cooperation on other matters; nor does the evidence indicate that lend-lease was restored on August 25 because that cooperation was forthcoming. Furthermore, such an explanation flies in the face of the limited utility of such a temporary cutback. It ignores both the fact that lend-lease was terminated for substantial reasons apart from the status of Soviet-American relations and the realization by those involved that the official proclamation of V-J Day—and thus the end of lend-lease—was most likely just a few days away.

A better explanation can be found by examining the implementation of the general decision to end lend-lease for the Russian program. As this study has shown, continued lend-lease to Russia had fewer and fewer supporters as the months of 1945 wore on, bringing first victory over Germany, then concentration against Japan with the USSR still in the status of a neutral. In the weeks following V-E Day it was left to Harriman in Moscow to urge fulfillment of Russian supply requests while Crowley and General Wesson—at the source of supply in Washington—resisted. Under these conditions loadings for Russia were drastically reduced and procurement of future cargo was on a month-by-month basis. In addition, there was no 3-c agreement with Russia to provide payment for material in the pipeline at the end of hostilities, and, in the case of the USSR, efforts to conclude such an agreement had failed, largely because of the stubbornness of the Russians. In the termination procedures there was, to be sure, provision for payment for supplies in process, but experience to date had gravely weakened confidence that the Soviet Union would make such payment.

On the part of those who were to implement the cutoff decision for Russia there was thus a disposition to do so at the earliest possible opportunity. In accordance with this disposition, planning for termination begun in the USSR Branch of FEA in the first days of August was well advanced by the time of the explosion of the second atomic bomb, and was being translated into action in the days that followed. Within forty-eight hours of the surrender announcement—and before the decision to terminate lend-lease was actually made—the Russians were told that for them the program was ending. There was some hesitancy the next day—August 17—when the actual date of termination of all lend-lease was set for the still-to-be-announced day of surrender, but to Harry Truman the explanations of Leo Crowley, combined with the recently fractious behavior of the Russians and the evident imminence (within only a few days it then appeared) of the official surrender, must have been convincing. There seemed to be no good reason to stop procedures for ending the USSR program that were, after all, already under way, and many reasons not to do so. A week later, with V-J Day definitely set for a week hence, with a slightly improved climate warming Soviet-American relations, and with the Russians aware that they were being accorded separate and discriminatory treatment, the USSR's lend-lease status must have appeared both anomalous and potentially embarrassing; and so it was changed.[97]

Thus, the peculiar ending of lend-lease to Russia—much like its equally peculiar cutback three months earlier—can be accounted for largely by the manner in which it was implemented, a process characterized by prior commitments, inadequate guidance, and a legacy of fixed views and mixed motives. In the end the result was similar to what would have happened had the termination been carefully planned as an effort to employ economic leverage: it served as an additional unnecessary irritant in U.S.-USSR relations; it demonstrated pique more than firmness; and it gained no concessions from the Soviet Union. In fact, as Roosevelt had well understood, lend-lease was a dubious weapon for economic warfare, and this was especially the case at the moment of its termination. There was, however, in the American economic arsenal another weapon many felt had much higher potential. This was the extension of long-term credits for postwar reconstruction.

6
Russia's Two Requests
for Postwar Loans

During the first eight months of 1945 the USSR made two formal requests to the United States for large-scale credits for postwar reconstruction. The first—for $6 billion—was made early in January in Moscow. The second—for $1 billion—was proposed late in August in Washington. At about the same time as the first Russian request Secretary of the Treasury Henry Morgenthau, Jr. also set forth his own plan—authored principally by his assistant secretary, Harry Dexter White—for a $10 billion loan to the USSR. While Morgenthau's plan was never formally acted upon it did influence disposition of the first Soviet request and thus came to play a role in the vital implementation phase of the response to that request, a phase that was to prove just as decisive in the disposition of the second Soviet request.

The First USSR Request and the Morgenthau Proposal

On the evening of January 3, 1945, Ambassador Harriman called upon Foreign Commissar Molotov at the latter's request and received from him an aide-memoire that in Harriman's words was "extraordinary both in form and substance." Molotov referred to the statements of public figures in the United States on the desirability of large Soviet orders in the postwar period and stated that the Soviet Union considered it possible to place orders for manufactured goods and industrial equipment on the basis of long-term credits in the amount of $6 billion. These credits would also cover orders for goods and materials placed under lend-lease but not delivered before the end of the war, thus embracing what was intended by the proposed 3-c Agreement. The total period of the credits would be thirty years with amortization over the last twenty on a gradually increasing scale. Molotov further proposed that annual interest be fixed at 2-1/4 percent and that the United States grant to the USSR a discount of 20 percent on orders placed before the end of the war and falling under the credit.[1]

Three days later, after he had recovered from what he described as his "surprise at Molotov's strange procedure," Harriman telegraphed his reactions to the State Department. He first dismissed the unconventional character of the request, chalking it up to "ignorance of normal business procedures and the strange ideas of the Russians on how to get the best trade." He then expressed his opinion that since greater tolerance by the USSR would come only as its people achieved a more decent life, the United States should do everything possible through credits to help the Soviet Union develop a strong economy; but he added that "the U.S. Government should retain control of any credits granted in order that the political advantages may be retained and that we may be satisfied the equipment purchased is for purposes that meet our general approval." Furthermore, Harriman argued, "At an appropriate time the Russians should be given to understand that our willingness to cooperate wholeheartedly with them in their vast reconstruction problems will depend upon their behavior in international matters." Molotov had made it clear, Harriman said, that a large postwar credit would be very important in the development of future Soviet-American relations. Therefore the time had come, he suggested, for the government's policy to be crystallized so that the entire matter could be discussed with the Russians at the high level "meeting" (Yalta) then being planned.[2]

Three days earlier, on New Year's Day, Treasury Secretary Henry Morgenthau, Jr. had sent to President Roosevelt a letter—with a copy for the new secretary of state, Edward Stettinius—explaining that he had a plan for comprehensive aid to the USSR that was not lend-lease or any form of relief, but "arrangement that will have definite and long-range benefits for the United States as well as for Russia." He went on to explain that his plan would aid the Russians in their reconstruction and help iron out many of the difficulties the United States was having with the Soviet Union.[3] Morgenthau was actually responding to a request, made over a year earlier, by FDR; but the plan he presented, in its scope and substance, was a unique creature of the Treasury, the product of Morgenthau's own vision of the future world economic order and the internationalist philosophy of his chief assistants; and it was offered to FDR with the full prestige of its author's twelve years as a close, personal, and influential colleague.

What Morgenthau proposed—as set forth in a memorandum to the president ten days later—was a $10 billion credit to be used to purchase goods in the United States needed for Russian reconstruction. The loan was to be amortized over a period of thirty-five years, at an annual interest rate of 2 percent, with repayment to be chiefly in raw materials in short supply in the United States. In supporting such a loan Morgenthau put forward to FDR just two reasons: first, it would enable the United States to conserve its depleted natural resources by drawing on Russia's reserves; and second, it would be a major step in Roosevelt's program "to provide 60 million jobs in the post-war period."[4]

Within the first ten days of January 1945, Washington thus had two concrete proposals to consider for massive long-term credits to the Soviet Union—Molotov's for $6 billion and Secretary Morgenthau's for $10 billion. On January 2, Stettinius had asked Assistant Secretary William Clayton to recommend the position the State Department should take on Morgenthau's proposal. Two days later he received a reply from Emilio Collado, chief of the Division of Financial and Monetary Affairs, that reiterated the arguments of the OSS study of the previous September concerning the utility of credits and cautioned—largely on the basis of anticipated congressional reluctance—against Morgenthau's proposal.[5]

It was a week later that Morgenthau brought the details of his proposal to the White House and sought to personally convince Roosevelt that it should be adopted. On the morning of that day he and Stettinius together raised the question of

Russian credits with FDR. According to Morgenthau's recollection it was a difficult session. The president appeared to be "very tired," and Stettinius seemed anxious to prevent him from reading Morgenthau's proposal. Stettinius came away with the impression that Roosevelt did not wish to do anything further about the matter until he talked with Stalin personally, while Morgenthau was convinced that since FDR was not taking any finance people with him to the Big Three Conference nothing further would be done until he returned to Washington. At lunch Morgenthau expressed his disappointment to Admiral Leahy: "Both the President and Stettinius were wrong," he later recalled telling FDR's chief of staff. "If they wanted to get the Russians to do something they should say it the first thing. Do it nice. . . . Don't drive such a hard bargain that when you come through it does not taste good." Later that afternoon he continued over the telephone his argument with Stettinius: "this I feel very, very strongly . . . with all due respect to the President and you, I think you are a hundred percent wrong on the approach to Russia. And I think that the carrot should be put before their nose when you first get there and let them know there's going to be financial aid for them while they're at war and financial aid for them when the war is over."[6]

The matter was next considered at an interdepartmental meeting a week later, and in preparation for that session Emilio Collado drew up for Stettinius's use a long background memorandum on aid to the USSR. In general it called for stiffer terms and a much lower credit than the Treasury proposal, and it considerably played down the commodity purchase option which Morgenthau had reckoned as one of the major features of his plan. In speaking of U.S. interests in a credit to the USSR Collado argued that it was general policy to extend credits for sound economic development, but that U.S. export industries would not be aided as much as the Soviets suggested. However, there were also political considerations to bear in mind, and he went on to call attention to the American desire to improve overall diplomatic relations with the USSR in a variety of areas, including:

Soviet participation in the Dumbarton Oaks program . . . in economic collaboration such as the Bretton Woods proposals . . . in the United Maritime Authority; the establishment of a proper role for the United States in the Allied Control Commissions in Rumania, Bulgaria, Hungary, and, eventually, Germany; establishing a proper role for the U.S. in general economic relations with the reconstruction and development of Poland, Czechoslovakia, and the Balkan nations and establishing a proper basis in Iran.

Collado also included among U.S. interests several questions "outstanding for a very long time," including the Kerensky debt to the U.S. government and the claims of private citizens who had properties in the USSR. He acknowledged that the department's experience had shown that the specific balancing of claims against credits had not been a successful diplomatic technique, but he felt it might be more successful with the Russians and that in particular the large amount of credits suggested might improve the U.S. bargaining position in achieving the various political objectives it had vis-à-vis the Soviet Union.[7]

The outcome of the interdepartmental meeting was inconclusive (Clayton had earlier advised Stettinius not to attempt to reach any immediate decision on the Soviet loan question), but subsequent developments indicated rather clearly that it was the State Department's position, and not the Treasury's, that would prevail. On the following day a memorandum for Stettinius, incorporating the views of Clayton and "the political office," summed up the opinion of the department. It argued that a $10 billion credit at very low interest rates over a long period was not a wise way to deal with the Soviets and that "the offer of such a large credit would be regarded as a sign of political weakness rather than as a great concession for which they would make important diplomatic concessions to the United States." The memorandum suggested instead that consideration be given to the extension of a $1 billion credit— with details, such as the interest rate, to be discussed later—to be handled under the increased loan authorization to be requested for the Export-Import Bank.[8] That same day

Roosevelt confirmed to Stettinius that he preferred to delay the whole question of postwar financing until he saw Stalin personally and could discuss the matter with him. Two days later, with Harriman's concurrence, Clayton advanced to Stettinius the additional argument that "from a tactical point of view" it would be harmful to offer such a large credit so early and lose what appeared to be "the only concrete bargaining lever for use in connection with the many other political and economic problems which will arise between our two countries."[9]

Proposed United States Response

Although Morgenthau's $10 billion credit plan continued to be mentioned from time to time, by the end of January it was virtually a dead issue, a conclusion that seemed clear to Morgenthau from a conversation he had with Clayton at that time and which the State Department implicitly conveyed to Ambassador Harriman a day later on the eve of his departure for Yalta.[10] On that same day the Soviet $6-billion proposal, which was also virtually dead (though the Russians had not yet received a formal reply to it), suddenly became public knowledge. Either through a leak or through shrewd investigative reporting, James Reston of the *New York Times* learned of the Russian request and the *Times* made the story front page news. Possibly spurred by this revelation, which caused a considerable stir at the highest levels in Washington and some embarrassment to the U.S. Embassy in Moscow, Acting Secretary of State Grew immediately sent Chargé George Kennan instructions for a reply to the Russian proposal. Kennan was authorized to state, first, that it was necessary to segregate the financing of projects ordered under lend-lease from that dealing with projects for purely postwar purposes; second, that the U.S. government was studying ways of providing postwar credits but that it would be some time before the necessary legislation could be enacted and a determination could be made with respect to amounts that could be made available; and third, that it was the opinion of the government that long-term postwar credits represented an important element in future Soviet-American relations.

Finally, Kennan was advised that the substance of this message was being sent to Harriman at Yalta and since he might have discussions on the subject there, it was suggested that no action be taken on it "pending further instructions from him or the Department."[11] At the end of January 1945, further discussion of postwar credits to the USSR was thus in abeyance and all attention was turned to the Crimean resort of Yalta.

In preparation for the Yalta Conference a "Briefing Book Paper" had been prepared that summarized the major points of the message that Grew had sent to Kennan concerning postwar credits but offered no specific proposals. However, a note attached to this paper indicated that a decision would be made early in the following week either to give the president a "general background with alternative suggestions" on the matter or "to make interagency agreed recommendations."[12] As it happened, neither course was taken and the matter was never formally raised in any of the Big Three discussions. Two passing references did indicate, though, that it was definitely on the minds of the Soviet leaders. When, at a dinner hosted by Roosevelt on the first day of the conference, the president was being kidded about whether he had actually ordered 500 bottles of champagne from Moscow, Stalin interjected that he would give them to him on a long-term credit of thirty years. The following day, at a luncheon meeting of the foreign ministers, when the subject of economic matters relating to Germany came up, Molotov stated his government's expectation that reparations would be received from Germany and his hope that the United States would furnish the USSR with long-term credits. Stettinius replied that the U.S. government had studied the question and that he was ready to discuss it at any time in Moscow or Washington.[13]

Back in Washington, consideration of the matter continued, both in the various executive departments concerned and with the Russians. Early in February Acting Secretary of State Grew informed Soviet Chargé Nikolai Novikov that Molotov's credit request of Janaury 3 was receiving "careful consideration" and that a response would be made "as soon as possible." There then followed the exchange of messages previously described in which Novikov asserted that his government was counting on

Molotov's proposal to also cover lend-lease goods with a postwar use and Grew replied that these constituted a separate and distinct matter to be covered by the proposed 3-c Agreement. Throughout this exchange the Russians were assured that their credit proposal was being given "careful consideration," but at the end of March, when they were told that the 3-c Agreement proposals offered them earlier had lapsed, they were also informed that their request of January 3 would necessitate additional appropriate legislation by the Congress that would require "a considerable amount of time to effectuate."[14]

While these communications were being exchanged progress continued to be extremely slow in implementing the decisions taken almost a year before to repeal the Johnson Act and increase the lending authority of the Export-Import Bank. The president had indicated his support for legislation to effect these changes when he submitted his budget message to Congress in January, and a month later, in a message urging prompt congressional action on the Bretton Woods agreements, Roosevelt stated that he would shortly be making proposals regarding the Export-Import Bank and the Johnson Act. However, despite the strong endoresment of such cabinet members as the new secretary of commerce, Henry Wallace, these proposals moved slowly in the administration's cumbersome wartime bureaucracy.[15] In late March Oscar Cox sent a memorandum to FEA Director Crowley concerning his efforts to "poke along" the Bureau of the Budget to get final clearance on the necessary legislation, and early in April James Reston, in a front page article in the *New York Times* reporting uneasiness in the capital over Russian relations, cited as a major Soviet grievance the failure of the U.S. government to respond to its request for postwar credits. Almost as if replying to Reston, Secretary Stettinius on the day following his article assured the Council on Foreign Relations in a public address that very soon Congress would be asked to expand the lending authority of the Export-Import Bank and repeal the Johnson Act.[16]

By that date, however, there was indeed a growing "uneasiness" in Soviet-American relations, a development acutely described in the two strongly worded messages Harriman sent from Moscow in early April in which he argued that the selfish interests of the Soviet government must force the United States to use its economic influence more positively. With specific reference to economic aid, he felt that the Russians regarded the continued generous and considerate attitude of America as a sign of weakness. They must be disabused of the notion, Harriman warned, that they can have U.S. help on their own terms, and when they failed in their actions to take American interests into account then the United States should indicate its displeasure in ways that would definitely affect their interests.[17]

On the day Harriman sent his second message, Acting Secretary of State Acheson cabled him a query that allowed Harriman to make specific recommendations on postwar credits in the context of his maturing views on Soviet-American relations. Acheson requested detailed comment on Morgenthau's all-but-dead $10 billion credit proposal, and Harriman responded at length in a message sent from Moscow on the afternoon of April 11, the eve of the day that turned out to be Roosevelt's last. He first stated that he agreed with the State Department's negative stand regarding Morgenthau's proposal but disagreed with the department's assessment (based on the September 1944 OSS report) of Russia's interest in foreign credits. He felt that the Russians had plans for a large-scale expansion of industrial production, would buy abroad on credit, and had carefully calculated their needs for purchases from the United States at a maximum of $6 billion. He was therefore inclined to discard the conclusion that the USSR would be able "to take a highly independent position, since two billion dollars in credits would speed up by only three or four months its reconstruction program." On the basis of his analysis Harriman felt credits should be extended and that the best means for doing so was the Export-Import Bank, provided that the United States retained the power to restrict or reduce such credits as it saw fit. Finally, Harriman concluded, the Soviet government should be encouraged to feel that the United States was favorably disposed toward assisting its reconstruction but that "we should at all times make it plain that our cooperation is dependent upon a reciprocal cooperative attitude of the Soviet government on other matters."[18]

It is difficult to determine how influential Harriman's opinion had become in the formation of Roosevelt's Russian policy by April 11, 1945. Attention was paid it, and it was, to be sure, highly valued; but it was only one of several competing views in an anarchic structure designed by a chief executive who kept his own counsel and seemed at times able to occupy all sides of an issue. Economic leverage for political purposes was a tactic not unknown to Roosevelt; but throughout the war he had eschewed the application of economic power to influence Soviet behavior on the grounds that it probably would be counterproductive. In the second week of April his pique at the Kremlin's contumacy had reached an unprecedented high and he must have been tempted to follow to the letter Harriman's advice; but instead he urged patience and sought to quiet the alarms of his Moscow ambassador. It is idle to speculate how long he would have continued to follow such a course. Within twenty-four hours fate gave a nudge to the kaleidoscope of history and the old pattern was gone forever. Roosevelt was dead, Truman was president, and Harriman's influence was in rapid ascent.

The New President and His Advisors

On April 13, the weekly "Digest of Problems Before the State Department" noted that "outside of questions relating to other areas [Eastern Europe], the most important present problem connected with our relations with the Soviet Union is that of the extension of credits."[19] On the same date the new president was informed of the Soviet credit request in a special report from Stettinius on the major foreign policy problems then before the United States. Truman's reaction at the time is not known, and in fact he later denied knowledge of the Russian request; but he has recorded in his *Memoirs* his support for the use of the Export-Import Bank, and possibly the International Bank, as a better means to assist the reconstruction of Europe than an extended lend-lease program.[20]

The impending visit to Washington at the end of April of Foreign Commissar Molotov brought the Soviet loan request to the forefront, and Charles E. Bohlen, assistant to the secretary of state for White House liaison, included it in a list of nine questions that might be raised in the ensuing discussion. Bohlen advised Stettinius to inform Molotov that his request of January 3 was being given "careful consideration" but that legislation by Congress would be required. Furthermore, Bohlen recommended that it might be advisable to point out to Molotov that Congress would doubtless be influenced by prospects for Soviet-American collaboration and that in addition "Congress reflects public opinion and that public opinion in this country has been greatly concerned over developments in Eastern Europe since the Crimea Conference."[21] In the State Department Emilio Collado authored another detailed recommendation for Stettinius and Assistant Secretary Clayton on the subject of reconstruction credits to the Soviet Union. Collado recommended legislative arrangements to put the Export-Import Bank in a position to begin negotiations with the Russians "shortly after the conclusion of the San Francisco conference, if political conditions are favorable" on a long-term credit of $1 billion. He further advised that the rate of interest be based on other long-term loans of the bank, that controls be established to assure that funds would be expended on U.S. reconstruction goods, that no commodity purchase arrangement be included, and that consideration of any future additional credits be handled, in part at least, through the International Bank set up at Bretton Woods. These recommendations were approved by Clayton and turned over to Under Secretary Grew by Stettinius; no immediate decision was made on them, however, pending the imminent arrival in Washington for consultations of the one American who had the most recent contact with the Soviet leadership, Ambassador Averell Harriman.[22]

The Secretary's Staff Committee held two long meetings with Harriman, on April 20 and 21, mainly exchanging views over the full range of U.S. relations with the Soviet Union. In discussing the question of postwar credits Harriman strongly agreed with both Grew and Clayton that this was "the greatest element in our leverage," for he felt that the Soviet Union needed heavy machinery and machine tools from the United

States as well as American know-how in many other fields. The best procedure for such credits, Harriman believed, was to adopt first a trial one-year arrangement rather than make a commitment for a period of several years. As for the timing of negotiations, he felt they should start promptly but that once begun it would be quite satisfactory to let them "drag along." Harriman concluded his comments by emphasizing again, as he had increasingly in his messages from Moscow during the previous eighteen months, that in its relations with the USSR the United States must be "resourceful and firm."[23]

Firmness was the keynote of President Truman's approach when he met Foreign Commissar Molotov in the White House three days later. Concerning the Yalta agreements regarding Eastern Europe, especially Poland, the meeting produced a particularly heated exchange. The Soviet request for postwar credits was not specifically raised, but Truman clearly had it in mind when he warned Molotov that legislative appropriations were required for any economic measures in the foreign field and that these in turn depended on public support, a fact that he hoped his Russian visitor would keep in mind "in considering the request that joint British and American proposals [regarding Poland] be accepted."[24]

In San Francisco at the United Nations Conference, when Senator Vandenburg was told by Stettinius of this tough stand taken by Truman and that future aid to Russia would depend upon USSR cooperation with the United States, he hailed it as "the best news in months," adding, "FDR's appeasement of Russia is over."[25] But at least one advisor with whom Truman was to counsel often during the next several months was alarmed at the rough reception Molotov had received from the new president. Joseph E. Davies, one-time U.S. ambassador to Russia and unabashed supporter of the Soviet regime, met with Truman on the last day of April and urged patience and understanding with the USSR. Davies specifically referred to reports that the United States could use a "strong arm" with the Soviet Union in order to get its way since the Russians needed $6 billion to reconstruct their country, and he advised Truman that such a course would not work with the Russians and would only worsen relations.[26]

In the first weeks in an office for which he was ill-prepared, Harry Truman thus found himself not only beset by staggering problems of war and peace but also beseeched by a congeries of advisors whose selection had been another man's choosing. As he sought to retrieve the reins of power so suddenly fallen and assert his own direction on the galloping course of events he listened with patience if not with full perception to the counselors of his predecessor. Those matters that demanded immediate decisions received them. Others, like the Soviet credit proposals, could be put off and were.

This then was the uncertain state of Washington policy in early May 1945 on the question of postwar credits to Russia. The Treasury's plan for a $10 billion loan had made no headway and was effectively dead—in part because of its source, but even more because it was considered economically and politically infeasible. Yet the spirit that inspired Morgenthau's proposal—that such a gesture was vital to insure Russian cooperation and also aid domestic economic needs—was not dead and still influenced many who found it entirely consistent with the aims and policies of Franklin Roosevelt. But this spirit dimmed and flickered uncertainly in an atmosphere of deteriorating Soviet-American relations that even then some attributed to the failure of the United States to unequivocally promise postwar aid. There was, too, an added dilemma in this state of affairs: those who believed in the efficacy of economic leverage felt they had the means to mitigate fractious Soviet behavior, while those who dispensed the funds (senators and congressmen) cited such behavior as the best reason for keeping their coffers closed. Thus Molotov's proposal for a $6 billion loan was seen by some as an opportunity and by others as a wasteful extravagance. Added to this was the doubt raised that Russia really needed credits for reconstruction, and from this the conclusion that they carried little or no leverage. Finally, from this point it could be argued, as Counselor of Embassy George Kennan did from Moscow in December 1944, that credits not necessary for civilian reconstruction could, if granted, be used to support and enhance a military capability that would be employed in ways potentially detrimental to the United States.[27] Hence a further torturous dilemma arose: if the withholding of credits carried the possibility of influencing Soviet behavior favorably toward the interests of the United States, then the eventual granting of them also held the possibility of improving Russia's ability to behave in ways inimical to those interests.

There was no easy or ready resolution to those conflicting views in the spring of 1945. Moreover, they were exchanged in an American capital that was at the same time beset by the gravest problems of war and peace and bereaved by the loss of the man who for twelve years had singularly attended to them. In the final analysis there was no immediate reply to the first Soviet request for postwar economic assistance because none was immediately required and none was possible.

Hopkins's Visit to Moscow and the Reply to the First USSR Request

Five days after the surrender of Germany a *New York Times* article pointedly noted that there had been "complete silence" on the progress of negotiations for a postwar credit to the USSR. Two weeks later Cox reminded Crowley that the Russians had been told for some time that the administration would have to get authorization from Congress to extend credits to them for reconstruction purposes, and added: "The Soviet Union unquestionably doubts whether we really mean business on this matter." Cox then suggested the immediate preparation of legislation that would permit the granting of $6 billion in credits to the USSR. There was impatience also in the American Embassy in Moscow. Harriman was content to let credit negotiations "drag along" once they had started, but he believed that they should begin soon and that in the meantime the Russians should not be left in the dark about American views on this question. At the end of May he cabled the State Department that Molotov had requested a reply to his note of January 3. "I do feel," advised Harriman, "that some reply or explanation is due the Soviet Govt. . . . and would appreciate being informed so that I can officially advise Molotov of our position in regard to his note." A day later Ambassador Andrei Gromyko, acting head of the Russian delegation at the San Francisco conference, publicly stated that there had been no reply to the Soviet Union's $6 billion credit request; and on June 3 the *New York Times* reported that "some Washington circles" had expressed the view that the request had been "tabled."[28]

By that date the climate of Soviet-American relations, chilled by the disputes that had steadily worsened since Yalta, was experiencing a noticeable warming. This change was occurring in the course of preparations to hold a new heads-of-government conference. As part of these preparations—and in the hope of achieving preliminary agreement on some of the more difficult issues troubling Soviet-American relations—Truman had sent Harry Hopkins as his personal envoy to Stalin. Hopkins more than justified the president's confidence, if not entirely his expectations concerning the Big Three meeting. First, he quickly mollified Stalin on four matters that had been troubling the Soviet leader: admission of Argentina to the San Francisco Conference, French representation on the Reparations Commission, the disposition of the German fleet, and the manner in which lend-lease to the USSR had been curtailed. Stalin in turn satisfied Hopkins on the appointment of a representative to the Allied Control Council for Germany, on the date and place of the forthcoming heads-of-government meeting, and on the timing of Soviet participation in the war against Japan. Finally, on the central issue of Hopkins's visit— the future government of Poland—agreement was at length reached on a list of Poles to be invited to Moscow to consult regarding their government's composition.

In the wake of the evident success of Hopkins's mission there was a surge of optimism concerning the future of Soviet-American relations. The atmosphere was suddenly clear of the gloom that had pervaded it since the moment of surrender a month before, and in the White House Harry Truman radiated confidence. On June 1 Morgenthau met with the president just after Truman learned of the agreement concerning the new Polish government. "I just put across all by myself the most wonderful thing without any help from Stettinius," Truman boasted. "I just finished talking to Harry Hopkins, and I am the happiest man in the world over what I have been able to accomplish." A few days later Col. Bernard Bernstein, a former

Treasury lawyer on Eisenhower's staff, visited the chief executive and reported that Truman was looking forward to his meeting with Stalin. "If you could sit down with Stalin and get him to focus on a problem," the president told Bernstein, "Stalin would take a reasonable attitude." Furthermore, he felt that the American position was a strong one because the United States "didn't have to go to the Russians for anything, and the Russians very definitely had to come to us for many things."[29]

This same optimism and confidence was reflected in an informal news conference Truman held with the directors of the American Society of Newspaper Editors early in June. Russia was very much on the president's mind and he turned to it again and again during the meeting. He made clear to the newsmen that it was vital to try to understand the Russian point of view, to recognize that "the Russians are coming out of the dark ages—just twenty-five years ago" and that they needed to have "friendly states" around them. But this friendship could be obtained only by "legitimate means," he warned, and to do so the Russians would need America's friendship first. Here the United States had real leverage because, as Truman put it, "they need our friendship a darn sight more than we need theirs. . . . Russia has got all the resources and everything else that go to make a great nation. They have all the land that is necessary to make a great nation. And they are anxious to develop that, and yet they need our help in that a darn sight worse, and we will use that."[30]

Russia had asked for help five months earlier with a request for a $6 billion credit for postwar reconstruction. A decision had been made at the end of January authorizing a reply to the request, but implementation of that decision had been delayed by a combination of uncertainty and indecisiveness. In the improved atmosphere of Hopkins's successful visit to Moscow, action finally was taken. Wakening to criticism that was becoming increasingly public, and evidently of the opinion that changed circumstances no longer permitted the matter to drift unattended with the tide of events, the State Department moved on both the legislative and diplomatic fronts. On June 2, Acting Secretary Grew informed Harriman that the State Department and FEA Director Crowley were recommending that the president shortly request the Congress to expand the lending authority of the Export-Import Bank to $3.5 billion and eliminate its default restrictions. Of this amount "about a billion" would be available "for possible negotiation with the Soviets if events so warrant." Harriman was then told that with respect to Molotov's January 3 note the department's telegram number 183 of January 27 authorized him to reply (this was true, but this telegram had also suggested that no action be taken pending further instructions) and that he was again authorized to reply "with appropriate modifications in light of new conditions" (notably with withdrawal of the 3-c Agreement offer and the change in the Soviet Union's lend-lease status). Harriman made the long-delayed reply on June 9, five months and six days after Molotov's request. He told the Russian commissar that he had been instructed to say that his government "was of the definite opinion that long-term postwar credits constituted an important element in postwar relations between our two countries" and "that the enactment of necessary legislation for an extension of long-term credits for postwar projects was being actively pursued but that until it was enacted by Congress no agreement could be formalized with respect to such credits."[31]

Thus was implementation finally completed in Moscow of a policy made months before in Washington; a formal reply was at last made to the first Russian aid request. In the interim it had been delayed and altered because of the changing international climate, different assessments of Soviet capabilities and intentions, lack of agreement on the efficacy of U.S. economic power to advance American interests with the USSR, and the absence of a clear means for doing so. In the end the reply that was made—under growing pressure to do so—was positive, but conditional and noncommittal; it must have suggested to the Russians that $6 billion on any terms was much more than they could hope to expect from the new American administration.

Expansion of the Lending Authority of the Export-Import Bank

In June 1944, FDR had given his approval to legislation to expand the limited lending authority of the Export-Import

Bank and repeal the default provisions of the Johnson Act, which had prevented government loans to the USSR. But for months the matter had lain dormant in the State Department, awaiting completion of work on the parallel but higher priority Bretton Woods proposals; then it had been delayed further by objections from the Treasury Department and the bank itself. Finally, Hopkins's successful mission, and Senator Taft's insistence that it was necessary to have plans available for the Export-Import Bank in order to give proper consideration to the Bretton Woods legislation then already before the Congress, roused the administration to action. In mid-June Brent Spence, chairman of the House Banking Committee, brought up the government's bill. This measure gave the Export-Import Bank the status of an independent agency of the government, raised its lending authority from $700 million to $3.5 billion, and totally repealed the Johnson Act.[32]

Administration leaders knew that in committee testimony the senators and representatives would want an indication of who was being considered for loans in the large expansion being requested. In anticipation of this there was an exchange of memoranda suggesting proposed breakdowns of the $2.8 billion increase and giving particular attention to the share being allotted for the USSR. At the bank itself President Wayne Taylor had received a memorandum from one of his associates estimating further Russian purchasing in the United States at about $5 billion and proposing initial "medium-term credits" of $1 billion. The author of the memorandum, Economic Advisor August Maffry, thought that the risk in such a loan would be "negligible" and that it would be "a profitable piece of business for the Bank and the country." He was not sure, however, about the "politics of this proposal." On the one hand he thought it might be "a very fine gesture" toward Russia; but on the other hand he was concerned lest it "affect the strategy being followed with respect to lend-lease shipments to Russia."[33] In the FEA, Deputy Administrator Oscar Cox had for several months been urging an initial credit of $2 billion to Russia as part of an overall loan of $6 billion. This was discussed with the Office of War Mobilization and Reconversion (OWMR) and in June the FEA sent to the

OWMR a detailed "Estimate of Minimum Needs of Other United Nations for Foreign Financing, 1945-1946" containing this figure.[34] OWMR Director Fred Vinson responded with his own firm plea for the bank's expansion in a memorandum prepared for President Truman but not sent because of Vinson's subsequent immediate appointment as secretary of the treasury succeeding the resigning Henry Morgenthau. In giving his views Vinson named no specific loan figure for Russia, but he included the following strong argument for the bank's expansion:

> The availability of such credits would strengthen your hand at the coming meeting of the "Big Three." The Soviet Union itself desperately needs outside assistance for its own reconstruction. But even more desperate, though less expansive, are the needs of those countries in eastern Europe which are occupied by Soviet troops. It is the objective of American foreign policy to secure the adoption of concerted action in these countries— action designed to provide genuine democracy and genuine victory for the inhabitants. In seeking to obtain these objectives of policy, our ability to extend financial aid is America's "ace in the hole."[35]

After consultation between key administrative personnel and the leaders of Congress the final projection of the bank's future loans was made in the State Department in the beginning of July. The earlier $6 billion Soviet request had long since been scaled down to $1 billion within the department, and it was this figure that Emilio Collado used in drawing up a memorandum for Assistant Secretary Dean Acheson's testimony on the proposed use of the bank's new funds. In addition to the billion for Russia, Collado proposed $300 to $400 million to finance the 3-c agreements with France, Belgium, and the Netherlands, $150 to $250 million for Latin America, $1,250 to $1,500 million for European reconstruction, and $100 to $150 million for other nations. Since the total ($2.8 to $3.3 billion) exhausted the bank's projected expansion, Collado noted that more Export-Import Bank funds would be needed for 1946 and after. Of these he estimated that "probably a further billion or two will be needed for the USSR." Finally, as the department had told Ambassador Harriman a month before, its estimates would not be made public but would be briefed to the appropriate congressional committees in executive session.[36]

Hearings began in mid-July before the House Committee on Banking and Currency. A Republican bill (introduced by Rep. Jesse Wolcott of Michigan) was put aside in favor of the administration bill and testimony was taken first from Leo Crowley. In his opening statement the FEA administrator— and by virtue of that post, chairman of the Export-Import Bank's board—put forth two major reasons for the bank's expansion. First, it was needed to support foreign trade and thus assist in maintaining manufacturing in the United States during the period of postwar reconstruction. Second, it was required in order to help the Allied nations in their postwar recovery, an effort that would ultimately generate more orders for U.S. goods and thus further stimulate the American economy. Crowley pointed out that the United States had no other means to extend immediate postwar recovery assistance. Lend-lease aid could not be used for reconstruction, UNRRA was strictly for relief, and the International Bank for Reconstruction and Development—which could eventually provide large-scale long-term credits for foreign countries— would not be in effective operation for another year or two. For both these reasons Crowley urged action on the bill "as rapidly as possible" and in any case before Congress's anticipated summer recess. In executive session he then presented the agreed estimate of how the bank's requested increase would be allotted.[37]

When the bill was brought to the floor of the House, most of the debate on it concerned a restrictive amendment offered by Rep. Everett M. Dirksen. The Illinois Republican saw economic credit as the one remaining weapon the United States possessed to insure the achievement of the freedom for which it had fought the war. He therefore suggested a clause to prohibit Export-Import Bank loans to any country that had not adhered to the first three principles of the Atlantic Charter or, having adhered, was not observing them. Since these principles dealt with territorial aggrandizement, territorial changes, and self-determination, Dirksen's amendment was aimed principally at Russia and Russian-occupied eastern Europe, where he felt these principles had been violated. But his suggested change received little support; members from both sides called it unworkable and urged its defeat, a fate it soon suffered on a division vote of 93 to 9. The House then voted on the entire bill and passed it decisively on another division, 102 to 6.[38]

The Senate Committee on Banking and Currency held hearings on the measure on July 17 and 18. The principal witness was again FEA Administrator Crowley, and his principal interrogator was a long-time critic of large-scale foreign lending, Republican Senator Robert Taft of Ohio. Even before Crowley had concluded his opening statement—essentially a reiteration of his testimony before the House committee—Taft was making pointed queries. The first of these concerned the French 3-c Agreement, and Crowley satisfied him by stating that no plans had been made for deliveries beyond December 31. Taft then turned the discussion to Russia and asked about rumors of a loan commitment of $1 billion for that country. Crowley denied there was such a commitment, but then went on to state his expectation that out of the Export-Import Bank's increased lending authority Russia could expect to get as "a reasonable amount . . . from 750 million to one billion dollars." He immediately added his request that this estimate be off the record, but Sen. Robert Wagner of New York, chairman of the committee, decided to leave it in, and Crowley acquiesced. The story made the front page of the *New York Times* the next morning, along with Taft's agreement that $1 billion was "a fair amount to be used in the next year to finance trade with Russia," and for the first time administration planning for a specific sum of postwar credit to the USSR was publicly known.[39]

During his testimony Crowley was also asked by Taft about the need for the Export-Import Bank in the light of the anticipated establishment of the International Bank. As before, Crowley replied that it would be some time before the International Bank was in operation and that even after its establishment the Export-Import Bank would be necessary because of its special purpose in financing American trade.

Taft then took Crowley's argument a step further and pointed out that while control of the International Bank was shared with other nations, the Export-Import Bank was exclusively a U.S. instrument. This led the FEA administrator to comment in turn that "there is a great advantage to us having something of our own." Taft replied: "In other words, this is a better bargaining method than any International Bank; isn't that right?" and he suggested that at the forthcoming Big Three meeting Truman should offer Stalin a billion dollar loan as a quid pro quo for the settlement of other matters. However, Crowley, who had been only an occasional advocate of the use of economic power as leverage in other matters, demurred from agreeing with the Ohio senator.[40]

On the floor of the Senate the most interesting comments— anticipated from the hearings—came again from Senator Taft. The Ohio Republican stated that he supported the bill, but that he did not believe that large-scale lending should be used to finance foreign trade. He agreed to the expansion of the bank, he said, because it seemed the only answer to the special problems of reconstruction and development then existing, but he hoped that this would be the last expansion of its capital and that Crowley would not be back in twelve months to ask for another increase. Taft informed his colleagues of his opinion that exclusive U.S. control of the Export-Import Bank made it a unique bargaining weapon and he urged again that Truman use it at Potsdam to get support for American policies. Taft also referred several times to Crowley's remark that up to a billion dollars of the bank's new increase would be earmarked for the USSR, an estimate in which the Democratic leader, Senator Barkley of Kentucky, concurred when he joined the debate toward its close to add his own support. With apparently unanimous approval the bill then passed the Senate by voice vote.[41]

Congressional action on the Export-Import Bank bill had made clear that there was strong bipartisan support for increasing the lending authority of the Bank and that this stemmed largely from fears that important segments of American industry would falter and fail without the foreign business that such an increase would bring. Testimony and debate on the bill had also shown that there was no substantial opposition to the designation of approximately $1 billion of the bank's enlarged lending power for a loan to the USSR; but it had revealed that there was stong support—especially from prominent Republicans—for the view that this and similar loans should be offered only in exchange for substantial concessions to U.S. policy preferences. President Truman's signature made the bill law on the last day of July, almost fourteen months after FDR had given his okay to the bank's expansion "as soon as practicable." With Truman's approval the way was finally clear for a new request by the Soviet Union for credits for postwar reconstruction.

The Second USSR Request

In Washington there had been little planning in anticipation of the Export-Import Bank's expansion. During July, while Congress was debating the bank's new status, its board chairman, Leo Crowley, was urged by both his FEA deputy, Oscar Cox, and Commerce Secretary Henry Wallace to draw up plans for credits to the USSR. Cox warned in mid-July, "If we don't really get on the ball we are likely to lose a great deal of Soviet postwar business for the United States," and a week later Wallace wrote that he hoped an early decision would be made on "specific steps for facilitating the financing on credit of the sizeable orders for equipment which the Government of the Soviet Union has placed or is interested in placing in the United States."[42] But Crowley was unmoved. At the end of the month he replied to a request from Sen. Claude Pepper of Florida for information on European reconstruction by stating that "No reconstruction program has yet been worked out for Europe." He noted that approval of the Bretton Woods agreements and expansion of the Export-Import Bank did "look, of course, toward European reconstruction, but," he added, "it is too early to say what programs will be developed."[43]

Clayton's early August report from London, with the danger to congressional approval of UNRRA's appropriation it conveyed in its news of the new Soviet request for funds, apparently spurred Washington to action. On the following day the State Department advised Clayton to tell the Russians in London that the Export-Import Bank was in a position to take up the question of a loan with their representatives in Washington. At the same time it directed Harriman to similarly inform the Kremlin, and on August 9 he reported that he had done so by letter of that date to Foreign Commissar Molotov.[44] There was no immediate response from the Soviet Embassy in Washington nor was it then informed of the bank's new status; but on August 16, when William McChesney Martin sent the Russians notice that lend-lease was terminated, he added a paragraph (on instructions from Crowley) mentioning the bank's facilities. Martin stated that cash purchases could be arranged for lend-lease items the Russians still desired, or it was possible, he went on, rather matter-of-factly, that "credit may be extended through the facilities of the Export-Import Bank. Your government may apply directly to the Bank for credit by writing to the Export-Import Bank of Washington, Washington 25, D.C., or discussions may be initiated through the U.S. Embassy in Moscow."[45]

This time the Russians responded quickly. Apparently still hopeful of discussing a sum of $6 billion they sent a delegation to Crowley on the day they learned of the lend-lease cancellation and asked for information about obtaining a credit.[46] Crowley turned the matter over to Martin who promptly washed his hands of it. "I am not familiar with the status of the USSR request for a six billion credit made to Mr. Harriman," wrote the acting executive of the Soviet Protocol Committee, "and what, if any, reference to this ought to be made at this time." He added that the State Department and the Export-Import Bank "will have to carry the ball here on in" because the protocol committee, except for the time required to complete its records, was "no longer necessary."[47]

During the following days information and expectations concerning Russian use of the Export-Import Bank circulated in Washington from a variety of sources. On August 17 Harriman reported to the State Department that Molotov had replied to his August 9 letter by stating that he had brought information about the bank's new status to the attention of his government. On August 20 Julius Krug, director of the War Production Board, complained to one of his associates about the absence of credit facilities to cover goods on order by foreign countries; then the following day he told Crowley: "With the cutback of lend-lease we find production going to hell in some of the important plants." On the same day Wayne Taylor, president of the Export-Import Bank, wrote William Martin that while the Russians had not yet taken up Martin's invitation to apply directly to the bank he expected to hear from a representative in the near future.[48] By that date, however, the question of Export-Import Bank credits to Russia was in the hands of the group expressly created to deal with all problems connected with American lending to foreign nations.

The public law approving U.S. participation in the economic organizations established at Bretton Woods, which Truman signed on July 31, 1945—the same date he authorized the Export-Import Bank's expansion—had also created the National Advisory Council on International Monetary and Financial Problems (NAC). The purpose of this council was to coordinate the policies and operation of all agencies of the government making or participating in foreign loans or engaging in foreign financial transactions. Its membership consisted of the secretary of the treasury, who served as chairman, the secretary of state, the secretary of commerce, the chairman of the Board of Governors of the Federal Reserve System and the chairman of the Board of Trustees of the Export-Import Bank.[49] On August 21, 1945, this new group held its first meeting. Chairman Fred Vinson discussed the responsibility of the NAC and suggested that it form an overall plan showing everything that was to be lent and spent abroad and received at home. The members agreed and the council decided to request the heads of all departments and agencies to submit programs of their expected foreign financial activities. The NAC then turned to the policies and operations of the Export-Import Bank. Its chairman, Leo Crowley, reported that the bank had under consideration several loans. These included $400 million in 3-c agreement loans for France, Belgium, and the Netherlands, and a $1 billion loan for the USSR. Crowley told the group he would continue negotiations on these loans but that the Export-Import Bank would make none of them "until the Council had an opportunity to pass on them."[50]

Since negotiations had not been completed on the loans Crowley discussed (in fact they had not even started in the case of the USSR), the NAC rendered no decision on them at its first meeting; nevertheless, consideration without objection by the government's highest policy body on foreign lending of the long-discussed sum of $1 billion for Russia tended to give that figure an authoritative endorsement. It was clear that negotiations could begin forthwith on postwar credits of that amount. All that was needed was a request by the Russians.

On August 28, Gen. Leonid G. Rudenko, chairman of the Government Purchasing Commission of the Soviet Union in the United States, met Leo Crowley and presented him with a memorandum requesting a billion dollar credit to purchase new equipment and supplies for postwar reconstruction. This was the sum that had been discussed at the highest levels of the State Department since early spring, it was the figure that was presented to Congress at the time of the Export-Import Bank bill hearings, and it was the amount that Leo Crowley— chairman of the bank—had suggested to the NAC at its first meeting as appropriate to meet the postwar needs of the USSR. The arguments offered for the loan (and for credits to other nations as well) had stressed its value in generating export business for the United States, thus helping to maintain employment and ease the transition from a wartime to a peacetime economy. It was also argued by some that the United States, undamaged at home and by far the strongest of the victorious Allies, had an obligation to assist those who had suffered and lost so much.

But in the context of Soviet-American relations that during the past six months had moved alternately from peaks of accommodation to valleys of suspicion, there were other important considerations. One of the strongest of these was the fear that a credit to Russia would be used not for postwar reconstruction but to help maintain wartime production. This possibility had been brought to Secretary Byrnes's attention in an analysis of Soviet industry made by the American Embassy in Moscow, and he regarded it so highly that he made it the substance of a circular telegram to State Department officers in all the major European capitals. "[Moscow Embassy] survey concludes," cabled Byrnes at the end of August, "that question of Soviet need for assistance from abroad is inextricably bound up with continued maintenance of war-time arms production and with political-military aims which that production is intended to further."[51] Byrnes also knew that a large loan constituted one of the few "high cards" he held in his hand in treating with the Russians. He was anxious, therefore, that the card not be played until he was able to determine both the best time to do so and what to seek in return. Immediately forthcoming in London was the first meeting of the Council of Ministers, the organization established by the Big Three in Potsdam to be the repository of the unresolved problems of that conference. This was too soon to allow adequate preparation for the introduction of a loan for bargaining leverage, but it would give Byrnes his first opportunity to test postwar Soviet attitudes.

On September 11, 1945, the day the London Council of Ministers meeting opened, the Soviet loan request began its course through Washington's new international economic bureaucracy. On that date it was one of several reconstruction credits "approved in principle" by the Board of Tustees of the Export-Import Bank. On the following day Leo Crowley transmitted the decisions of the bank's board to the NAC, recommending their prompt approval.[52] When the NAC then deferred action on the credits to await additional financial information from the countries involved, Crowley wrote again, urging speedy action. Anxious to avoid cancellation costs for material still in the lend-lease pipeline and fearful of a postwar depression, he recommended immediate approval of the applications already endorsed by the bank's board, including the billion dollar Russian request. The NAC considered Crowley's new request at its next meeting, on September 18, but again decided to postpone action, this time "until the issues and problems involved could be discusssed with the president."[53]

The discussion with the president took place three days later when Treasury Secretary Vinson, Assistant Secretary Clayton, and Crowley called on Truman to obtain his approval of the various loans the NAC had discussed at its first meetings. The memorandum they brought to the White House outlined the proposed loans and noted that the appropriate congressional committees had been informed by Crowley of the Export-Import Bank's intended use of its expanded lending authority. The memorandum's last paragraph dealt specifically with the loan for Russia:

> The EximBank loan to Russia has, as noted above, been approved in principle by the Bank and been considered by the Council. You will recall that the Russians were invited to enter into negotiations for the amount indicated. Those negotiations should go forward and we will so inform the Bank if you approve.

At the bottom of the document the president wrote: "Approved 9/21/45 Harry S. Truman."[54] At its next meeting at the end of September, the NAC noted this action and gave its own approval to all the loans proposed by the bank, but with the understanding that "the negotiations with the USSR were not to go forward until there was an opportunity to consult Secretary Byrnes."[55] Thus, within a month after Rudenko had made his request for a $1 billion credit from the Export-Import Bank, it had been approved in principle by the bank, the president, and the National Advisory Council. What remained was to implement the agreed action. Implementation, in the hands of Byrnes and his department, rested in turn on the answers to two questions: When was the best time to offer to start negotiations? and what should be asked of the Russians in return?

United States Preparation for Negotiations

The London meeting of the Council of Foreign Ministers gave Byrnes his first chance to assess the state of postwar Soviet-American relations. It was a chastening experience, but for the new secretary still not a completely disheartening one. The task of the council's initial meeting was to agree on the principles of the peace treaties to be written for Italy and the ex-enemy states of eastern Europe. But in the end, no agreements were reached and most of the ministers' time was spent in fruitless wrangling over procedural matters. Finally, on the second day of October, the council broke up in complete frustration, unable to agree even on a concluding protocol. Byrnes returned to Washington tired and distraught over the council's lack of success; but he was by nature an optimist and had unbounded confidence in his skills as a negotiator and conciliator. These were the traits that had carried him far in American political life and earned him notable success as a legislator in the U.S. Congress. And so, with that peculiarly American vision that so often regards the world as simply the domestic political scene writ large, he sought once again to ply his skills—this time in the Russians' own capital.

While Byrnes prepared for his next meeting with the Russians, his top aides in the State Department began compiling a list of desiderata to place before the Soviets in the course of negotiations on their credit request. As discussed earlier, for most of the war the United States had carefully refrained from seeking any specific quid pro quo for the shipment of lend-lease supplies to its Allies. It was understood that in the course of the various lend-lease settlements American negotiators would press for those concessions for freer world trade set forth in Article VII of the Master Agreements; but these discussions would take place after the war and after the delivery and utilization of all goods and materials. There was to be no withholding of supplies while fighting was under way in order to extract concessions for the future. As the war in Europe drew to a close this policy was increasingly challenged and finally discarded. The confused cutback of lend-lease to the USSR was an inept effort to signal the Russians that the unconditional lend-lease policy was over. The cut-off of lend-lease to Russia three months later, while not explicitly an attempt to exert pressure, was accomplished in a context that resulted in harsher treatment of the USSR than others and gave credence to the view that it was just such a pressure tactic. With regard to postwar loans for Russian reconstruction, the policy of extracting concessions for economic favors was clearer and less in dispute. This was not only because the restraints imposed by the necessity of maintaining wartime cooperation had been removed, but also because most of the discussion about loans took place during a time when the United States found its view of the postwar world increasingly challenged by the statements and actions of the Kremlin.

There were also many persuasive arguments in favor of using American economic power to achieve political objectives vis-à-vis the Soviet Union. The Russians evidently wanted a postwar loan. They had repeatedly raised the subject of credits and had advanced their own proposals for obtaining them. The United States had certain long-range economic objectives (expressed in Article VII of the Master Lend-Lease Agreements) for the achievement of which Soviet cooperation was necessary, and certain short-range political objectives (in Europe and Asia) that were being thwarted by Russian opposition. In the aftermath of World War II U.S. economic power was formidable, and its use to extract concessions and attain political goals was endorsed by both the Congress and the public. Finally, if the United States rapidly demobilized and withdrew its military power from abroad—as it said it would—its economic power would be the only viable means to influence the actions of others.

By the end of June 1945 these arguments had been accepted by the new administration and the use of reconstruction loans as a quid pro quo to obtain concessions on economic and political matters was becoming an acknowledged position of the State Department in its dealings with the countries of eastern Europe. This was seen particularly clearly in the case of Poland. A briefing book paper prepared in June for the forthcoming Potsdam Conference stated: "In assisting through credits and otherwise in the physical reconstruction of the Polish economy, we should insist on the acceptance by Poland of a policy of equal opportunity for us in trade, investment and access to sources of information."[56] In subsequent discussions with Polish leaders not only were these conditions insisted on, but other more far-reaching ones were added. In September the State Department listed additional economic concessions it wished the Poles to make in exchange for an Export-Import Bank loan. In October the American ambassador in Warsaw,

Arthur B. Lane, urged that the United States also attach political conditions to the granting of loans. In response, Byrnes instructed Lane that at his discretion he could point out that the early holding of free elections "would undoubtedly contribute materially to popular support in this country for any program of aid to Poland which might be under consideration."[57]

Elsewhere the same policy was recommended and, when the occasion arose, applied. The U.S. representative in Albania suggested economic assistance with the quid pro quo that the regime reduce the size of its army. A loan request was never received, but subsequently the State Department did tie recognition to assurances of free elections. When the U.S. ambassador to Yugoslavia related to President Truman at the end of August 1945 that he told Marshal Tito he could expect "no economic help" unless he carried out the Yalta agreements, the president replied, "You did the right thing." Three months later the acting chief of the Division of Southern European Affairs wrote a memorandum recommending no consideration of financial loans or credit unless political conditions in Yugoslavia improved. In the margin Byrnes penned: "I agree, J.F.B." When Czechoslovakia requested a $300 million Export-Import Bank credit in September 1945, the department suggested to the bank that it defer action on the request pending clarification of the Czech nationalization program.[58] Throughout the area the accepted policy for dealing with requests for economic assistance became one of determining, and then demanding, economic and political conditions favorable to the United States. Economic leverage had long been discussed as a potent force for exerting American influence; by the end of 1945 it seemed to many that in Eastern Europe it was the only force left to the United States.

It was with this background that the Russian application for a $1 billion Export-Import Bank loan prompted consideration of what the United States wanted in return. Early in September 1945 Acting Secretary of State Acheson informed Harriman in Moscow that economic conditions were being drawn up "for inclusion in any EximBank credits to Russia," and at the end of the month conversations were held within the department to determine what precisely should be requested from the USSR "precedent to the grant . . . of a loan." These conversations then led to inquiries outside the department as interested agencies were canvassed to determine what benefits they wished to obtain from the Soviet Union in exchange for financial assistance. A memorandum from the Operations Division (OPD) of the War Department indicates the broad scope of these inquiries. In October OPD informed G-2, G-4, and a designated distribution list that there had been "some indications that the USSR will seek financial or economic assistance from the United States." It went on to request the views of the addressee "as to agreements or concessions of military importance that might be obtained from the Soviets in connection with any financial discussions." These, the memorandum stated, would be incorporated into a single paper to be used by the secretary of war to advise the secretary of state.[59]

However, the State Department moved very slowly in its preparations for a response to the Russian credit request, and when Harriman cabled from Moscow at the end of November that he was "anxious to know urgently" about the status of negotiations for a Soviet Export-Import Bank credit, Clayton replied: "Dept. has been pursuing policy of not encouraging active discussions and at present matter is dormant."[60] There were apparently two reasons for the State Department's procrastination, each reflecting views that had been expressed since Molotov's initial request for reconstruction credits. First, there was the continuing apprehension of some in the department that credits would be used by Russia to maintain a strong military posture potentially inimical to the interests of the United States. Throughout the late summer and fall of 1945 this fear was regularly fed by press and economic reports from the U.S. embassy in Moscow. A late August résumé of developments in the Soviet press had reported a strong desire on the part of Russian leaders to improve living conditions but added that "there is no reason for believing that they will allow the Russian standard of living to rise at a rate which will interfere with aims which are more basic," including "the strengthening of [Russia's] military-economic potential." In mid-November Edward Page, Jr., first secretary of the embassy, sent a long report on international political conditions in the USSR that stated as one of its conclusions that "individual wants are being sacrificed to the aggrandizement of the economic-military might of the Soviet Union"; and at the end of December an economic review of the year prepared at the suggestion of George Kennan, and given to Byrnes in Moscow, concurred: "While [Soviet leaders] are not opposed in principle to a rise in the standard of living, economic-military potential must come first, in their opinion, and the standard of living of the Soviet people can always be raised later."[61] In some quarters in the State Department these reports were seen as vindication of the nonapproval of credits thus far and support for the continuation of such a "dormant" policy. A memorandum from the East European Branch to the chief of the European Division in early January 1946 illustrates this view. Quoting extensively from embassy reports since the previous August the author set forth the proposition that "our failure so far to grant credits to the USSR appears to be having the effect of forcing them to move more in the direction of a peacetime economy, rather than increasing their war potential."[62]

The second reason for delay on the part of the State Department was the desire of others in the department to make maximum use of the leverage credits offered. This meant first deciding just what should be sought in return for granting them, and second, selecting the opportune moment to make an offer. Under the circumstances extensive canvassing for the former necessarily postponed the latter, a situation that was further compounded by the uncertain course of Soviet-American relations during these months. Economic credits were not discussed at Potsdam, and Rudenko's request of August 28 had occurred too close to the opening of the London Conference to permit adequate preparation for raising the subject there. Thus, the next opportunity was the December Foreign Ministers Meeting in Moscow. In preparation for that meeting a memorandum was prepared for Byrnes's use that summarized the Russian proposal for a $1 billion credit, reminded him that it was considerably less than the USSR's earlier $6 billion request, and warned that the USSR would resist efforts to link the credit with other matters, including a

lend-lease settlement.[63] Additional messages were then sent to
the secretary at the beginning of the conference linking the loan
question to other matters; but at the meeting Byrnes mentioned
economic assistance in only the most general way. In his
opening statement he alluded to the American desire to "help
through economic means our friends abroad to restore the
damages of war." Later, in an effort to resolve directly with
Stalin political matters in the Balkan states, Byrnes told the
Soviet leader: "It is terribly important to settle this matter and
proceed with the peace treaties so that we can be in a position to
render them economic assistance."[64] There is no other record of
the subject being discussed. The Russians evidently did not
raise it, and Byrnes returned home with his economic card still
unplayed.

Nevertheless, as the new year began both sides continued to
express interest in the possibilities and opportunities offered by
the extension of credits, and these views prompted Emilio
Collado—still less than enthusiastic about the potential
leverage they carried—to summarize the entire question of
USSR economic matters in a memorandum addressed to his
seniors in the State Department. Collado first recapitulated the
developments that had occurred since Rudenko's August 28
credit request. He noted that the subject had not been raised by
the Russians at the London and Moscow conferences and that
"the Department's view is that when credit discussions take
place, they should involve a full discussion of all economic
matters between the two governments, including economic
problems relating to the Eastern European countries." He
noted that it would be difficult for the United States to extend a
reconstruction loan to the USSR if it continued to remain
outside the Bretton Woods institutions and he concluded by
recommending that the department continue to leave the
initiative for any further loan discussions in the hands of the
Soviets.[65] At the time Collado wrote his memorandum this was
also the position of Secretary of State Byrnes. As late as
February 5 he was still reported as "not yet prepared to act on
the loan." But three days later he changed his mind. He had just
participated in the bitter debates at the first session of the UN

Security Council concerning continued Soviet occupation in Iran, an episode—as he later wrote—that convincd him that the Soviet attitude was "hardening." Chastened by this experience and still smarting from what he judged to be unfair congressional criticism of his performance at Moscow, Byrnes decided on February 8 to use America's wealth to pursue its economic and political objectives vis-à-vis the Soviet Union.[66]

Work began immediately in the State Department to draw up a message incorporating the conditions that had been suggested by various other departments during the past several months. At about the same time the department's Coordinating Committee, which had been wrestling for some time with arguments for and against the use of economic pressure toward the USSR, produced an authoritative justification for Byrnes's new policy initiative. "Although it is a somewhat discredited theory that financial aid will solve all the United States' problems from commercial policy to freedom of the press," the committee wrote in mid-February, "there seems to be little question that American credits are the strongest bargaining lever we will have in the immediate future." The committee then recommended that "the appropriate officers of the geographic and functional divisions should prepare statements of what we are now or may soon be seeking from foreign countries in the way of political and economic rights and concessions and other things of value."[67]

Initial United States Response

For the Soviet Union this task, already well advanced, was completed on February 21. On that date the secretary of state transmitted to the chargé of the Soviet Union in Washington a formal reply to General Rudenko's memorandum of the previous August. Byrnes's note, drafted with Harriman's help, stated that the United States considered the requested credit "one among a number of outstanding economic questions" to be settled between the two countries. It proposed that "negotiations be initiated forthwith" on these issues, including the question of a credit, and it singled out nine in particular that should be covered:

1. Claims of American nationals against the USSR.
2. Concerted policies to assist the peoples of liberated Europe "to solve by democratic means their pressing economic problems."
3. Free navigation of international rivers.
4. Preliminary discussions of a treaty of friendship, commerce, and navigation.
5. Arrangements for the protection of copyrights.
6. Methods for giving effect to the terms of Article VII of the Soviet Master Lend-Lease Agreement.
7. General settlement of lend-lease obligations.
8. Civil aviation matters of mutual interest.
9. Discussion of other economic questions connected with the general aims of the proposed negotiations.

Byrnes's note then concluded by expressing the hope that the Soviet Union would send observers to the forthcoming initial meetings of the Boards of Governors of the International Monetary Fund and the International Bank for Reconstruction and Development.[68]

Russia's second request for postwar credits—like its first—had waited six months for a formal reply. On March 1 the State Department—apparently fearing public criticism of its procrastination—lamely explained that the long delay in responding had been due to the fact that the request had been "misplaced" during the transfer of lend-lease records from the defunct Foreign Economic Administration (terminated by executive order on September 27, 1945) to the newly established Office of Foreign Liquidation in State and "had turned up only last week."[69] While it is possible (though by no means certain) that the verbatim record of Crowley's August 28 meeting with Rudenko may indeed have been missing for a time, it is very clear that Rudenko's request, and all of its details, were well known. As the foregoing has shown, the Russian credit request was discussed and debated regularly by high officials of the State and Treasury Departments, the Export-Import Bank, and the National Advisory Committee during the six months it was alleged to have been lost.

While the long-delayed reply of February 21 was being

drafted in the State Department, American officials received what many considered convincing evidence and authoritative explanation of what they had interpreted during the past several months as a hostile new course in Soviet foreign affairs. On February 9, the eve of elections for a new Supreme Soviet, Generalissimus Stalin—in accordance with established practice in these matters—had made a speech in support of his candidacy. The central theme of the speech was that the war just concluded (like the earlier world war) was the inevitable product of crises inherent in international capitalism, and that in winning it the Soviet social order had demonstrated its stability and superiority. The strong implication of Stalin's remarks was that the continued existence of international capitalism made future wars likely. To be prepared for such contingencies Stalin proposed at least three more five-year plans to provide "a new mighty upsurge in the national economy" so that the socialist homeland would be "guaranteed against all possible accidents."[70]

This was not a sudden new theme in Soviet postwar utterances. In August 1945, Presidium Chairman Mikhail Kalinin had warned: "The victory achieved does not mean that all dangers to our state structure and social order have disappeared. Only the most concrete, most immediate danger . . . has disappeared"; and in November, commemorating the anniversary of the Bolshevik Revolution, Molotov had reminded his audience that "while we live in a 'state system' and roots of fascist and imperialist aggression have not yet finally been pulled out of the earth our vigilance in relation to possible new victories of peace should not weaken."[71] But Stalin's expression of these sentiments made them authoritative dicta, and, uttered in February of 1946, they seemed to provide an instant explanation of Soviet behavior of the past several months. In the setting of Russia's intransigence in Iran, its intervention in eastern Europe, and its efforts to extend its influence in the Far East, Stalin's speech was regarded as the Rosetta Stone with which the course of postwar Soviet foreign policy could be deciphered. The speech was widely reported. Excerpts from it appear in all the major documentary archives, and it is discussed in the memoirs of almost every important figure of the day. There is little doubt that it influenced thinking in all echelons of the American government on virtually every aspect of relations with the Soviet Union. Byrnes regarded it as "a far more reliable guide . . . than the statements made to visiting Americans and foreign correspondents." According to Walter Millis, editor of Forrestal's diaries, "this speech and the program it laid down came close to convincing [Forrestal] that there was no way . . . in which democracy and communism could live together." Millis also quotes Justice William O. Douglas's comment to Forrestal that the speech was "the Declaration of World War III." Charles E. Bohlen, Soviet expert and State Department liaison with the White House, counted it among the "origins of the cold war." Elsewhere in the department it created considerable interest. The editors of the *Foreign Relations* series state that the speech "called forth much comment within the Department of State," and they quote the following memorandum of February 11 by the director of European affairs: "Stalin's speech of February 9 constitutes the most important and authoritative guide to postwar Soviet policy . . . it should be given great weight in any plans which may be under consideration for extending credits or any other form of economic assistance to the Soviet Union."[72]

In response to a request for comment on this speech a second major document of the winter of 1946 was produced, one destined to be equally important in explaining and directing the course of postwar Soviet-American relations. A few days after Stalin spoke the State Department asked its embassy in Moscow for an "interpretive analysis" of the Soviet leader's remarks. At that moment Averell Harriman had just relinquished his post as ambassador and his designated successor, Gen. Walter Bedell Smith, had not yet arrived in the Russian capital. The embassy was in the hands of its chargé, George F. Kennan, an energetic and enthusiastic student of Soviet affairs who was in his second Moscow tour and had already filled the telegraphic channels with lengthy scholarly commentaries on Russian behavior. With historical insight, trenchant analysis, and perfervid emphasis Kennan produced an 8,000-word five-part dissertation on the Soviet outlook and its implications for

American policy. This document, which Kennan later styled as "The Long Telegram" was the precursor to his famous "Mr. X" *Foreign Affairs* article eighteen months later. It depicted the "natural and instinctive urges of Russian rulers" as "increase of military police power of Russian State, . . . isolation of Russian population from outside world, and . . . fluid and constant pressure to extend limits of Russian police power." This historic pattern, Kennan believed, would be continued by the present leaders in the Kremlin through an internal policy of intensive military-industrial development and an external policy of advancing wherever possible the limits of Soviet power. He described at length the worldwide apparatus available to the USSR to advance its cause and the manner in which that apparatus would be used to undermine the Western powers; then he summarized the "practical deductions" to be drawn from his analysis. These included the recognition that "we have here a political force committed fanatically to the belief that with the U.S. there can be no permanent *modus vivendi*, that it is desirable and necessary that the internal harmony of our society be disrupted, our traditional way of life be destroyed, the international authority of our state be broken." There was encouragement, however, in the realization that "Soviet power . . . is highly sensitive to the logic of force . . . it can easily withdraw—and usually does—when strong resistance is encountered at any point. Thus, if the adversary has sufficient force and makes clear his readiness to use it, he rarely has to do so." Kennan recommended thorough understanding of the Communist movement, education of the American people to the "realities of the Russian situation" and the presentation of a "positive and constructive picture" of the kind of world the United States would like to see in the future.[73]

Kennan's long telegram received almost as much attention in official Washington circles as the speech by Stalin that spurred its composition. If Stalin's exhortation was the summons to a new contest for the future destiny of the world, then Kennan's long telegram appeared to be the appropriate response to that challenge. Copies of the message were distributed throughout the administration; Truman himself read it. Navy Secretary Forrestal saw in it both confirmation of the position he had

been taking on Russian relations and answers to questions he
had been asking about Soviet ideology, and he made it required
reading for top officers of his department. Under Secretary of
State Acheson recalled it later as a "truly remarkable dispatch"
that "had a deep effect on thinking within the government."[74]
For Kennan it brought instant recognition and a reputation
that changed his life profoundly, propelling him into
positions of influence and authority within the State Department. In his memoirs he shrewdly observes that the key to the
wide acclaim given his message was the "subjective state of
readiness on the part of Washington officialdom" at the time.[75]
Six months earlier it would have been premature, six months
later redundant; but in the climate of events of late February
1946, it was received as an accurate barometer of the changing
state of Soviet-American relations and a perceptive forecast of
the storms that lay ahead.

On the last day of that month Secretary Byrnes completed his
own conversion to the ranks of those who believed that the best
approach to assume with the USSR was one of firmness.
Chastened by a long talk with visiting ex-Prime Minister
Winston Churchill and stiffened further by a tough foreign
policy speech from Republican Senator Arthur Vandenberg,
Byrnes delivered a major address to the Overseas Press Club in
New York on February 28. In words that he later described as
"intended for the Kremlin," he said:

> All around us there is suspicion and distrust, which in turn
> breeds suspicion and distrust. Of some others that cannot be
> said. We have covenanted not to use force except in defense of
> law embodied in the policies and principles of the Charter. We
> intend to live up to that covenant. . . . We have a responsibility
> to see that other powers live up to *their* covenants. And that
> responsibility we intend to meet.[76]

A week later, at a small college in Fulton, Missouri, Byrnes's
views were seconded by the most prestigious living statesman
of the day. With President Truman on hand to introduce him
and applaud his words, Winston Churchill comprehended
with customary eloquence the current world situation. Using

publicly for the first time his striking metaphor of the iron curtain, he depicted all of East Europe "from Stettin in the Baltic to Trieste in the Adriatic" lying in the dark shadow of Soviet domination, and he called upon the "fraternal association of the English-speaking peoples" to provide the "overwhelming assurance of security" that would halt the curtain before it closed around more lands, East and West.[77]

These signal utterances of February and March 1946, did not immediately usher in a complete change in America's foreign relations. The doctrine that cooperation with Russia for future peace was necessary could not so quickly be discarded, nor could the opposite view be instantly adopted; in the late winter of 1945-1946 the dramatic events of the new diplomatic turn that was to come—the Truman Doctrine and the Marshall Plan—were still more than a year away. But the words of Kennan, Byrnes, and Churchill provided clarity where heretofore there had been confusion and uncertainty. The vacillation that had characterized U.S. foreign policy during the six months since V-J Day was ending and a new course was being set that would be maintained for more than a decade and a half. In the months that followed, America, its conscience cleared by the rectitude of its intentions, took its first tentative steps onto the uncharted field of the Cold War.

Russia's Reply and the Subsequent Exchange

It was in the context of this clear but slowly forming consensus that the Soviet reply to the note of February 21 was received in Washington in mid-March. In their answer the Russians agreed to discuss the terms and conditions of a long-term credit and the fourth, sixth, and seventh issues mentioned in the American note. These were the conclusion of a treaty of friendship, commerce, and navigation; methods for giving effect to Article VII of the Master Lend-Lease Agreement; and the general settlement of lend-lease obligations. The Russians stated that they did not consider it expedient to connect any of the other questions with the discussion of a credit, but they did express a willingness to consider them separately at a time and place agreeable to both parties.[78]

Although the Soviet reply agreed to connect the credit

discussion with three matters considered particularly important by the American administration, its failure to include the
other questions, especially those relating to matters in eastern
Europe (issue two), was viewed with keen disappointment. In
the State Department Elbridge Durbrow, emboldened by recent
events to be firmer than ever in his attitude toward the
Russians, characterized the note as "entirely unsatisfactory
since it did not respond to all of the issues raised." Emilio
Collado, however, felt that some movement could be made
toward the Soviet position and he suggested separate discussion of issue three (free navigation of international rivers) and
issue eight (civil aviation). He obtained Durbrow's agreement,
and after several weeks of discussion and drafting, a reply was
cabled to the Russians over Byrnes's signature in mid-April.
The U.S. Government expressed its satisfaction with the
USSR's willingness to consider issues four, six, and seven in
connection with discussion of a credit and suggested that issues
three and eight be treated separately in talks to begin on June 1,
1946. But on issues one (claims of American nationals), two
(policies in eastern Europe), five (protection of copyrights),
and nine ("discussions of other economic questions") the reply
was insistent. These questions were "so closely related," the
American note said, with those already agreed to be discussed in
connection with the loan "that it would be virtually impossible
to discuss the one group of questions without the other."[79]

During the two-month period of this Soviet-American
exchange the Export-Import Bank continued to commit its
limited funds and the president, keenly sensitive to election-
year Republican criticism of excessive spending for foreign
purposes, continued to delay a specific request to Congress for
the further expansion of the bank's lending authority that
probably would be needed to make the projected billion dollar
loan to Russia. Early in April Alexander Gerschenkron, chief
of the Foreign Areas Section of the Board of Governors of the
Federal Reserve System, advised John Hazard that the bank's
funds would probably be exhausted by credits for the French
and Chinese and that this would mean no money for the USSR.
A week later Commerce Secretary Henry Wallace (a strong
supporter of the Russian loan) was warned by one of his
assistants that if the bank did not receive an additional

authorization it would not be in a position to provide both the one billion "earmarked for the USSR" and meet its other commitments. The National Advisory Council took note of this situation early in May and decided to amend its action of the previous September approving a one billion dollar Export-Import Bank loan to the USSR. Recognizing the near exhaustion of the bank's funds the council added to its statement of the previous fall the following caveat: "The approval of the above-mentioned loan is conditioned upon negotiations not being completed by the Export-Import Bank until adequate additional lending authority is conferred upon the Bank by Congress."[80]

In mid-May Nikolai Novikov (newly promoted to the rank of ambassador) paid an anxious call on the State Department to express his concern over reports he had heard of rapidly depleting Export-Import Bank funds. Dean Acheson explained to him that the sum of $1 billion had never been "specifically set aside" for the Russians and that the bank's available capital had indeed fallen below this sum. But, Acheson added, the president had asked Congress for $1.25 billion additional capital for the bank (something that at that point Truman had only said he intended to do), it was anticipated that Congress would approve such an increase before its adjournment, and, if so, there would then be funds available should negotiations bring about agreement on a loan. Thus reassured, the Russians responded a few days later to Byrnes's message of the previous month. The Soviet note began by reiterating the USSR's readiness to start negotiations on a credit together with issues four, six, and seven of the original U.S. note of February 21. The Russian reply also stated a readiness to begin negotiations separately, as proposed by Byrnes, on navigation of international rivers and civil aviation. On the remaining issues (numbers one, two, five, and nine), the Russians professed to see no direct connection with those already enumerated, but they did nevertheless agree "to exchange in a preliminary fashion opinions on these questions *during negotiations mentioned above* [emphasis added]."[81]

Congress's Debate on the British Loan

The Soviet note did represent an effort, however small, to

move in the direction of the American position. But this compromise did not impress Washington, then in the midst of a great debate over another foreign loan to a wartime ally, this one for $3.75 billion to Great Britain. The unexpectedly swift ending of the war with Japan followed by the equally swift ending of lend-lease had left England, in the words of one British historian, "the greatest debtor in the history of the world."[82] The English were burdened with enormous financial obligations, not only to the United States, but to the Allies and neutrals from whom they had made heavy purchases to continue the war. Export of manufactured goods was Britain's traditional means for settling foreign obligations and purchasing supplies for its industries and its people. But in the fall of 1945 English manufacturers were tooled for war, not for the export trade. It would be months before they could fully convert, and in the meantime the British people would have to eat and their creditors would have to be satisfied. The only solution was a large injection of foreign capital and the only source was the United States.

In September Lord Keynes had traveled once more to Washington to plead Britain's economic case. This time he sought an act for the postwar period equal in generosity to the lend-lease program that had funded the war. His goal was a grant-in-aid of $6 billion. But Keynes misread the American mood and underestimated the degree to which American negotiators felt constrained by it. To them a grant-in-aid to succor and salvage the British Empire seemed as likely of public approval as a new declaration of war. In the end Keynes and his delegation had to settle for a loan of $3.75 billion amortized over fifty years with an annual interest charge of 2 percent. There were sweeteners, however. Repayment would not begin until 1951 (making the interest in effect only 1.6 percent), and annual interest charges could be waived during periods when the British trade balance fell below specified prewar levels. For these, and for the loan itself, the U.S. delegation demanded and received important concessions designed to crack the imperial preference system and further a multilateral trade that would open new markets for American goods.[83]

The Anglo-American Financial and Trade Agreement was

signed in Washington on December 6, 1945; six weeks later President Truman transmitted it to the Congress and it was taken up as a Senate Joint Resolution implementing the purposes of the Bretton Woods Agreement. Hearings were held first in the Senate, and for ten days its Banking and Currency Committee took testimony from government officials and leaders of business, finance, labor, and agricultural groups. Spokesmen for the administration stressed the economic gains to be obtained from the agreement. Treasury Secretary Vinson, the chief American negotiator of the loan, depicted its benefits in glowing terms: "The financial agreement will open the markets of England and many other countries to our exporters. This means more exports for our farmers and manufacturers, more jobs for our workers, more profits for business, and a higher income for all our people." Under Secretary of State Dean Acheson warned that without the loan Britain would have no choice but to form its own empire bloc, excluding the United States and every other country from its trade; and Assistant Secretary Clayton argued that approval of the agreement would assure British participation in the international economic institutions set up at Bretton Woods. Even Commerce Secretary Wallace, not notably a strong supporter of England, urged favorable action on the resolution as a necessary step to "creating a peaceful world trading community."[84]

These arguments were met in committee principally by the objections of its second ranking Republican, Sen. Robert Taft. Taft replied that the British did not need such a big loan, that large-scale foreign lending would promote inflation, and that in any event the purposes which the agreement was intended to serve were supposed to be accomplished through the Bretton Woods institutions. While some of his colleagues supported Taft in certain of these points, majority sentiment in the committee was clearly favorable to the agreement. The committee report, issued early in April, discussed the testimony it had heard, replied to objections that had been raised against the agreement, and concluded that its approval would further America's international economic policy by aiding British recovery and opening up markets to U.S. exporters on nondiscriminatory terms.[85]

On the floor of the Senate the loan agreement encountered

much greater opposition. When it was first taken up, majority leader Barkley announced that he wanted to see it brought to a vote after two or three days of debate. However, both proponents and opponents of the resolution quickly dashed this hope. Each senator was anxious to explain his position at length and some, like Senators Langer of North Dakota and Bilbo, Democrat from Mississippi, seemed intent on filibustering the resolution to death. Since defeat by a coalition of Republicans and southern Democrats was a distinct possibility, the positions of certain GOP leaders were anxiously awaited. The first of these to set forth his views was the party's leading spokesman on foreign affairs, Senator Arthur Vandenberg. On the day of his departure as a member of Secretary Byrnes's delegation to the Paris foreign ministers meeting the Michigan Republican addressed the Senate on the loan agreement. He confessed that the British loan had perplexed him "more than any other problem in all my eighteen years," but after much study he had "come to the reluctant but firm conviction . . . that the joint resolution should pass for the sake of America."[86]

Vandenberg believed that the loan was necessary for America's export industries, that it would forestall a surge of restrictive trade alliances and bloc arrangements, and that without it Bretton Woods would be "all but nullified." But these arguments did not end the debate. For two more weeks lengthy speeches were made for and against the loan and numerous additional amendments were offered, including one by Senator Taft to reduce the amount of the loan to $1.25 billion and another to require "permanent acquisition" of wartime-leased British bases before any payments on the loan could be made to England. Finally, the pressure of other legislation brought an end to the debate and the commencement of voting on the resolution and its amendments. Taft's proposal mustered only 16 yeas against 50 nays and was easily defeated, but the acquisition of bases amendment lost by the much narrower margin of 40 to 45—a dramatic indication of the support this idea had continued to attract since it was first put forth at the beginning of the war. On May 10, after all further attempts at amendment had failed, the resolution was passed by a roll call vote of 46 to 34. In the end it was the Republican split over the measure that saved it. Republican senators voted for and against the resolution 17-18; the Democrats voted 29-16. Had six more Republicans voted in opposition the Senate would have killed the British loan.[87]

Four days later the Senate-passed resolution was referred to the House Committee on Banking and Currency, which at once began its own round of hearings on the bill. The economic points for and against the loan agreement were rehearsed and repeated as before; but a new argument was added with growing intensity. Reports of Russia's occupation policies in eastern Europe, its slow and reluctant withdrawal from Iran, the unyielding posture of Molotov and his associates in the early postwar negotiations—all these were taking their toll among those who had advocated friendship with Russia. For many the only alternative appeared to be strong friendship with the United Kingdom. In this context the British loan came to be viewed not just as a support for England but more importantly as a bulwark against Communist Russia. Vandenberg had implied this when he warned his colleagues before he left for Paris: "If we do not lead . . . some other great and powerful nation will capitalize our failure, and we shall pay the price of our default."[88] By early May this argument was being made more explicitly. Rep. Christian Herter, Republican of Massachusetts, wrote to Assistant Secretary of State Clayton after a dinner tendered by the latter to sway a number of Republican legislators toward the loan: "I find that the economic arguments in favor of the loan are on the whole much less convincing to this group than the feeling that the loan may serve us in good stead in holding up a hand of a nation whom we may need badly as a friend because of impending Russian troubles." Clayton replied: "I am sure you are right in your analysis of the reaction of our friends the other evening on this British loan."[89]

In the House committee's hearings and in its report on the resolution this argument commanded increasing attention. In his testimony before the committee Secretary Vinson alluded to the existence of two economic blocs in the world, one British-American and the other Russian. He asserted that this situation had been brought about by Russia's refusal to join the Bretton Woods institutions, and he left little doubt that in these circumstances the loan was essential to strengthen the British-American bloc. "I feel," said Vinson, "that the Anglo-American financial agreement is in the interests of capitalism, that is, in the interests of free enterprise. It is in the interest of the kind of an economy, and the kind of a life, that we want here in the United States." Another prominent witness made the point even clearer. Charles E. Dewey, a former congressman and member of the Banking Committee, returned in the role of vice president of the Chase National Bank to tell his ex-colleagues: "This loan, to me, will be the means, and probably the last chance we have, of bringing back to our side very willing nations who might, due to force of circumstances and difficulties, slip under the general influence of the Russian ideology of government."[90] In its report the committee specifically endorsed the views of Vinson and Dewey, quoting statements by both. A minority dissented from supporting the loan, but their arguments—mostly economic—carried little weight with the majority and seemed less significant in the light of heightened perception of the threat from the East.[91]

Debate on the floor of the House was long and vigorous and for a time sufficiently hostile to the loan as to raise serious doubts about the resolution's eventual passage. All the economic arguments for and against the loan were heard again, but it was the loan's appeal as a means to halt the spread of Communism that finally proved decisive. From the first day of the House's consideration it was argued that the loan was needed to maintain the system of free enterprise in world trade and support "the only other great democracy in the world."[92] This theme was heard repeatedly during five days of debate on the measure, and in the end it overcame the doubts of many who for various reasons had never been conspicuous supporters of Great Britain. Rep. Sol Bloom of Brooklyn, chairman of the House Foreign Affairs Committee and a vehement critic of England's Palestine policy, declared: "I know that this loan is going to help my country. As an American I am going to vote for that which is in the best interest of my country."[93] Majority Leader John McCormack, representing the Irish-Americans of South Boston, clearly felt that the major argument for the loan was its value as an anti-Soviet measure. On the next to the last day of debate he told his colleagues: "We should not allow feelings on our part related to the past, or past disagreements, to influence our judgement. . . . If we close our eyes . . . if our public officials charged with responsibility fail through indifference, uncertainty, or fear to do the things we ought to do in our own national interest, then we leave those countries who look toward Washington with friendly eyes no other alternative but to be subjected to the sphere of influence of Moscow."[94] Others, including minority leader Jesse Wolcott and Speaker Sam Rayburn, echoed McCormack's views. With this late wave of support the tide turned toward the loan. The House vote, on July 13, was by the fairly comfortable margin of 219 to 155. Once again the Republican split was critical. Exactly one-third of the minority party's votes were in support of the resolution. Had slightly more than half of these gone the other way the loan agreement would not have been approved.

The Final Disposition of the Second USSR Request

The debate over the British loan provided a revealing account of congressional sentiment toward foreign loans in general and the possibility of a loan to the USSR in particular. The British loan had not been popular with the Congress. It was viewed by many as an unnecessary extravagance, and it was approved by the Senate only because a slight majority of those voting were convinced that on balance American economic interests would be furthered by it. In the House it appeared that its passage was assured only by the additional argument that the loan was necessary to keep England from falling into the arms of Russia. In both houses the loan was regarded as an exceptional measure made palatable only because of Britain's leading role in world commerce and its unique and long-standing relationship with the United States. These conditions applied to no other country and thus no other was likely to be granted similar assistance. Under these circumstances a large loan to even a friendly and cooperative Russia in 1946 would have found few strong supporters in the Congress. For a Russia that Congress regarded with growing hostility—so much so that one of its houses actually saw the extension of a loan to another ally as a means to blunt the threat it posed—the extension of economic aid seemed all but impossible.

In the White House and in the State Department, during the long struggle over the British loan, these congressional sentiments were clearly perceived and understood. At the end of May, a memorandum from the Office of Financial and Development Policy in the State Department proposed to Assistant Secretary Clayton that the government either take advantage of the latest Russian reply to "break off gracefully" the loan discussions or postpone requesting $1.25 billion in additional lending authority "until we have a clearer picture of the likelihood of successful negotiations with the USSR." This view apparently also froze further consideration of Russia's request to make a $100 million purchase of surplus property. In April the Russians had accepted with only slight changes U.S. conditions for this transaction; but by the end of May there had been no reply from the State Department on the matter. To an inquiry from another branch of the department, John Hazard of the Office of Foreign Liquidation replied that the agreement "had been held up due to the Secretary's feeling that matters with the USSR should be a little clearer before proceeding."[95]

By the middle of June, when matters were still no clearer but when congressional views expressed in the British loan debate were growing much stronger, Byrnes evidently decided to find out just how badly the Russians wanted a loan. He therefore sent a note to Ambassador Novikov that simply repeated the American position set forth in its message of mid-April. The Soviet concession on discussing issues one, two, five, and nine was noted, but it was dismissed as insufficient. "The Government of the United States must reaffirm the view, expressed in its note of February 21, 1946," Byrnes wrote, "that the settlement of all questions enumerated in that note is necessary to provide a sound basis for the mutually beneficial development of economic and financial relations between the United States and the Union of Soviet Socialist Republics."[96] This did not terminate the discussion of credits, but it had the effect of forcing the Russians to either accept American conditions for a loan or break off further consideration of the matter. At the same time, President Truman did his part to convince the Soviet Union that a slim possibility for a loan still existed. When he was asked at a press conference on June 14 if he still planned to request from Congress a $1.25 billion increase in the Export-Import Bank's lending authority, he left the matter open by replying, "I have not yet got to the point where I can consider that."[97]

June 14 was also the day that the House Banking and Currency Committee reported out the resolution approving the British loan agreement. Since testimony before the committee had shown the growing strength of the argument that the loan was necessary to strengthen the capitalist system in general and Britain in particular, many representatives who normally would have opposed the loan were persuaded to back it as a bulwark against Communist expansion. If such an argument was adding support to the resolution, then it was clear that a request to expand the lending authority of the Export-Import Bank—when that expansion would be used for a loan to the USSR—would meet a hostile reception, occasion a bitter debate, and ultimately fail of passage. Such an outcome would be unwelcome to any administration at any time; in the summer preceding a difficult congressional election it was tantamount to courting disaster. These points became even clearer during the bitter debate on the British loan that followed in the House. Against them Truman could balance neither political nor economic reasons sufficient to continue to offer long-term credits to Russia. When the loan finally passed on July 13 and the United States had not yet received from the Soviet Union a reply to its note of a month before, the president made up his mind to terminate consideration of any similar large loan to Russia. An exchange at his press conference five days later made this evident. When a reporter asked if he planned to request from Congress additional authorization for foreign loans, Truman replied, "I have no such intention." When pressed further regarding his earlier proposal for a $1.25 billion expansion of the Export-Import Bank, the president replied that he thought it would come up in the next Congress. Finally, when asked specifically if there was any plan at all for an early request for a loan to Russia, Truman answered, "Not that I know of. I haven't heard about it yet."[98]

It remained only to take the necessary steps consonant with Truman's decision and withdraw as gracefully as possible from further discussions with the Russians about long-term credits. These activities extended over the next two months. First, the project to sell to Russia $100 million of surplus property was terminated. As late as June 29, Thomas McCabe, foreign liquidation commissioner in the State Department, had been instructed to proceed with negotiations on this matter on the basis of the Soviet Union's April proposals; but on July 24 McCabe was informed that Secretary Byrnes had decided that he "did not wish to raise the matter at this time."[99] Then, when Truman met the press early in August to discuss his budget for 1947, he again made it clear that he was not including at that time a request for $1.25 billion in additional funds for the Export-Import Bank.[100] Finally, since the Soviet loan was linked with a number of other issues, further discussion on these matters required uncoupling them from the question of long-term credit. The most important of these was the settlement of lend-lease because under the provisions of the Master Agreement such settlement envisioned agreement to terms and conditions of international trade beneficial to the interests of the United States. In September Assistant Secretary Clayton therefore proposed to Byrnes that the USSR be requested to begin lend-lease settlement discussions at an early date "apart from any discussion [of a] billion dollar loan." He added that such discussions should cover matters under the Soviet Master Lend-Lease Agreement, including Article VII. "Remoteness of loan prospect and other conditions of which you are aware," Clayton concluded, "commend this course." Byrnes concurred, adding that he hoped the question "would be pressed vigorously," and on September 14 the Soviet chargé in Washington was duly notified.[101]

With this message all further efforts to implement the presidential approval given one year before of a long-term billion dollar credit to the USSR for postwar reconstruction were formally terminated. Truman's remarks at his July press conference had undoubtedly made clear to all—including the Russians—that the loan was dead. The message of September 14 to the Soviet chargé was merely the last nail in the coffin.

Implementation: The Neglected Phase
of the Policy-making Process

The decisions to end aid to Russia in 1945 and 1946 contributed to the coming of the Cold War. They were not the main causes; these lay deeper, in differences of culture, history, and political ideology, in the inevitable disputes of great power rivalry, and in the bitter controversies that emerged from the war that had just been won. Yet these decisions did contribute to accelerating and widening the course of the Cold War, and they did foreclose opportunities to slow its pace and narrow its controversies. The lend-lease cutback at the end of the war in Europe was interpreted by the Russians as a crude effort to force them to change the policies they had been pursuing in the nations they had fought and freed from Nazi rule; their response was to tighten more firmly their hold on these areas and to gird themselves for a new round of hostility from the West. The lend-lease cutoff at the end of hostilities with Japan and the subsequent decisions on the Russians' credit requests, together with the halting of reparations deliveries, probably convinced them that in their reconstruction they would have to rely entirely on their own resources, and that in so doing they would have to make special efforts to maintain and improve a large defense establishment. Each of these decisions, with successively diminishing force, was a cause of the Cold War, and each, with successively increasing impact, was a symptom.

But this was not the intention of U.S. policy makers. As this study has shown, in each case the implementation phase of the policy-making process significantly affected the outcome of that process. In the May 1945 cutback of lend-lease to the USSR, implementation resulted in a signal to the Russians far stronger and more abrasive than that intended by Truman and his advisors. In the August 1945 lend-lease termination, implementation caused the Russians to receive treatment more discriminatory than that accorded other recipients. This did not disadvantage the Soviets substantially more than if they had been treated the same as others, but it did make clear that they were being dealt with less favorably, an outcome that was neither envisioned nor intended. In both these cases the decisions that were made had to be modified when the consequences of their implementation became known. This in turn not only embarrassed the American administration at a critical time but also created an appearance of uncertainty and ineptitude in its foreign policy-making. In the case of the replies to Russia's two requests for credits for postwar reconstruction, long delays in implementation, and finally the manner of implementing the reply to the second request, aborted the opportunity to further the policy goals that the responses had sought. As a result, the policy of trying to obtain concessions in return for credits was never tested and a potentially important avenue of communication with the Soviet Union was closed. In all four decisions, results differed from intentions, new misperceptions were created, and old misunderstandings were renewed.

Such an interpretation of these decisions challenges the views of both orthodox and revisionist historians of the origins of the Cold War who have tended to depict them as generally consistent outcomes of the clearly expressed preferences of informed national leaders. Such explanations make it possible to impute motives, trace cause and effect, and fix responsibility. They lend weight to assertions that the Cold War was "caused" by one or the other side and that blame for its coming can be securely fixed; and these assertions become in turn the heart of accusations that serve to prolong and intensify that which they are explaining.

Thus, scholars and participants who collectively have been grouped under the rubric of "orthodox" concerning their view of the origins of the Cold War view its onset—with varying degrees of emphasis—as a consequence of Russian expansion and Communist aggression opposed by Western efforts designed to halt and contain these parallel movements. In this explanatory context the decisions on lend-lease and loans to Russia are viewed either as appropriate responses in the face of Soviet misbehavior or as casualties of a struggle whose causes lie almost exclusively in the deliberate acts of the USSR.

George F. Kennan has written:

> Far from disapproving the cancellation of lend-lease after the termination of our military partnership with Russia in 1945, I considered . . . that barring some satisfactory political understanding with the Soviet Union, we should have considered at least an extensive curtailment of this program at the time of the Warsaw uprising, in the summer of 1944.[1]

Herbert Feis disavows any special U.S. intent to penalize the Soviet Union in the May 1945 lend-lease cutback, but he argues that the decision was influenced by the fact that "the American government was accumulating grievances about what it deemed certain sharp Soviet practices."[2] In the most thoroughly researched account of lend-lease to Russia, George C. Herring discusses the importance of domestic pressures on Truman and concludes that his administration "did not employ lend-lease systematically to achieve its foreign policy goals." But still he states: "He [Truman] intended the cutback in aid to indicate to the Kremlin U.S. displeasure with its actions and to make clear that the USSR could not defy American wishes with impunity."[3] Martin F. Herz explains that the Russian request for a $6 billion loan "became tangled up in a legal argument in Washington" and he credits the story that in February 1946 the second Russian loan request was "discovered, having been lost for six months."[4] William H. McNeill also gives credence to the story that the second loan request was "lost," and adds that when the proposal was found the American government replied by explaining the situation and following "the identical procedure which had been followed in the negotiation with Great Britain and other Allied countries; but the Russians chose to interpret it as a clear case of American financial aggression."[5] Arthur Schlesinger, Jr., in his survey of Cold War origins, cites suspicion, accident, and misunderstanding as factors in these decisions, then adds, "Actually the American attempt to settle the fourth lend-lease protocol [the reference is probably to the abortive 3-c Agreement] was generous and the Russians for their own reasons declined to come to an agreement. It is not clear, though, that satisfying Moscow on any of these financial scores would have made much essential difference."[6]

Others who have examined these and other decisions concerning the origins of the Cold War, and written of them in a manner more critical of the United States, are frequently labeled "revisionist" because they have reached very different conclusions from the traditional or "orthodox" perspectives of those cited above. Such writers, again with widely varying emphases, lay the blame for the Cold War on the deliberate actions of the Western Allies, particularly the United States. They depict the Soviet Union as essentially defensive in the immediate postwar period, concerned mainly with security and the enormous tasks of reconstruction. In their view it was the West that was aggressive, seeking to advance capitalist rule to the very doorstep of the USSR, thus reducing the Kremlin's policy alternatives and forcing it to assume a tough defensive posture. In their opinion the decisions examined here were purposefully taken to exert pressure on the Soviet Union and further weaken it in a time of need. They are variously described as evidence of a newly assumed hard-line policy or as carefully conceived acts of economic coercion.

William A. Williams, frequently considered the "dean" of American revisionist historians, wrote in 1958 that while the great crusade against communism did not begin until the end of 1946, still "as one insider remarked, 'the strong view prevailed' from the very beginning. . . . Thus, for example, further lend-lease allocations and shipments to Russia were cancelled in May 1945."[7] Lloyd C. Gardner, one of Williams's students at the University of Wisconsin, has concluded, "Yet it was impossible . . . to deny that most American policymakers wanted to use further financial or economic aid as a diplomatic tool."[8] Gar Alperovitz sees strong evidence of coercive motivation in both the cutback and cutoff of lend-lease to Russia: "The primary motivation for the timing of the Lend-

Lease cutback is to be found in the prevailing concepts which guided the showdown strategy," and "It is now beyond question that Truman's famous 1945 Lend-Lease cutoff was made to increase the President's political leverage against the Soviet Union in connection with such issues [internal political matters in Eastern Europe]."[9]

Walter LaFeber extends the showdown strategy to include the loan decisions as well as those on lend-lease: "Having failed to budge the Russians in face-to-face negotiations, even when backed by atomic bombs, the State Department next tried to buckle Stalin's iron fence with economic pressure."[10] Gabriel Kolko adds: "The principle of using economic aid as an instrument of political and economic policy, and above all as a means to introduce stability and stop communism, meant a final shattering of the last shred of Russian hope for an American loan," and Thomas G. Paterson, in a detailed examination of the loan decisions, concludes:

> A considerable amount of evidence suggests that the United States' refusal to aid Russia's postwar construction through a loan similar to that granted Britain in early 1946 may have contributed to a continuation of a low standard of living for the Russian people, with detrimental international effects; to a harsher Russian policy toward Germany and Eastern Europe; and to unsettled and inimical Soviet-American relations.[11]

This study has offered a different explanation. While not ignoring the preferences of authoritatively placed individuals, it has focused attention on the actions that followed to implement these expressed preferences. In so doing it has discovered that in these decisions policy outcomes differed widely from policy goals, that in the process of implementation both institutional rules and the preferences of implementors influenced the content of policy and the pace of its consideration. The result was less the product of deliberate design and more the residual of numerous attitudes and goals, each held with varying degrees of tenacity and each advocated with varying degrees of force. This is not to submit to a neo-Rankean view of history that absolves all national decision makers of ultimate responsibility for their decisions, but it is to argue that responsibility is diffused; it falls on some more than on others, but not entirely on one or on one single group.

Yet there still must be responsibility in public policy making, and an important part of that responsibility is to make policy outcomes more consistent with policy goals. What then are the implications of this examination of policy implementation and the lessons to be learned for the achievement of this aim? The first is simply that those who carry out policy decisions, the implementors, can greatly influence the content, timing, and impact of those decisions. Implementors have their own values and attitudes, their own loyalties to serve, and their own goals to achieve, and these differ from those of more senior decision makers. At the same time, their expertise, their activities in gathering and processing information for their superiors, and their day-to-day involvement in operations give them enormous power in shaping policy outcomes. According to Graham T. Allison and Morton Halperin, "The action channel for major foreign policy decisions can be usefully divided into that portion which leads to decisions by senior players and that part which follows from those decisions."[12] With regard to those who carry out the second part of the "action channel," Allison and Halperin have written:

> In some cases, players responsible for implementing decisions will feel obligated to implement the spirit as well as the letter of the decision. Even in such cases, the action may differ from the action that the senior players thought would result from their decisions. This is in part because actions are carried out by large organizations according to existing routines, in part because decisions do not usually include an explanation of what the action is intended to accomplish, and in part because when specifying details junior players may distort the action.[13]

The decisive influence of implementors was seen in all four decisions examined in this study. In the decision to cut back lend-lease to the USSR, zealous wording in the operative documents by State Department officials long convinced of Russian hostility was complemented by the zealous action of American generals long chagrined at the policy of unquestioningly feeding Russia's apparently limitless appetite for equipment and material. The result was an outcome far stronger than that intended by senior policy makers. In the August 1945 cutoff of lend-lease, the influence of the implementors of the decision was similar. The attitudes of those authoritatively placed in the implementation part of the "action channel" (notably Leo Crowley, the director of the FEA, and General Wesson, director of its USSR Branch) were such that steps were under way to terminate Russian lend-lease even *before* the atomic explosion at Hiroshima. As a result, instructions to do so were written before Japan's surrender and delivered to the Russians before Truman's decision to terminate the entire program, an outcome that meant far different treatment for the Soviet Union than that accorded other lend-lease recipients.

The long delays in replying to Russia's two requests for credits for postwar reconstruction were also attributable in part to the attitudes and activities of subordinate bureaucratic players. Particularly important in these cases was the inability of these players to reach consensus on important aspects of the loan question and present agreed positions to their seniors. These aspects included Russia's need for credits, the value and wisdom of using credits to extract political and other concessions, the nature of the concessions to be requested, and the possible disadvantages to U.S. security of extending a loan. As long as disagreement continued on these matters in lower levels of the executive bureaucracy, implementation was delayed on agreement already achieved in principle to extend credits to the USSR.[14]

Critical in all four cases was the latitude allowed implementors in carrying out prescribed policy. As long as implementors have different preferences and differently ranked priorities than policy makers—as they often do—then the probability that implementation will not accurately reflect policy makers' intentions will increase directly with the latitude allowed implementors. If latitude is sufficiently wide then it is the preferences of the implementors that will be carried out.[15] Realizing this, policy makers must either narrow latitude, be prepared to accept the consequences of permitting it, or—finding these options unacceptable—withdraw the decision.

The second important implication that arises from this study concerns the influence on implementation of the institutions and organizations through which policy decisions are processed. The existence and activities of such organizations, with their established rules and routines, can cause decisions to be handled in ways unsuspected and unintended by senior policy makers. On the other side of the coin, the absence of a suitable organization can deprive a decision of a mechanism and sponsors for its implementation and thus render it stillborn. Richard C. Snyder and his colleagues have argued the importance of what they call "the organizational context" in explaining foreign policy decision-making processes and have deplored the absence of its inclusion in previous studies of international politics.[16] Taking their work several steps further, Graham Allison has made "Organizational Process" the focus of the second of his three models of the foreign policy-making process. Concerning the importance of organizations and their procedures in the processing of foreign policy, Allison has written:

> At any given time, a government consists of *existing* organizations, each with a *fixed* set of standard operating procedures and programs. The behavior of these organizations— and consequently of the government—relevant to an issue in any particular instance is, therefore, determined primarily by routines established in these organizations prior to that instance.[17]

In the decisions concerning the ending of lend-lease to Russia, implementation was influenced by both the institutions and rules of the lend-lease program in general and the specific organization and procedures set up for the USSR in particular. The Lend-Lease Act provided the means—through contracts made in accordance with its Section 3-c—for the uninterrupted flow of supplies following the termination of hostilities. Interpretation of the act and its successive renewals also established the practice that lend-lease would be extended only to cobelligerents. When the war in Europe ended, the USSR was neither covered by a 3-c agreement nor was it a cobelligerent with the Allies against Japan. Thus, its legal standing as a lend-lease recipient was effectively undermined; and in August, when the Pacific war ended with the Soviet Union still not covered by a 3-c pact, it had no standing at all as a recipient. In addition, the special organization (the President's Soviet Protocol Committee) and the special procedures (the annual Soviet Supply Protocols) that had been established to speed supplies to Russia and circumvent its reluctance to provide normal justification for its requests, created both a disposition (in the minds of those administering the program) and the means to quickly cut it back and terminate it. Finally, although procedures had been established to run the entire lend-lease program while the war was on, none had been established to reduce it gradually, or in stages, once the war ended. Thus organizational rules and procedures presented senior policy makers with only two immediate choices at the end of hostilities: continue the program as it was or terminate it.

In the case of the extension of credits to Russia, it was the absence of an organization and appropriate procedures that contributed to the failure to implement approved policy. The United Nations Relief and Rehabilitation Agency (UNRRA) was restricted to a narrow interpretation of relief and rehabilitation, the Bretton Woods institutions (the International Bank and the International Monetary Fund) were months from being in operation, and direct loans to Russia were effectively prohibited by the Johnson Act. Only the Export-Import Bank provided a possible vehicle for a loan, but its lending power was very small and it, too, fell under the restrictive clauses of the Johnson Act. Thus, until the bank's lending power could be expanded and its default provisions removed, neither Roosevelt at Yalta nor later Truman in Washington (at the time of Molotov's visit in May 1945) could make a meaningful reply to the January 1945 Soviet request for a six billion dollar credit. Later, when the bank was finally in a position to make the requested loan, implementation of approval to do so was hindered first by the postwar resignation and dispersal of those who had been most actively involved in discussions about the loan and second—while the request was delayed—by the steady disbursal of most of the bank's increased funds.

From these decisions it is clear that organizational structure and routine greatly shape policy implementation. While these might be seen as establishing restraints on bureaucratic activity and insuring consistent results, they also constrain initiative and adaptation when situations change and organizations are restructured. In such cases there is no longer an acknowledged forum with agreed procedures, and implementation either halts entirely, is delayed, or is carried out in ways not anticipated by policy makers.

A third implication of the examination of the efforts to implement these four decisions is that considerable influence is exercised on implementors by those who are outside the executive foreign policy-making process. In these decisions the most important nonexecutive policy makers were the members of the U.S. Congress, both collectively in their committee and law-passing roles and individually as spokesmen for foreign policy positions. In lend-lease matters Congress had no direct role concerning recipients of assistance. It did not determine which nations would receive aid, and it did not determine when, with regard to whom, and under what conditions assistance could be ended. It did, however, hold the power of annual extensions of the program (after its first two years); it did appropriate its funds (as part of the annual National Defense Appropriations Bills); and it could by concurrent resolution terminate it.

Concerning foreign loans, congressional powers were also general rather than specific. The Congress could create international lending organizations, establish some restrictions on their transactions, and, through appropriations, set limits on the total of the loans they made; but until it took up the British loan agreement early in 1946, it did not concern itself with loans to particular countries and the precise amounts of such loans. Nevertheless, in the programs it established and renewed the Congress did manage to make known to those who staffed them its specific views and preferences; and these implementors—for reasons of both conviction and self-interest—attended carefully to expressions of congressional opinion and adjusted their programs accordingly. In this way Congress exercised on the implementation of such programs what Stanley Hoffman has aptly termed its "deterrent power," restraining initiative and innovation in both new and established programs.[18]

Those who implemented the cutback of lend-lease to Russia were responding in part to what they felt were congressional preferences. This was certainly true of Leo Crowley, and it is clear that he had conveyed this same feeling to the generals in the USSR branch of the FEA who implemented the cutback. In committee hearings and in debates on the floors of both houses, prominent senators and congressmen, through their questions and comments, had made clear their view that lend-lease aid should be extended only to nations who were cobelligerents with the United States against a common enemy. While this was never written into the legislation that extended the Lend-Lease Act, it was considered by many who managed the USSR program to represent the intent of the Congress. Thus the ending of Russia's cobelligerent status when Germany surrendered provided a strong and convincing rationale for immediately cutting back the Soviet aid program. Even more clearly Congress had conveyed the impression that lend-lease should end when hostilities ended and should not be used for purposes that did not support actual war-fighting. To some of the implementors of lend-lease policy this was regarded as a virtual mandate to terminate the program at the moment of victory and guard carefully against its use for purposes of rehabilitation and reconstruction. To the program's leaders—particularly Leo Crowley—prompt termination was the necessary redemption of prior promises and a valued opportunity to demonstrate that congressional confidence in their stewardship had been well placed.

The influence of the Congress on the implementation phase of the Soviet loan decisions was most clearly seen in the handling of the second Russian credit request. Although Congress had enlarged the lending powers of the Export-Import Bank and removed its default provisions in July 1945 with full understanding that these measures would make possible a billion dollar reconstruction loan to the Soviet Union, influential members had made clear their opinion that this was exceptional legislation created because of exceptional circumstances and that large-scale foreign lending was best considered an emergency measure rather than a regular foreign policy activity. These views became even more pronounced during the extended debate and final close passage of the British loan resolution, and when the debate—in its later stages—became a forum for the expression of anti-Soviet views, those who were to implement the agreed policy of loaning a billion dollars in postwar credits to the USSR knew that their efforts had been dealt a decisive blow. They also knew that with the war's end Congress was demanding and regaining its role as a foreign policy-making partner with the executive and that to oppose that effort—on an issue where the stakes were relatively low and the prospects for controversy relatively high—would be to invite both defeat and collateral damage to other legislative programs.[19]

Thus it is necessary to be aware that implementors often have different relationships with third parties than do policy makers. This is particularly true in the American system of government where power is separated and implementors in one branch pay careful attention to the opinions and preferences of those in other branches, as in the case of office holders and staff members in the executive who look to the Congress for their charter and their funds. Implementors' loyalties, therefore, often are divided; they look in more than one direction for support and guidance, and their implementation of policy varies accordingly.

A fourth implication derived from this study concerns the importance of the external setting to the implementation of foreign policy decisions, particularly as it is perceived by those who are tasked to do the implementing. In recent years scholars of the foreign policy-making process have devoted increasing attention to the importance of foreign policy-makers' perceptions of the external setting to their decision-making process. Synder and his associates consider "external conditions, objects, events and other actors" to be one of the two main categories of limitations on decision making (the other being limitations having their sources within the system) and they state: "The important point here is that these factors are mediated—or gain their significance—from the perceptions and judgments of the decision-makers."[20] Joseph H. de Rivera has stressed the importance of perceptions and attitudes in understanding the making of foreign policy and has warned that "it is difficult even to intellectually grasp the fact that *we construct* the reality in which we operate."[21] Robert Jervis has made a detailed examination of the construction of reality by foreign policy makers, explaining their processes of perception as well as several categories of common misperceptions.[22]

In each of the decisions examined in this study, perceptions of the external setting influenced implementation of the decisions. In the early years of the war, Russia was perceived as a beleaguered ally in desperate need of aid. Impressions of the USSR as the implacable foe of Western capitalism were set aside for the duration, and for the most part the difficulties in dealing with its alien and suspicious bureaucracy were forgiven by the common need to pursue the greater goal of defeating Nazism. But when the tide turned in the Allies' favor, old impressions returned with it, augmented by the seemingly insatiable Soviet appetite for supplies of all kinds. Thus, at the moment of victory over Germany the image of Russia held by those implementing the decision to cut back lend-lease was heavily colored by impressions of greed and ingratitude. In the months that followed, perceptions of Soviet intransigence in the disputes that developed between Russia and its Western allies served to reinforce this image and contributed importantly, in the cutoff of lend-lease, to a virtual repetition of the singularly abrupt and abrasive treatment the USSR had received in the earlier cutback. These images reflected the expectations of those who held them, expectations that were built of difficult direct experiences with the Russians that seemed to reconfirm earlier attitudes sublimated by the call of duty. For top policy makers these images were mitigated by the larger context in which they were perceived as well as by the greater awareness of the need to overcome them and the consequences of not doing so. But at the level of policy implementation there was neither context nor awareness to inhibit actions guided by current perceptions.

In the matter of the extended responses to Russia's two requests for credits, implementation was especially affected by the great changes that occurred during this period in perception of the external setting. These changes were particularly important in delaying the responses, and in so doing they significantly influenced their content. Uncertainty about Russian intentions contributed in part to U.S. failure to respond immediately to Molotov's January 1945 request for a $6 billion credit; hope of influencing these intentions largely determined the timing of the response that was finally made. When Hopkins's mission to Moscow in June briefly warmed the climate of Soviet-American relations with apparent progress on the troubling question of the future government of Poland and other issues in dispute between the two nations, Acting Secretary of State Joseph Grew gauged the moment appropriate to reply to Molotov's request, albeit with an answer that could only indicate interest and promise attention when Congress had made means available for the desired loan. By the time means were available and the Russians had made their second request, perception of the state of Soviet-American relations had changed again. Old disputes had been rekindled and new ones had flared up, and once more uncertainty over Soviet intentions paralyzed American policy making on the question of a loan to Russia. While officials in the State Department delayed the response to Russia's second request, awaiting clarification of its intentions, their image of the USSR was slowly reshaped by their reading of Russian hostility in Eastern Europe and stubbornness at the Foreign Ministers Conferences of London and Moscow. Thus, when the response was finally made to the second credit request, its content and tone reflected more the stance of a hard-bargaining adversary and less the view of an understanding ally seeking a desirable arrangement mutually beneficial to both parties. When in the following months events seemed to reinforce this image—and the analysis of George Kennan gave them a convincing and coherent explanation—follow-on exchanges of diplomatic messages about the loan took on an increasingly uncompromising cast and finally terminated the discussion by restricting it almost entirely to American-preferred conditions.[23]

Implementors view the world differently because they see it from a different perspective. They share neither the larger view of policy makers nor their responsibility for the policies they make. Instead, theirs is a microcosmic view of the policy-making process, involving detailed knowledge of specific issues and direct contact with their opposite numbers. As a result, implementors frequently view their environment with less detachment and more passion than policy makers. Because of their closer contacts and greater knowledge they are deeply convinced of their views and less willing to change them. Thus, when implementing policies that are not congruent with their view of the external setting they seek to alter them or, failing that, to delay them. Delay, in turn, often means that options thought to be open become closed.[24]

The fifth and final implication revealed by the examination of the implementation phase of these decisions deals with the importance of feedback to successful implementation of public policy decisions. Idealized models of the public policy-making process almost always include feedback as a final or penultimate step in the process. In his "Optimal Model of Public Policymaking," Yehezkel Dror makes feedback the model's last phase, dividing it into three categories:

1. Immediate feedback about the policy that is being executed aimed at stimulating remaking of the policy;
2. Immediate feedback about the policy that is being executed aimed at stimulating changes in the way the policy is being executed;
3. Learning feedback which is aimed at all the meta-policymaking, policymaking, and post-policymaking phases, and intended to improve their future operation in the light of current experience.[25]

For the foreign policy decision-making process, John Lovell explicitly links implementation and feedback and warns that "successful performance hinges upon adequate monitoring of actions and of subsequent changes in the situation."[26]

In the decisions discussed here feedback failures critically influenced policy implementation. Had there been adequate and timely feedback of the actions taken by the Soviet Protocol Committee's subcommittee on May 12 to implement the decision to cut back lend-lease to the USSR, policy makers would have quickly realized (as they eventually did) that the output of their decision was going to be far stronger than they had intended, and they then could have altered the subcommittee's actions. In the same way, both planning for the cutoff of lend-lease to Russia in August 1945 and the cutoff itself were undertaken by lower-level bureaucrats in a series of actions that were largely unknown to senior policy makers whose expectations and subsequent actions would be substantially affected by what their subordinates had done.

In the loan decisions lack of feedback was equally critical. Had there been prompt feedback from the U.S. Embassy in Moscow about the State Department's instructions regarding its reply to the first Soviet loan request, then the Department might have realized the inadequacy of its instructions, directed that some kind of reply be made, and spared itself the embarrassment (as well as the consequences of whatever opportunities were lost) of responding six months late. In the reply to the second request, lack of adequate feedback was even more serious. In this case, activity and discussion concerning the loan request occurred in several arenas, but implementation of agreed policy concerning a reply to the request was held up pending consultation with Secretary Byrnes. Yet there is no evidence that Byrnes was regularly kept appraised of developments concerning the loan request. Not until February 1946 was a decision made to reply, and by that date an again embarrassed State Department had to explain its six-month delay with the lame and hardly credible excuse that the Soviet request had been "misplaced."[27]

The role of feedback in the implementation phase of the policy-making process is perhaps the most important of the lessons to be learned from the study of these four decisions. The absence of feedback not only keeps the policy maker in the dark concerning how and with what results his policies are being implemented, but it has an additional pernicious consequence. Without feedback the policy maker tends to assume his policies are being carried out as directed; however, this is often not the case, with results (ranging from confusion to the very opposite of what is intended) that compound the policy makers' problems. While it is a truism that feedback is essential to the successful completion of policy making, the historical record indicates that only rarely are feedback channels explicitly considered in the design of policy.

In 1945 and 1946 failure to understand the extent to which implementation affected the outcome of the policy decisions discussed here had two serious consequences for American foreign policy. First, it added to the suspicion and mistrust that developed between the two great victors of World War II as they confronted each other with differing goals and policies for the lands they had conquered and liberated. As a result, whatever possibilities existed for reaching understandings that would have ameliorated these differences, or at least reduced the level of confrontation over them, were made that much more difficult of achievement. Thus, the course of the Cold War was made wider and deeper—harder to slow and all but impossible to reverse. Second, this failure forfeited important opportunities. At the most, these were opportunities to gain concessions on desired U.S. policy goals in exchange for economic assistance which the USSR did need and did want. This was less so for the lend-lease decisions, where important constraints limited possibilities, but more so for the credit request decisions where the possibilities were far greater. At the least, opportunities were lost to open channels of communication and create bonds of indebtedness, economic and moral. Pursuing these opportunities would have involved only small risks; it might have brought great gains. Not doing so deprived the world of the chance to find out.

Today, and in the future, failure to understand the importance of implementation can have even greater consequences. The nations of the world are more interdependent than they were three decades ago, and they are growing more so each year. Bureaucracies of modern nations are larger and more complex; communication within them is slow and often imperfect. Yet the power at their disposal in implementing decisions is very great. Foreign policy decisions made today—particularly by powerful nations—will affect more people more deeply, for longer periods of time, than ever before. Undesired and unexpected implementation of these decisions can raise levels of confrontation and lead to conflict, with results that will be damaging and perhaps even irreversible.

Improving the implementation of foreign policy decisions will not make bad decisions good, nor will it end conflict and everywhere increase cooperation; but it can make policy outcomes more consistent with policy goals, and in so doing improve the quality of foreign policy decision-making. It is with this hope that this study began, and it is with this hope that it ends.

Notes

Preface

1. Thomas B. Smith, "The Policy Implementation Process," *Policy Sciences* 4 (1973):197-209, and Donald S. Van Meter and Carl E. Van Horn, "The Policy Implementation Process: A Conceptual Framework," *Administration and Society* 6 (1975):445-488.

2. Morton H. Halperin, *Bureaucratic Politics and Foreign Policy* (Washington: The Brookings Institution, 1974), chap. 13, and Joseph Frankel, *The Making of Foreign Policy: An Analysis of Decision Making* (London: Oxford University Press, 1963), chap. 15.

3. Jeffrey L. Pressman and Aaron B. Wildavsky, after thorough search, state that they "have been unable to find any significant analytic work dealing with implementation," *Implementation* (Berkeley: University of California Press, 1974), p. 166; Eugene Bardach reports that his own search "has turned up relatively little that they [Pressman and Wildavsky] did not already find," *The Implementation Game: What Happens after a Bill Becomes a Law* (Cambridge, Mass.: MIT Press, 1977), p. 310.

4. Graham T. Allison, *Essence of Decision: Explaining the Cuban Missile Crisis* (Boston: Little Brown and Co., 1971), p. 267.

5. Truman in his interview with Krock, *New York Times*, 15 February 1950, p. 1; Dean Acheson, *Present at the Creation: My Years in the State Department* (New York: Norton, 1969), pp. 28, 106, 122; Charles G. Ross to Arthur Krock, 17 October 1945; Edward R. Stettinius, Jr., *Roosevelt and the Russians: The Yalta Conference*, ed. Walter Johnson (Garden City, N.Y.: Doubleday, 1949), p. 121; Albert Z. Carr, *Truman, Stalin and Peace* (Garden City, N.Y.: Doubleday, 1950), chap. 1; Philip E. Mosely, *The Kremlin and World Politics: Studies in Soviet Policy and Action* (New York: Vintage Books, 1960), p. 156.

6. Exponents of the former, or "revisionist" position, include: William A. Williams, *The Tragedy of American Diplomacy* (Cleveland: World, 1959), p. 169; Lloyd C. Gardner, *Economic Aspects of New Deal Diplomacy* (Madison: University of Wisconsin Press, 1964), pp. 315-18; Gar Alperovitz, *Atomic Diplomacy: Hiroshima and Potsdam* (New York: Random House, Vintage Books, 1965), pp. 35-40 and *Cold War Essays* (Garden City, N.Y.: Doubleday, Anchor Books, 1970), p. 98; Gabriel Kolko, *The Politics of War: The World and United States Foreign Policy, 1943-1945* (New York: Random House, 1968), pp. 333-40, 397-98, 499-502. Among exponents of the latter, more "orthodox" view are: Herbert Feis, *Churchill, Roosevelt and Stalin: The War They Waged and the Peace They Sought* (Princeton University Press, 1957), p. 647; Martin F. Herz, *Beginnings of the Cold War* (Bloomington: Indiana University Press, 1966), pp. 167-68; William H. McNeill, *America, Britain and Russia: Their Co-operation and Conflict, 1941-1946*, Survey of International Affairs, 1939-1946 (London: Oxford University Press, 1953), p. 691.

Chapter 1

1. Quoted in Warren F. Kimball, *The Most Unsordid Act: Lend-lease, 1939-1941* (Baltimore: Johns Hopkins, 1969), p. 96.

2. No complete account of lend-lease has been published. The following paragraphs rely especially on Kimball's fine study of the origins of lend-lease, *The Most Unsordid Act*. A briefer version of the program's inception appears in chaps. 8 and 9 of William F. Langer and S. Everett Gleason, *The Undeclared War, 1940-1941* (New York: Harper, 1953). Descriptions by participants and close observers are found in John Morton Blum, *From the Morgenthau Diaries*, 3 vols. (Boston: Houghton-Mifflin, 1964-1967), vol. 2, *Years of Urgency, 1938-1941* (1965), chap. 6; Edward R. Stettinius, Jr., *Lend-Lease: Weapon For Victory* (New York: Macmillian, 1944), pt. 2, and Robert E. Sherwood, *Roosevelt and Hopkins: An Intimate History*, rev. ed. (New York: Harper, 1950), chap. 10.

3. Kimball, *The Most Unsordid Act*, pp. 77, 93.

4. Sherwood, *Roosevelt and Hopkins*, p. 222.

5. Winston Churchill, *The Second World War*, 6 vols. (Boston: Houghton-Mifflin, 1948-1953), vol. 1, *Their Finest Hour* (1949), pp. 558-67.

6. Kimball, *The Most Unsordid Act*, pp. 151-52.

7. "History of Lend-Lease," pt. 1, chap. 4, p. 10, Record Group

169, "Records of the Foreign Economic Administration," Box 3139 (hereafter cited as FEA Records with box numbers).

8. U.S., Congress, *An Act further to Promote the Defense of the United States, and For Other Purposes*, Public Law 11, 77th Cong., 1st Sess., 1941, in U.S., *Statutes at Large*, vol. 55.

9. Pierre Renouvin and Jean-Baptiste Duroselle, *Introduction to the History of International Relations*, trans. Mary Ilford (New York: Frederick A. Praeger, 1967), p. 253; Robert E. Osgood, *Ideals and Self-Interest in America's Foreign Relations: The Great Transformation of the Twentieth Century* (Chicago: University of Chicago Press, 1953), p. 417.

10. U.S. Congress, House, Committee on Foreign Affairs, *Extension of Lend-Lease Act: Hearings . . . on H.R. 1501*, 78th Cong., 1st Sess., 1943, p. 1 (Congressional hearings will hereafter be cited with house of Congress, committee name, short title of bill, and bill number and date, viz. House, Committee on Foreign Affairs, *Hearings, Extension of Lend-Lease* (H.R. 1501), Jan. 29, 1943.

11. Assistant Secretary of State Acheson's preference for a two-year extension is indicated in ibid., Feb. 3, 1943, p. 95. Truman's assertion in his *Memoirs* that "one of the difficulties [with lend-lease] was the fact that we could never get Congress to authorize lend-lease for the duration of hostilities" is thus very misleading, and his statement in the following paragraph that it was the Senate Finance Committee "through which the lend-lease legislation went" is simply incorrect (Harry S. Truman, *Memoirs*, 2 vols. [Garden City, N.Y.: Doubleday & Co., 1955-1956], vol. 1, *Year of Decisions* [1955], pp. 231-32).

12. House, Committee on Foreign Affairs, *Hearings*, Extension of Lend-Lease (H.R. 1501), Jan. 29, 1943, pp. 33-34.

13. Ibid., p. 35.

14. Memorandum, Stettinius to Roosevelt, Dec. 22, 1942, Confidential File (hereafter cited as CF), "Lend-Lease (1941-1944)," Franklin D. Roosevelt Library, Hyde Park, N.Y. (hereafter cited as FDR Library).

15. House, Committee on Foreign Affairs, *Hearings*, Extension of Lend-Lease (H.R. 1501), Jan. 29, 1943, pp. 38-43.

16. U.S. Congress, House and Senate, *Congressional Record*, 78th Cong., 1st Sess., 1943, 89, pt. 3: 1846, 1853 (*Congressional Record* will be hereafter cited only with date and page numbers).

17. Entry of Oct. 21, 1943 in the record of State Department activities kept by Stettinius for Hull during the latter's absence at the Moscow Conference, Cordell Hull Collection, Container 83, Library of Congress; critical views of lend-lease at the time by members of

Congress appear in *Congressional Record*, Oct. 11, 1943, pp. 8213-15, and Oct. 12, 1943, pp. 8251-64.

18. House Committee on Foreign Affairs, *Hearings*, Extension of Lend-Lease (H.R. 4254), Mar. 2, 1944, p. 24, and Mar. 8, 1944, p. 122.

19. Ibid., Mar. 2, 1944, pp. 24-25.

20. U.S. Congress, House, Committee on Foreign Affairs, *Second Extension of Lend-Lease: Report to Accompany H.R. 4254*, 78th Cong., 2nd Sess., Mar. 30, 1944, H. Rept. 1316, p. 2 (Congressional reports will hereafter be cited by House of Congress, committee name, bill title, report number, and date).

21. *Congressional Record*, May 8, 1944, p. 4097.

22. House, Committee on Appropriations, *Hearings*, Defense Aid Appropriation Bill for 1945 (H.R. 4937), May 5, 1944, p. 30.

23. Senate, Committee on Appropriations, *Hearings*, Defense Aid Appropriation Bill for 1945 (H.R. 4937), June 8, 1944, p. 18.

24. House, Committee on Foreign Affairs, *Hearings*, Extension of Lend-Lease (H.R. 2013), Feb. 8, 1945, p. 37.

25. Diary of Henry L. Stimson (hereafter referred to as Stimson Diary with volume number and date), vol. 50, Feb. 14, 1945. Sterling Memorial Library, Yale University, New Haven, Conn.

26. House, Committee on Foreign Affairs, *Hearings*, Extension of Lend-Lease (H.R. 2013), Feb. 14, 1945, p. 83; Stimson Diary, vol. 50, Feb. 14, 1945.

27. Leland M. Goodrich and Marie J. Carroll, eds., *Documents on American Foreign Relations* (Princeton, N.J.: Princeton University Press, 1939-   ), vol. 7, *July 1944-June 1945* (1947), pp. 302-9.

28. House, Committee on Foreign Affairs, *Hearings*, Extension of Lend-Lease (H.R. 2013), Mar. 5, 1945, pp. 139-41.

29. Ibid., pp. 147-51.

30. House, Committee on Foreign Affairs, *Report, Third Extension of Lend-Lease*, H. Rept. 259, Mar. 6, 1945, pt. 1.

31. Ibid., pt. 2.

32. A description of the writing of the amendment and Cox's evaluation of it are in a copy of a memo Cox sent to Roosevelt, Mar. 12, 1945, Oscar S. Cox Papers, Box 63, FDR Library.

33. *New York Times*, Mar. 14, 1945, p. 7.

34. Senate, Committee on Foreign Relations, *Hearings*, Extension of Lend-Lease (H.R. 2013), Mar. 28, 1945, pp. 12-13.

35. Ibid., pp. 13-25.

36. Stettinius Papers, Box 233, Alderman Library, University of Virginia, Charlottesville, Va.; Grew, Morgenthau, and Crowley, in a memo to FDR the day after Vandenberg's testimony, had indicated

their intention to so delay the conclusion of further 3-c Agreements, *Foreign Relations of the United States: Diplomatic Papers*, 1945, vol. 4, *Europe* (Washington: U.S. Government Printing Office, 1968), p. 97 (this series will hereafter be cited as *Foreign Relations* with year and volume number).

37. Senate, Committee on Foreign Relations, *Report*, Extension of Lend-Lease, S. Rept. 178, Apr. 5, 1945.

38. *Congressional Record*, Apr. 9, 1945, p. 3218.

39. Ibid., pp. 3219-23.

40. Ibid., Apr. 10, 1945, pp. 3232-46 for the debate on Taft's amendment, the vote for which is recorded on pp. 3246-47. In his *Memoirs* Truman lends credence to the erroneous view that his vote was necessary to defeat the amendment (vol. 1, *Year of Decisions*, pp. 46 and 98). Had Truman voted yea, the amendment would have passed, but since the final tally was a tie, it stood defeated without his vote.

41. The conclusion of the debate and final vote is in *Congressional Record*, Apr. 10, 1945, pp. 3247-55.

Chapter 2

1. Raymond H. Dawson, *The Decision to Aid Russia, 1941: Foreign Policy and Domestic Politics* (Chapel Hill, N.C.: University of North Carolina Press, 1959), pp. 15-17. Dawson's study, on which the first part of this chapter relies heavily, is an excellent account of the influence of the domestic political process on Roosevelt's decision to extend lend-lease assistance to Russia.

2. Sherwood, *Roosevelt and Hopkins*, p. 304; Langer and Gleason, *The Undeclared War*, p. 538.

3. Sherwood, *Roosevelt and Hopkins*, pp. 306-8; Blum, *From the Morgenthau Diaries*, 2:259-60; Max Freedman, ed. and comp., *Roosevelt and Frankfurter: Their Correspondence, 1928-1945* (Boston: Little, Brown, 1967), pp. 613-15.

4. Quoted in Dawson, *Decision to Aid Russia*, p. 121.

5. Welles's assurances to Oumansky are in *Foreign Relations 1941*, 1:769-72.

6. Memorandum of conversation between Welles and British Ambassador Lord Halifax, quoted in Dawson, *Decision to Aid Russia*, p. 142.

7. Ibid., pp. 149-55 for a description of Roosevelt's activities at this time.

8. Quoted in Langer and Gleason, *Undeclared War*, pp. 560-61

9. Ibid., p. 561.

10. *Foreign Relations 1941*, 1:815-17.

11. *Pravda*, August 6, 1941; P. N. Pospelov, ed., *Istoriia velikoi otechestvennoi voiny Sovetskogo Soiuza, 1941-1945* [History of the Great Fatherland War of the Soviet Union, 1941-45], 6 vols. (Moscow: Voennoe izdatel'stvo, 1960-1965), 2:182. This history, the most definitive Soviet work on World War II completed to date, will hereafter be cited as *Istoriia* with appropriate volume number and page. There is apparently no single work published in the USSR dealing with lend-lease. Brief articles appear in the first and second editions of *Diplomaticheskii slovar'* [Diplomatic Dictionary] (Moscow: Gosudarstvennoye Izdatel'stvo Politicheskoi Literatury, 1948-1950), 2:11-14, and 2d ed., 3 vols. (1960-1964), 2:174-176. A good summary of lend-lease to Russia is included in I. A. Gladkov, ed., *Sovetskaia ekonomika v period velikoi otechestvennoi voiny, 1941-1945* [The Soviet Economy in the Period of the Great Fatherland War, 1941-1945] (Moscow: Izdatel'stvo "Nauka," 1970), pp. 476-84.

12. *Foreign Relations 1941*, 1:841-42; *Istoriia*, 2:188-89.

13. The complete texts of all four protocols were published by the Department of State after the war in *Wartime International Agreements: Soviet Supply Protocols* (Washington: U.S. Government Printing Office [1947]); details of the Harriman mission, including Foreign Commissar Molotov's insistence on a signed protocol, are described in W. Averell Harriman and Elie Abel, *Special Envoy to Churchill and Stalin 1941-1946* (New York: Random House, 1975), chap. 4.

14. Dawson, *Decision to Aid Russia*, pp. 151-52; Sherwood, *Roosevelt and Hopkins*, p. 395.

15. *Foreign Relations 1942*, 3:743.

16. Acheson, *Present at the Creation*, p. 34.

17. Department of State, *Soviet Supply Protocols*, p. 3.

18. These decisions are described in Marvin D. Bernstein and Francis L. Lowenheim, "Aid to Russia: The First Year," a case study in Harold Stein, ed., *American Civil-Military Decisions: A Book of Case Studies* (Birmingham: University of Alabama Press, 1963), pp. 126-67. The continuation of the AA-1 priority for Russia is discussed in a letter from WPB Chairman Julius Krug to FEA Administrator Leo T. Crowley, May 15, 1945, Julius A. Krug Collection, Container 5, Library of Congress, Washington, D.C.

19. Robert W. Coakley and Richard M. Leighton, *United States Army in World War II, The War Department, Global Logistics and Strategy 1943-1945* (Washington: U.S. Government Printing Office, 1968), p. 672.

20. The problems that arose in fulfilling the First Protocol are discussed in Bernstein and Lowenheim, "Aid to Russia: The First Year," especially pp. 121-38. A description of the operation of lend-lease to Russia throughout the war, dealing mainly with quantities shipped and the routes along which they travelled, is contained in Robert H. Jones, *The Roads to Russia: United States Lend-Lease to the Soviet Union* (Norman: University of Oklahoma Press, 1969); George C. Herring, Jr., in his excellent study, *Aid to Russia 1941-1946: Strategy, Diplomacy and the Origins of the Cold War* (New York: Columbia University Press, 1973), presents a broader historical treatment of lend-lease to Russia, including a comprehensive account of its diplomatic aspects.

21. From a letter dated Nov. 12, 1941, quoted by R. A. Winnacker in correspondence of Sept. 4, 1945, Stimson Papers, Box 423, Sterling Memorial Library, Yale University, New Haven, Conn.

22. Directive to Maritime Commission quoted in *Foreign Relations 1941*, 1:864; Hopkins's note with Roosevelt's notation is reproduced in Sherwood, *Roosevelt and Hopkins*, p. 399.

23. Soviet ship requests are from *Foreign Relations 1941*, 1:863-64; cargo and tonnage figures are in U.S., Department of State, *Report on War Aid Furnished by the United States to the USSR June 22, 1941-September 20, 1945* (Nov. 25, 1945), pp. 14-15; data on critical items are from Dept. of State, *Soviet Supply Protocols*, p. 3, and *Istoriia*, 2:365 (based on documents in the Archives of the Soviet Ministry of Foreign Trade).

24. Sumner Welles, *Seven Decisions That Shaped History* (New York: Harper and Bros., 1951), pp. 140-41; Richard M. Leighton and Robert W. Coakley, *United States Army in World War II, the War Department, Global Logistics and Strategy, 1940-1943* (Washington: U.S. Government Printing Office, 1955), p. 115. Even a normally careful historian like Herbert Feis exaggerated greatly the effect of the early First Protocol supplies when he wrote, "what was sent had been of real, perhaps vital, use to the Russians during the following winter," *Churchill, Roosevelt and Stalin*, p. 17.

25. *Foreign Relations 1941*, 1:865.

26. Figures on ship sailings and arrivals are from Dept. of State, *Report on War Aid*, pp. 14-15; the story of the northern route convoys has been dramatically told by Samuel E. Morison, *History of United States Naval Operations in World War II*, 15 vols. (Boston: Little, Brown and Co., 1947-1962), vol. 1, *The Battle of the Atlantic: September 1939-May 1943* (1947), chap. 7 and pp. 358-75, and S. W. Roskill, *History of the Second World War: United Kingdom Military Series, The War at Sea, 1939-1945*, 2 vols. (London: Her

Majesty's Stationery Office, 1956), vol. 2, *The Period of Balance,* chap. 5.

27. Dept. of State, *Report on War Aid,* pp. 14-15.

28. Figures compiled from ibid., pp. 11-15, 18; Leighton and Coakley, *Global Logistics 1940-1943,* p. 559; *Istoriia,* 2:365; *Pravda,* June 11, 1944, p. 1.

29. Leighton and Coakley, *Global Logistics 1940-1943,* p. 561.

30. The JCS estimates and the Roosevelt-Molotov conversations are described in ibid., pp. 561-63 and in Sherwood, *Roosevelt and Hopkins,* pp. 556-78; a record of the conversations held and the messages exchanged regarding the visit is in *Foreign Relations 1942,* 3:566-94.

31. Quoted in Robert W. Coakley, "The Persian Corridor as a Route for Aid to the USSR" in U.S. Dept. of the Army, Office of the Chief of Military History, Kent R. Greenfield, ed., *Command Decisions* (Washington: U.S. Government Printing Office, 1960), p. 239.

32. *Foreign Relations 1942,* 3:715.

33. *Foreign Relations: The Conferences at Washington, 1941-1942, and Casablanca, 1943,* pp. 707-19.

34. Ibid., pp. 805-7.

35. The detailed schedule is in Leighton and Coakley, *Global Logistics 1940-1943,* p. 588.

36. Standley sent a summary of his remarks to the State Department the following day (*Foreign Relations 1943,* 3:631-32). A longer account of the incident is set forth in his memoirs, written with Adm. Arthur A. Ageton, *Admiral Ambassador to Russia* (Chicago: Henry Regnery, 1955), chap. 20.

37. *New York Times,* Mar. 9, 1943, p. 5.

38. Quoted in Paul Willen, "Who Collaborated With Russia?" *Antioch Review* 14 (1954):274.

39. Quoted in Sherwood, *Roosevelt and Hopkins,* p. 706.

40. Churchill, *Second World War,* vol. 4, *The Hinge of Fate,* p. 755.

41. Figures computed from Leighton and Coakley, *Global Logistics 1940-1943,* Appendix D., p. 731.

42. Messages exchanged regarding the formulation of the Third Protocol are in *Foreign Relations 1943,* 3:737-81; the full protocol is in Dept. of State, *Soviet Supply Protocols,* pp. 49-85.

43. Changing Soviet requirements are discussed in Leighton and Coakley, *Global Logistics 1943-1945,* pp. 674-75; a table depicting these changes appears in McNeill, *America, Britain and Russia,* p. 238.

44. Leighton and Coakley, *Global Logistics 1943-1945*, pp. 676-78; Dept. of State, *Report on War Aid*, p. 4.

45. *Foreign Relations 1944*, 4:1053.

46. Ibid., pp. 1132-34.

47. The Fourth Protocol is in Dept. of State, *Soviet Supply Protocols*, pp. 87-156.

48. U.S., War Department, Army Service Forces, International Branch, *International Aid Statistics, World War II* [1946], pp. 39-40.

49. American efforts to obtain Soviet participation in the war against Japan are discussed in "The Entry of the Soviet Union into the War Against Japan," mimeographed press release (Washington: Department of Defense, Oct. 19, 1955); MILEPOST is discussed on p. 37, ibid., and in Leighton and Coakley, *Global Logistics 1943-1945*, pp. 687-94. The list of supplies constituting Annex III is in Dept. of State, *Soviet Supply Protocols*, pp. 141-46.

50. Dept. of State, *Report on War Aid*, p. 14.

51. Leighton and Coakley, *Global Logistics 1943-1945*, pp. 680-81.

52. Henry L. Stimson and McGeorge Bundy, *On Active Service in Peace and War* (New York: Harper and Bros., 1948), p. 641.

53. Henry H. Arnold Collection, Container 43, jacket no. 90, Library of Congress, Washington, D.C.

54. Soviet historians have steadily maintained that the second front in Europe could have been opened long before it was. A summary of this argument appears in a recent short history of the war intended for mass circulation, P. A. Zhilina, ed., *Velikaia otechestvennaia voina, 1941-1945: kratkii nauchno-populiarnyi ocherk* [The Great Fatherland War, 1941-1945: Short Popular-Scientific Essay] (Moscow: Politizdat, 1970), pp. 477-81.

55. Such sentiments were strongly expressed at meetings before and during the Casablanca Conference, *Foreign Relations 1943: The Conferences at Washington and Casablanca*, pp. 507, 551, 632-33, 709; similar views are contained in Leighton and Coakley, *Global Logistics 1940-1943*, chaps. 20 and 21 and Coakley and Leighton, *Global Logistics 1943-1945*, chap. 27, and in the Arnold Collection, Containers 39 and 130.

56. Expressions of such views are found in the minutes of the meetings of the President's Soviet Protocol Committee, FEA Records (USSR Branch), Box 93, and in Records of the Office of the FEA Administrator, FEA Records, items 128, 129, and 134. (Because lend-lease to Russia was still unsettled in the years following World War II, records of the USSR Branch were segregated from the general records of the FEA and kept for many years in the State Department. When

they were finally retired to the National Archives and Records Service, they were accessioned to Record Group 59 (General Records of the Department of State) rather than Record Group 169 (FEA Records). They will hereafter be cited as Records of the USSR Branch (FEA) with appropriate box number. In addition, the writer has learned of these attitudes in correspondence with Maj. Gen. Sidney P. Spalding, U.S.A., Ret., former head of the Supply Section of the U.S. Military Mission in Moscow (letter of Mar. 22, 1970) and Maj. Gen. John Y. York, USAF, Ret., former executive of the President's Soviet Protocol Committee (letters of Mar. 8 and 10, 1970).

57. *Foreign Relations 1944*, 4:1039-40. The views of Deane and Kennan are expressed in John R. Deane, *The Strange Alliance: The Story of Our Efforts at Wartime Co-operation With Russia* (New York, Viking Press, 1947), especially chap. 7, and George F. Kennan, *American Diplomacy, 1900-1950* (New York: New American Library, Mentor Books, 1952), pp. 85-86 and *Memoirs: 1925-1950* (Boston: Little, Brown, 1967), pp. 211, 266-67.

58. President's Secretary's File (hereafter cited as PSF), FDR Library.

59. Stanislaw Kot, *Conversations with the Kremlin and Dispatches from Russia*, trans. and arr. by H. C. Stevens (London: Oxford University Press, 1963), p. 5.

60. Jones, *Roads to Russia*, p. 242.

61. Arnold Collection, Container 130, folder "SAS 452.1 Russia."

62. The Russian commitment not to transfer goods without U.S. consent was contained in a letter of Nov. 7, 1941, from Soviet Chargé Andrei Gromyko to President Roosevelt, *Foreign Relations 1941*, 1:858-59 and in the Master Lend-Lease Agreement signed with the USSR; over two dozen messages were exchanged concerning this matter during 1944 and 1945, *Foreign Relations 1944*, 4:1082-1158 and *Foreign Relations 1945*, 5:945-1016.

63. These matters are discussed in John R. Deane, "Negotiation on Military Assistance, 1943-1945" and John N. Hazard, "Negotiating Under Lend-Lease, 1942-1945" in Raymond Dennett and Joseph E. Johnson, eds., *Negotiating with the Russians* (Boston: World Peace Foundation, 1951), pp. 3-28, 31-46.

Chapter 3

1. Among the economists were: J. B. Condliffe, "Implications of Lend-Lease: Economic Problems in the Settlement," *Foreign Affairs* 21 (1943):494-95 and Arthur D. Gayer, "The Problem of Lend-

Lease: Its Nature, Implications and Settlement" in *American Interests in the War and Peace* (New York: Council on Foreign Relations, April 1944), pp. 23-24. A list of sources indicating that "by mid-1944, businessmen and foreign traders were lobbying vigorously for the return of trade to normal commercial channels" is in George C. Herring, Jr., "The United States and British Bankruptcy, 1944-1945: Responsibilities Deferred," *Political Science Quarterly* 86 (1971):264, fn8.

2. The remarks of Crowley, Acheson, and Stettinius during 1944 have been discussed and referenced in chapter 1 above. Further statements by Crowley early in 1945 emphasizing this position are in FEA Records, Box 1050 (Feb. 16 and Mar. 1, 1945) and Box 773 (Mar. 22, 1945).

3. *Foreign Relations 1941*, 1:757-58.

4. McNeill, *America, Britain and Russia*, pp. 24-25, 779.

5. Cable of Dec. 5, 1941 from Secretary Hull, *Foreign Relations 1941*, 1:194-95; this decision is discussed by Langer and Gleason, *The Undeclared War*, pp. 553-57 and by Sumner Welles (who disagreed with it), *Seven Decisions*, pp. 123-45.

6. Soviet Protocol Committee Records, Box 5, FDR Library (part of Record Group 220, "Records of Committees, Commissions and Boards"); letter to the writer from Maj. Gen. Sidney P. Spalding, USA, Ret., Mar. 22, 1970.

7. *Report to the Congress on Lend-Lease Operations* [no. 4], Mar. 11, 1942, p. 33. (The first of these quarterly reports was issued June 10, 1941; thereafter they appeared irregularly and with varying titles through No. 45 of December 31, 1963. They will hereafter be cited as *Report to the Congress*, with number and date.)

8. George M. Fennemore, "The Role of the Department of State in connection with the Lend-Lease Program" (typewritten manuscript prepared in the Division of Research and Publication, U.S. Dept. of State, Apr. 3, 1943), pp. 249-50.

9. *Congressional Record*, Mar. 8, 1943, pp. 1664-65, Mar. 11, 1943, p. 1853.

10. Standley and Ageton, *Admiral Ambassador to Russia*, p. 308.

11. Arnold's memo and comments on it are in the Arnold Collection, Container 39; the statement of the Operations Division's Policy Committee is quoted in Maurice Matloff, *Strategic Planning for Coalition Warfare, 1943-1944, United States Army in World War II* (Washington: U.S. Government Printing Office, 1959), p. 282.

12. Ibid., and Coakley and Leighton, *Global Logistics 1943-1945*, pp. 675-76, where the Protocol Committee ruling is quoted.

13. These changes, and the difficulties that led to them, are discussed in Standley and Ageton, *Admiral Ambassador to Russia*, chaps. 21 and 28 and in Deane, *Strange Alliance*, chap. 6.

14. *Foreign Relations 1944*, 4:802-3.

15. Deane to JSC, Jan. 17, 1944; this message, and two others on this question, are referred to in *Foreign Relations 1944*, 4:1038 (fn. 26), 1055 (fn. 50) and 1062 (fns. 59 and 62) with the notation "not found in Departmental Files." These and other messages concerning this matter are in the Soviet Protocol Committee Records, Box 21.

16. York's memos are in ibid., York to the Secretary, JSC, Jan. 18, 1944, and York to Leahy, Jan. 21, 1944; the cable to Moscow is in *Foreign Relations 1944*, 4:1055-56.

17. Ibid., pp. 813-19.

18. Ibid., p. 951.

19. Quoted in Matloff, *Strategic Planning 1943-1944*, p. 497.

20. Arnold to Hopkins, Sept. 30, 1944 and Hopkins to Arnold, Oct. 17, 1944, Arnold Collection, Container 43.

21. Soviet Protocol Committee Records, Box 21, FDR Library. In Walter Millis, ed. and E. S. Duffield, collab., *The Forrestal Diaries* (New York: Viking Press, 1951) there are numerous references to both Forrestal's views on Russia and his preoccupation with the realistic use of U.S. power. On Sept. 2, 1944, he wrote to Palmer Hoyt: "I find that whenever any American suggests that we act in accordance with the needs of our own security he is apt to be called a God-damned fascist or imperialist, while if Uncle Joe suggests that he needs the Baltic Provinces, half of Poland, all of Bessarabia and access to the Mediterranean, all hands agree that he is a fine, frank, candid and generally delightful fellow who is very easy to deal with because he is so explicit in what he wants" (p. 14); on Nov. 29, 1944, he suggested to Harry Hopkins that lend-lease negotiations then being conducted with the British be used to "facilitate" progress in the International Civil Aviation Conference where resistance was being met from Great Britain (p.19).

22. Stimson Diary, vol. 49, Dec. 31, 1944 and vol. 50, Feb. 13, 15, 1945 (however, Stimson did later change his mind about using the atomic bomb to obtain concessions from Russia).

23. In this case Roosevelt succeeded; within a week Salazar authorized renewal of the construction. *Foreign Relations 1944*, 4:76-78, 81; Stimson Diary, vol. 48, Oct. 8, 12, 1944.

24. Acheson to Stettinius, Jan. 11, 1945, Stettinius Papers, Box 243.

25. Deane, *Strange Alliance*, pp. 157, 160, 294, and 298; York to the JCS, Soviet Protocol Committee Records, Box 21.

26. *Foreign Relations 1945*, 5:817-20.

27. *Foreign Relations 1941*, 1:790-93.

28. Harry L. Hopkins Papers, Box 306, FDR Library (Stettinius forwarded Harriman's letter to Hopkins).

29. Spalding to Hopkins, May 5, 1943, Box 18, Records of the President's Soviet Protocol Committee.

30. Stettinius's memo to the president is in the Oscar S. Cox Papers, Box 80, FDR Library; FDR's approval (with his reservation) is indicated in a Cox to Crowley memo, Nov. 22, 1943, FEA Records, Box 1071.

31. Ibid., Cox to Crowley, Jan. 1, 1944, FEA Records, Box 767; Cox to Hopkins, Jan. 15, 1944, Hopkins Papers, Box 323.

32. Cox's arguments were incorporated in a letter to Harriman (Cox Papers, Box 80) that was not sent but did serve as the draft for a Hopkins message to Harriman (*Foreign Relations 1944*, 4:1043-46).

33. The Stettinius-Crowley memo, with the enclosed message to Harriman, is in *Foreign Relations 1944*, 4:1059-62; the original (CF, "Lend-Lease," Box 1-c, FDR Library) contains Roosevelt's pen and ink notation, "O.K. FDR." The draft agreement is in *Foreign Relations 1944*, 4:1087-94; the financial terms were suggested to Hull by Morgenthau on Mar. 22, 1944, Dept. of State Records, 861.51/3042.

34. Summaries of the talks between Acheson and Stepanov are in ibid., pp. 1106-49; a brief description appears in Dean Acheson, *Present at the Creation*, pp. 85-86; additional information was given to the writer by Mr. Acheson in a letter of July 17, 1969.

35. In a memo of Aug. 18, 1944 to Dean Acheson, Emilio Collado, chief of the Division of Financial and Monetary Affairs, expressed his doubts regarding "the extension of some of the concessions which treasury is being urged to make in order to please the Russians," *Foreign Relations 1944*, 4:1118-19.

36. Ibid., pp. 1135-47.

37. Ibid., p. 1072.

38. Dept. of State, *Soviet Supply Protocols*, pp. 111-12.

39. Hazard to Spalding, Letter No. 303, Aug. 8, 1944, Records of the Military Mission in Moscow, in Box 84 of Records of the USSR Branch (FEA); information concerning reduced procurement of industrial equipment during this period has also been obtained from entries in the "Day Journal" kept by John N. Hazard, especially for the following 1944 dates: July 29, Aug. 15, 17, 18, and Nov. 15 (manuscript in the possession of its author).

40. Records of the USSR Branch (FEA), Box 93.

41. This cable to Harriman and his own memo are both in Records

of the Military Mission in Moscow, in Box 84 of Records of the USSR
Branch (FEA); a further message of Aug. 17 to Harriman from the
secretary of state repeated this instruction, *Foreign Relations 1944*,
4:1115-18.

42. This letter, which was evidently the only direct warning ever
given the Russians concerning the possibility of the automatic
cessation of lend-lease upon the termination of hostilities with
Germany, was apparently not found by the usually thorough
researchers of the State Department's *Foreign Relations* series. It is in
Records of the Military Mission in Moscow, in Box 84 of Records of
the USSR Branch (FEA).

43. Harriman to Mikoyan, Sept. 18, 1944, ibid.

44. *Foreign Relations 1944*, 4:1114-15. Hazard, fluent in Russian,
had several such conversations during this period; memoranda of
these are in the Records of the USSR Branch (FEA), Box 89. He also
elaborated on these matters in an interview with the writer, May 28,
1969.

45. *Foreign Relations 1944*, 4:1125. These attitudes were further
encouraged by the views of certain leading American officials and
businessmen who either visited the Soviet Union during this time or
met with Soviet representatives in Washington. Prominent among
these were Eric Johnston, president of the U.S. Chamber of
Commerce, who visited the USSR in June 1944, to discuss future trade
possibilities, and Donald Nelson, former chairman of the War
Production Board, who visited Moscow in September 1944, en route
to China as head of the U.S. Economic Mission to that country.
Nelson went so far as to send a message to Hopkins via diplomatic
channels strongly endorsing Mikoyan's view that long-term industrial equipment should not be excluded from lend-lease financing
pending agreement on a 3-c pact (ibid., p. 1129).

46. Ibid., p. 1121.

47. Morgenthau's "no-interest" proposal is discussed in U.S.,
Congress, Senate Committee on the Judiciary, Subcommittee to
Investigate the Administration of the Internal Security Act and Other
Internal Laws, *Morgenthau Diary (Germany)*, 2 vols., 90th Cong.,
1st Sess., Nov. 20, 1967, 1:704-5, 2:866-68, 879-83, 866 (hereafter cited
as *Morgenthau Diary [Germany]*); he finally withdrew it on Jan. 23,
1945 in the face of strong State Department opposition, ibid., pp. 907-
8 and *Foreign Relations 1945*, 5:966.

48. Hazard, "Day Journal," Dec. 5, 1944.

49. *Foreign Relations 1945*, 5:942-44.

50. Ibid., pp. 977-79, 980-81.

51. The discussion of the withdrawal of the 3-c Agreement is noted in Hazard, "Day Journal," entries for Mar. 15, 16, 19, and 21, 1945; Harriman's concurrence with the withdrawal is in *Foreign Relations 1945*, 5:988-89; FDR's approval and the aide-memoire informing the Russians is in ibid., pp. 991-93.

52. Richard M. Leighton and Robert W. Coakley, *Global Logistics and Strategy, 1943-1945*, p. 656.

53. Quoted in ibid., p. 657 where there is an extended discussion of this directive on pp. 656-61. Roosevelt's approval, given on May 10 and apparently—as later events indicated—without full understanding of its implications, is mentioned in ibid., p. 658 and in a memo from York to Hopkins, Aug. 11, 1944, Soviet Protocol Committee Records, Box 18. That this approval was not widely known is seen in an FEA response to a query about it that indicated no knowledge of its existence (note on memo from Capt. Puleson, USN, to Frank Coe, May 15, 1944, FEA Records, Box 1058).

54. Copies of these memoranda are in FEA Records, Box 1058.

55. Memo, York to Hopkins, and draft of memo, Hopkins to the president, both Aug. 14, 1944, Soviet Protocol Committee Records, Box 18.

56. Henry Morgenthau claimed that Hopkins was the source of Roosevelt's information and the author of FDR's subsequent directive (*Foreign Relations, Conferences at Malta and Yalta, 1945*, p. 136), but according to Robert Sherwood, Roosevelt's need for Hopkins's counsel at this time was not so great and Hopkins's influence over FDR was waning (*Roosevelt and Hopkins*, p. 814); evidence of "cautious soundings at a high level in Washington" by the British is given in H. Duncan Hall, *North American Supply, History of the Second World War*, United Kingdom Civil series, edited by Sir Keith Hancock (London: Her Majesty's Stationery Office & Longmans, Green & Co., 1955), p. 441.

57. Part of this letter is quoted in *Foreign Relations 1944*, 4:1132; a copy of the entire letter is in Records of the USSR Branch (FEA), Box 89.

58. Roosevelt to FEA Administrator Crowley, Sept. 29, 1944, in Goodrich and Carroll, eds., *Documents on American Foreign Relations*, 7:466.

59. The circumstances surrounding this agreement are related from Morgenthau's notes in Blum, *From the Morgenthau Diaries*, vol. 3, *Years of War, 1941-1945*, pp. 306-16.

60. Hull's reaction is in Cordell Hull, *Memoirs*, 2:1613-18; Stimson's doubts are in Stimson and Bundy, *On Active Service*, pp.

592-93 and Stimson Diary, vol. 48, Sept. 20, Oct. 9, 13, and 18, 1944 (Crowley's doubt is also indicated in the last two entries); the objections of the military chiefs are mentioned in the *Diary of William D. Leahy*, vol. 10, Oct. 24, 1944 (hereafter cited as Leahy Diary with volume number and date) Leahy Collection, Container 11, Library of Congress, Washington, D.C.), and the War Department's opposition at the time is discussed in memo for Judge Vinson, May 26, 1945, Record Group 250, "Records of the Office of War Mobilization and Reconversion," Box 118 (hereafter cited as OWMR Records, with box number).

61. Keynes's statement is quoted from a volume in the official British history of the war in Herring, "United States and British Bankruptcy," which also has a good discussion of the domestic political pressures affecting Phase II, pp. 270-72. Roosevelt's instruction to Crowley is in James F. Byrnes, *Speaking Frankly* (New York: Harper and Bros., 1947), p. 184; Roosevelt also told Admiral Leahy that he wished "lend-lease to Great Britain to be conducted as heretofore, and that additional commitments be not made," Leahy Diary, vol. 10, Nov. 18, 1944. The Roosevelt-Churchill messages (which were not referred to in Churchill's memoirs and have not been published in the *Foreign Relations* series) concerned shortages in food allocations and are in OWMR Records, Box 176.

62. *Foreign Relations 1944*, 4:1051.

63. Minutes of the 7th meeting of the President's Soviet Protocol Committee, May 10, 1944, Soviet Protocol Committee Records, Box 5.

64. The meeting is described in a memo of May 17, 1944 in Records of the President's Soviet Protocol Committee, Box 4, FDR Library and in Hazard, "Day Journal," May 17, 1944.

65. Minutes of the 8th meeting of the Protocol Committee, Aug. 7, 1944, Records of the USSR Branch (FEA), Box 93; Wesson's proposal at this meeting is in Records of the USSR Branch (FEA), Box 94.

66. The minutes of the meeting of the Subcommittee on Supplies (Sept. 8, 1944), the War Department revision (dated Aug. 15, 1944) to Wesson's proposal, and Wesson's final version of his proposal sent to Crowley on Sept. 11, 1944, are in Records of the USSR Branch (FEA), Box 94.

67. Hull to Roosevelt, Sept. 13, 1944, PSF, "Lend-Lease," FDR Library; Roosevelt to Hull, Sept. 30, 1944, PSF, Box 62.

68. *Foreign Relations 1945*, 5:944.

69. These suggestions are mentioned in Hazard to York, Dec. 28, 1944, Soviet Protocol Committee Records, Box 4.

70. Notes on Executive Policy Committee Meeting, Feb. 1, 1945, FEA Records, Box 1050.

71. Teleprint, Hutchins to Cushing, Feb. 26 and 27, 1945, Record Group 248, "Records of the War Shipping Administration," Box 61 (Hereafter cited as WSA Records, with box number).

72. Hazard, "Day Journal," Mar. 20 and 22, 1945; General York's opposition to the withdrawal of the 3-c Agreement offer is stated in ibid., Mar. 19, 1945.

73. Draft memo for the president, Apr. 6, 1945, Soviet Protocol Committee Records, Box 4; draft memo for the president, Apr. 14, 1945, Records of the USSR Branch (FEA), Box 89.

74. Memoranda, York to Hopkins, Apr. 18, 1945, Soviet Protocol Committee Records, Box 17; opposition to Wesson's views in the FEA is indicated in memo, Howard to Cox and Wesson, Apr. 18, 1945, Records of the USSR Branch (FEA), Box 89.

75. *Foreign Relations 1945*, 5:845.

76. Deane's concurrence with Harriman and his request for support from General Marshall and the JCS are discussed in Leighton and Coakley, *Global Logistics 1943-45*, p. 694; Crowley's agreement is indicated in memo, York to Hopkins, Apr. 26, 1945, Soviet Protocol Committee Records, Box 4; Wesson revealed his activities with the War Production Board in minutes of the 23rd meeting of the Protocol Subcommittee on Supplies, May 16, 1945, Records of the USSR Branch (FEA), Box 94.

77. This memo, undated but evidently prepared on Apr. 24, 1945, is in Records of the USSR Branch (FEA), Box 93.

78. Memo, York to Hopkins, Apr. 26, 1945, Soviet Protocol Committee Records, Box 4.

79. Harriman's recommendation against a new 3-c Agreement and reactions to this in the FEA are in memo, Fetter to Collado, Apr. 26, 1945, General Records of the State Department, 861.24/4-2645; the withdrawal of Wesson's draft memoranda and subsequent reconsideration of the whole matter during the following week are indicated in Hazard, "Day Journal," Apr. 26, May 4 and 5, 1945 and in notes on copies of the memoranda in Soviet Protocol Committee Records, Box 4.

80. Hazard to Spalding, letter no. 662, Apr. 30, 1945, Records of the Military Mission in Moscow in Records of the USSR Branch (FEA), Box 84.

81. *New York Times*, Jan. 10, 1945, p. 10.

82. References to Crowley's assurances regarding the termination of lend-lease are in footnote 2 above; Crowley described his last

conversation with Roosevelt in an interview with the writer, Aug. 21, 1968, Chicago, Ill.

83. Patterson to Roosevelt, March 24, 1945, copy in Arnold Collection, Container 117.

84. Truman to Jones, Truman to Stimson, Apr. 17, 1945, OWMR Records, Box 131.

Chapter 4

1. Roosevelt to FEA Administrator Crowley, Sept. 29, 1944, in Goodrich and Carroll, eds., *Documents on American Foreign Relations* 7:467.

2. Perkins to Hopkins, Dec. 22, 1942, Hopkins Papers, Box 317.

3. Barnes to Roosevelt, Aug. 14, 1944, James M. Barnes Collection, Container 26, Library of Congress, Washington, D.C.

4. Currie to Roosevelt, Sept. 8, 1944, Official File (hereafter cited as OF) 396, FDR Library.

5. Elliott Roosevelt, ed., *F.D.R., His Personal Letters*, 4 vols. (New York: Duell, Sloan and Pearce, 1950), 4:1546-47.

6. This position is cogently summarized in the Fortnightly Report of the State Department's Division of Commercial Policy, Oct. 30, 1944, Cordell Hull Collection, Container 89B, Library of Congress, Washington, D.C.

7. Langer and Gleason, *The Undeclared War*, p. 557.

8. Ernest F. Penrose, *Economic Planning for the Peace* (Princeton, N.J.: Princeton University Press, 1953), pp. 181, 187, 189.

9. Memos, Stettinius to Hopkins, June 24, 1942 and Cox to Hopkins, Dec. 8, 1942, Hopkins Papers, Box 317; Lippmann in the *Washington Post*, Jan. 25, 1943, p. 4; Winant to Hull, Mar. 24, 1943, Hull Collection, Container 82. Many others shared these views, as indicated by Penrose, *Economic Planning for the Peace*, pp. 157, 190; H. Bradford Westerfield, *The Instruments of America's Foreign Policy* (New York: Crowell, 1963), p. 274; and Leo T. Crowley (who himself did not), interview with the writer, Aug. 21, 1968.

10. Sen. Hugh Butler, "Lend-Lease for War Only? A Finance Committee Member Discusses the Public Interest in a $63 Billion Program," *Nation's Business*, May 1943, pp. 43 ff.

11. Condliffe, "Implications of Lend-Lease," 494-504; articles in business and trade periodicals are also noted in Herring, "The United States and British Bankruptcy," p. 264, fn. 8.

12. National Opinion Research Center (NORC), University of

Denver, Colo., *Report*, No. 5, Aug. 1942, and No. 8, Mar. 1943; Hadley Cantril, *Public Opinion, 1935-1946* (Princeton, N.J.: Princeton University Press, 1951), pp. 411-13.

13. *Foreign Relations 1942*, 3:580.

14. Memo, Stettinius to Acheson, Oct. 12, 1943, Stettinius Papers, Box 215.

15. Memo, Rostow to Taft and Acheson, Feb. 18, 1944, "General Records of the Department of State," 861.50/997.

16. Records of the USSR Branch (FEA), Box 94; this position was vigorously supported by FEA Administrator Crowley, who later assured Secretary of the Navy Forrestal (and others who inquired) that he would never knowingly permit lend-lease funds to be used for rehabilitation, Crowley to Forrestal, July 31, 1944, FEA Records, Box 794.

17. Various State Department memos dealing with reconstruction financing are included in FEA Records, Box 1050.

18. The origins and initial development of the Export-Import Bank are described in Hawthorne Arey, *History of Operations and Policies of Export-Import Bank of Washington* (Washington, D.C.: Government Printing Office, 1953), pp. 4-22; a Soviet version of the origins of the Bank is set forth in I.A. Ornatskii, *Esportno-Importnyi Bank SShA* [Export-Import Bank of the USA] (Moscow: Izdatel'stvo IMO, 1959), chap. 1; Pierson's testimony is in Senate, Committee on Appropriations, *Hearings*, Defense Aid Appropriation Bill for 1945 (H.R. 4937), June 8, 1944, p. 56.

19. Cordell Hull, *Memoirs*, 2 vols. (New York: Macmillan Co., 1948), 1:303-4; Memo to Wesson, Sept. 18, 1944, Records of the USSR Branch (FEA), Box 89.

20. FEA Records, Box 1050; Hull to Roosevelt, June 2, 1944, OF 5528, FDR Library.

21. Quoted in William L. Neumann, *After Victory: Churchill, Roosevelt, Stalin and the Making of the Peace* (New York: Harper and Row, Colophon Books, 1967), p. 89.

22. *Foreign Relations: The Conferences at Cairo and Tehran, 1943*, p. 15.

23. Nelson recounted his talks in Moscow in Donald M. Nelson, *Arsenal of Democracy: The Story of American War Production* (New York: Harcourt, Brace, 1946), chap. 21.

24. Hull, *Memoirs*, 2:1247-48.

25. *Foreign Relations 1943*, 1:703-81; notes and drafts for the preparation of the conference documents are in the Hopkins Papers, Box 321, and the Hull Collection, Boxes 79-80.

26. *Foreign Relations 1943*, 1:754.
27. Ibid., 3:781-86.
28. Ibid., pp. 786-87, 788-89.
29. "Economic Loans" was included in a list of items to be discussed at Tehran, Hopkins Papers, Box 321; the Roosevelt-Stalin exchange is in *Foreign Relations: The Conferences at Cairo and Tehran, 1943*, pp. 483-84.
30. Roosevelt to Harriman, Dec. 1, 1943, OF 220, FDR Library.
31. *Quoted in Gardner, Economic Aspects of New Deal Diplomacy*, p. 313.
32. Harry L. Hopkins, "What Victory Will Bring Us," *American Magazine*, 137 (Jan. 1944):21.
33. *Foreign Relations 1943*, 3:722-23.
34. *Foreign Relations 1944*, 4:1032-37.
35. Ibid., pp. 1038-39.
36. Ibid., pp. 1042-48.
37. Ibid., pp. 1048-55.
38. Ibid., pp. 1059-1062; Oscar Cox also wrote a long letter to Harriman explaining in detail each article of the 3-c Agreement, Records of the USSR Branch (FEA), Box 84.
39. *Foreign Relations 1944*, 4:1063-65, 1076-77 and Records of the USSR Branch (FEA), Box 84.
40. Hull, *Memoirs*, 1:295.
⁻41. Sumner Welles, *The Time for Decision* (New York: Harper and Bros., 1944), p. 334.
42. Crowley's views are quoted in Gardner, *Economic Aspects of New Deal Diplomacy*, pp. 313-14; negotiations between U.S. firms and the USSR at this time are described in *Foreign Relations 1944*, 4:1078-79, General Records of the State Department, 861-50/1008 and Hazard, "Day Journal," May 17, 1944.
43. *Foreign Relations 1944*, 4:959-60.
44. General Records of the State Department, 861-50/1003.
45. *Foreign Relations 1944*, 4:1129-30, 980-90, 992-98.
46. The State Department's copy of the OSS study was closed to researchers at the time records were examined for this study. The description here is from a memo to Bernard Baruch from Sam Lubell, March 1945, in the Bernard Baruch Papers, Princeton University Library, Princeton, N.J. The phrases quoted here appear in quotes in this source.
47. Hazard, "Day Journal," Nov. 6, 1944.
48. *Foreign Relations 1944*, 4:1150-51.
49. Stettinius Papers, Box 233.

Chapter 5

1. The messages exchanged between Roosevelt and Stalin, and FDR's exchange with Harriman, are in *Foreign Relations 1945*, pp. 737-57; details of the dispatch of these messages and their drafting are found in Map Room Papers, Boxes 7 and 23, FDR Library, and are discussed in William D. Leahy, *I Was There* (New York: Wittlesey House, McGraw-Hill, 1950), pp. 328-36 and in Charles E. Bohlen, *The Transformation of American Foreign Policy* (New York: Norton, 1969), pp. 72-73.

2. *New York Times*, Sept. 1, 1944, p. 26.

3. Truman, *Memoirs*, 1:328.

4. Quoted from Truman's Washington's Birthday address at Jefferson City, Missouri, Feb. 22, 1945, *Congressional Record*, March 1, 1945, pp. A911-19.

5. Memo of conversation by Charles E. Bohlen, *Foreign Relations 1945*, 5:256-58; Truman's account, based on the Bohlen memo but containing additional details, is in his *Memoirs*, 1:79-82; Leahy's account is in his book, *I Was There*, pp. 351-2.

6. Churchill, *Second World War*, vol. 6, *Triumph and Tragedy*, p. 501.

7. *Foreign Relations 1945*, p. 253.

8. Hazard to Spalding, May 7, 1945, Records of the Military Mission in Moscow in Records of the USSR Branch (FEA), Box 84.

9. Truman, *Memoirs*, 1:227-29; in the second volume of his *Memoirs* (2:103) Truman, evidently referring to this incident, describes it as the "termination" of lend-lease, which clearly it was not.

10. Truman's misrecollections in this and other matters discussed in this study have been an important source of error in the works of historians of this period. Among those who have accepted his account of this incident are: Feis, *Churchill, Roosevelt and Stalin*, pp. 647-48 and *Between War and Peace: The Potsdam Conference* (Princeton, N.J.: Princeton University Press, 1960), pp. 26-28; Herz, *Beginnings of the Cold War*, pp. 167-68; Gar Alperovitz, *Atomic Diplomacy: Hiroshima and Potsdam*, p. 36; and Adam B. Ulam, *Expansion and Coexistence: The History of Soviet Foreign Policy, 1917-1957* (New York: Frederick A. Preager, 1968), p. 348. William P. Gerberding refers to Truman's act as a "symbolic episode, the very day of the German surrender," *United States Foreign Policy: Perspectives and Analysis* (New York: McGraw Hill, 1966), p. 149. Gerberding and several other historians, including the following, also go further than

Truman's version and erroneously assert that his action "cut-off," "terminated" or "canceled" lend-lease; Walter LaFeber, *America, Russia and the Cold War 1945-1966* (New York: Wiley, 1967), p. 22; Arthur Schlesinger, Jr., "Origins of the Cold War," *Foreign Affairs* 46 (1967):44; and William A. Williams, *The Tragedy of American Diplomacy* (Cleveland: World Publishing Co., 1959), p. 169.

11. At a meeting of top War Department officials on Apr. 30, 1945 the opinion was expressed that with regard to financial matters "the British are trying to pull our leg." (Stimson Diary, vol. 51, Apr. 30, 1945.).

12. The post–V-E Day reduction of lend-lease to Britain is discussed in Leighton and Coakley, *Global Logistics 1943-45*, pp. 663-68, Herring, "United States and British Bankruptcy," pp. 274-76, and Blum, *Morgenthau Diaries*, 3:446-51.

13. Stettinius Papers, Box 292.

14. *Foreign Relations 1945*, 5:998.

15. In a telephone conversation later in the day Stettinius asked Truman if he had liked Harriman's suggestion "of getting tough on lend-lease shipments." Truman replied, "I agree with that entirely." Memo of telephone conversation, May 10, 1945, Stettinius Papers, Box 244.

16. Memo of May 11, 1945, to the chief of staff and the assistant secretary, War Department General Staff, in Record Group 165, "Records of the War Department General Staff," Box 530, OPD 400.3295 USSR 19 Apr 1942, sec. 3.

17. Memo of May 13, 1945, to Gen. Hull, ibid.

18. Memo of May 11, 1945, to the chief of staff, ibid.

19. The quoted words are from Durbrow's memo of Feb. 3, 1944, *Foreign Relations 1944*, 4:813-19.

20. Durbrow's role in the final drafting of the memo is indicated in Hazard, "Day Journal," May 11, 1945; the evidence for the additional wording is from General Lincoln's memo of May 13, 1945, to General Hull and his Memorandum for the Record of May 14, 1945, Record Group 165, "Records of the War Department General Staff," Box 530, OPD 400.3295 USSR 19 Apr. 1942, sec. 3 and Box 142, OPD 336TS case no. 92. The new wording was also discussed in a phone conversation between General Hull and General York on May 12, 1945, Transcript of Telephone Conversation, ibid., Box 530, OPD 400. 3295 USSR 19 Apr. 1942, sec. 3.

21. Hazard, "Day Journal," May 11, 1945.

22. Wesson's call to Mack is mentioned in ibid. and discussed in Morgenthau Diary, Box 846, p. 106. Morgenthau had told Truman in

a memo of Apr. 20, 1945 (repeated on May 9, 1945), that "the treasury believes that the entire lend-lease program should be surveyed and overhauled as soon as possible after V-E Day," Morgenthau Presidential Diary, vol. 7, p. 1559, FDR Library.

23. Jonathan Daniels, *The Man of Independence* (Philadelphia: Lippincott, 1950), p. 271; Leo T. Crowley interview with the writer, Aug. 21, 1968, Chicago, Ill.

24. Memo to the Secretary by Daniel Bell, May 11, 1945, Morgenthau Diary, Box 846, p. 109, FDR Library.

25. Grew to Stettinius, Apr. 22, 1945, Grew Papers, "Letters," vol. 123, Houghton Library, Harvard University, Cambridge, Mass.

26. Truman, *Memoirs*, 1:216; Memo to President Truman, May 5, 1945, *Foreign Relations 1945*, 3:277-78; Minutes of Secretary's Staff Committee Meeting, May 9, 1945, General Records of the State Department, lot 122 (rev.) Box 13147; Grew Papers, "Conversations," vol. 7. The height of Grew's disenchantment with the Soviet Union was reached a week later when, by his own account, he arose at 5:00 a.m. after a sleepless night and wrote for his private use a memo expressing his innermost thoughts. These included: "A future war with Russia is as certain as anything in this world can be certain. . . . The most fatal thing we can do is to place any confidence whatever in Russia's sincerity. . . . As soon as the San Francisco Conference is over, our policy toward Soviet Russia should immediately stiffen, all along the line." Joseph C. Grew, *Turbulent Era: A Diplomatic Record of Forty Years*, 2 vols. (London: Hammond, 1953), vol. 2, pp. 1445-46.

27. Minutes of Secretary's Staff Committee Meeting, May 11, 1945, General Records of the State Department, lot 122 (rev.), Box 13147.

28. Memo of telephone conversation, May 11, 1945, Grew Papers, "Conversations," vol. 7 (excerpt printed in *Foreign Relations 1945*, 5:999, fn. 47). The Russians had learned that when refused by one agency they could often obtain what they wanted by appealing to other agencies or individuals with a different perspective on their problems. Among their favorite targets were Morgenthau, Oscar Cox, and Harry Hopkins. Examples of this activity are cited in *Morgenthau Diary (Germany)*, 2:904-6, 909-10, 933-34 and in Memo, Wesson to Crowley, July 14, 1944, FEA Records, Box 819. The whole problem is comprehensively examined by John Hazard in "Negotiating under Lend-Lease, 1942-1945," in Dennett and Johnson, eds., *Negotiating with the Russians*, pp. 39-42.

29. Memo or Telephone Conversation, May 12, 1945, Grew Papers, "Conversations," vol. 7.

30. Stettinius, *Roosevelt and the Russians*, pp. 318-19.

31. *Foreign Relations 1945*, 5:999, fn. 47.

32. In an exclusive interview with Arthur Krock in Feb., 1950, President Truman characterized his action to "abolish" lend-lease at that time as a "mistake" and implied that the reason for the mistake was that he had no staff and no cabinet of his own (*New York Times*, Feb 15, 1950, pp. 1, 5).

33. *Foreign Relations 1945*, 5:999-1000.

34. Ibid., pp. 1000-1.

35. These minutes, on which this description of the meeting's discussions and decisions is based, are in Records of the USSR Branch (FEA), Box 94.

36. In correspondence with the writer General York recalled that the policy of unconditional aid to the Russians without demanding full justification of their needs had grown increasingly unpopular with many in the military. "After V-E Day," he wrote, "our supply people were 'fed up' and eager to cut off the Soviet pipeline." Letter of Mar. 8, 1970.

37. Memos, General Shingler to surgeon general and chief of ordnance, May 12, 1945, Record Group 160, "Records of Headquarters Army Service Forces," Box 308, 400.312 Requirements USSR, vol. 3, Apr. 1, 1945–Apr. 19, 1946; Record of Conversations of Director of War Production Board, Krug Collection, Container 47.

38. Memo, Coe to Mack, May 12, 1945, Morgenthau Diary, Book 846, p. 151. (The opening sentence of this memo, in caps, reads: "The following is very confidential and should be handled accordingly.")

39. J. M. Johnson, director, Office of Defense Transportation, to J. J. Pelley, president, Association of American Railroads, May 12, 1945, WSA Records, Box 18.

40. Copies of cables containing these various orders to War Shipping Administration representatives in the major ports of the world are in Soviet Protocol Committee Records, Box 17; a memo of May 14, 1945 from Hutchins to York summarized all the actions taken on May 12 regarding shipping and requested York's "confirmation" (which he gave) that these were in accord with the decisions of the Committee (ibid., Box 4).

41. Hazard, "Day Journal," May 12, 1945; memo for members of the President's Soviet Protocol Committee [May 15, 1945], Records of the USSR Branch (FEA), Box 93. The sequence of events involving a typical case that day is recounted in a letter of May 14, 1945 from Willis Armstrong to the administrative assistant of the Defense Supplies Corporation in which Armstrong confirmed three phone

calls made from Washington on May 12 regarding a cargo of alcohol for a Soviet tanker in San Francisco. The first call carried instructions to cease pumping the alcohol, the second to pump out what was already on board, and the third to proceed with the loading of the vessel as originally planned (ibid., Box 153).

42. Memorandum of Conversation, May 12, 1945, Grew Papers, "Conversations," vol. 7.

43. Acquisition of the story by AP from the docks is discussed in James F. Roche to Crowley, May 17, 1945, FEA Records, Box 841.

44. Memo to telephone conversation, May 12, 1945, Grew Papers, "Conversations," vol. 7.

45. Quoted in *New York Times*, May 13, 1945, p. 10; full text is in Records of the USSR Branch (FEA), Box 89.

46. Memo for the Record, May 14, 1945, Record Group 165, "Records of the War Department General Staff," Box 530, OPD 400.3295 USSR Apr 1942, sec. 3.

47. Minutes of Meeting on Soviet Lend-Lease Program, May 14, 1945, Records of the USSR Branch (FEA), Box 93.

48. Two different sets of minutes exist for this meeting. One, the "official" minutes, recorded by the committee's secretary, John Hazard, is in ibid.; the other, taken by an unknown recorder and somewhat more candid in its description of the differences of opinion that were expressed, is in Soviet Protocol Committee Records, Box 4.

49. This summary is from Memo for the Commanding General, Army Service Forces, from General Edgerton, May 17, 1945, Record Group 160, "Records of Headquarters Army Service Forces," Box 5.

50. Sherwood, *Roosevelt and Hopkins*, pp. 894-97; *New York Times*, Feb. 15, 1950, p. 5; and ibid., Aug. 5, 1949, p. 1; Adam Ulam also concludes that the "suspension of Lend Lease . . . was interpreted in Moscow as a means of pressuring the USSR" (*Expansion and Coexistence*, p. 384).

51. In conversations of May 14 and 15, 1945, John Hazard learned that the British had not been consulted regarding the post–V-E Day cutback and that the Russians had learned about it from a firm in New York before being officially notified by the U.S. government ("Day Journal," May 14, 15, 1945).

52. These feelings emerged strongly from interviews and correspondence between the writer and participants, including the following: interview with William McChesney Martin, Apr. 2, 1969, Washington, D.C.; interview with John N. Hazard, May 28, 1969, New York, N.Y.; letters from Maj. Gen. John Y. York, USA (ret.),

Mar. 8, 10, 1970, and telephone interview with General York, Mar. 31, 1970; letter from Maj. Gen. Sidney P. Spaulding, USA (ret.), Mar. 22, 1970.

53. *Foreign Relations 1945*, 5:1004-5, 1009-10.

54. Memo of Hopkins's second conversation at the Kremlin, May 27, 1945, *Foreign Relations: the Conference of Berlin (Potsdam) 1945*, 1:32-36.

55. *Foreign Relations 1945*, 5:1007-8; the additional Russian requirement for the last six months of 1945 totaled 1.8 million tons and consisted of military supplies, machinery and equipment, raw materials, foodstuffs and miscellaneous products, ibid., p. 1003, fn. 54 and Soviet Protocol Committee Records, Box 4.

56. *Foreign Relations 1945*, 5:1012-14. Three days after this message, and following a long meeting with Mikoyan, Deane and Harriman reported improved cooperation with the Russians and set down in more detail their reasons for support of most of the items on the May 28 list (ibid., pp. 1016-18).

57. Quoted in Gardner, *Economic Aspects of New Deal Diplomacy*, 317.

58. Coordinating Committee Minutes, meetings of May 19 and 24, 1945, General Records of the State Department, Lot 122 (rev.) S/S-S, Box 59.

59. The attitudes of Leahy and Crowley are mentioned in Coakley and Leighton, *Global Logistics 1943-45*, p. 697; Crowley's position is discussed in Hazard, "Day Journal," June 7, 1945, and fully presented in his memo of June 12, 1945 to the secretary of state (*Foreign Relations 1945*, 5:1023-25).

60. Wesson to Crowley, Aug. 2, 1945, Records of the USSR Branch (FEA), Box 819. The difficulties the Russians had in purchasing even supplies for cash is shown in Hazard, "Day Journal," Aug. 1, 1945.

61. George Woodbridge, *UNRRA: The History of the United Nations Relief and Rehabilitation Administration*, 3 vols. (New York: Columbia University Press, 1950), 2:233; Penrose, *Economic Planning for the Peace*, pp. 210-12; Minutes, Secretary's Staff Committee Meeting, Aug. 8, 1945, General Records of the State Department, Lot 122 (rev.), Box 13147.

62. Notes on Executive Policy Committee Meeting, Aug. 7, 1945, FEA Records, Box 772.

63. "History of Lend-Lease," pt. 1, chap. 11, pp. 18-19, FEA Records, Box 3139.

64. Hazard, "Day Journal," Aug. 10, 1945; "Daily Reports," Aug. 10-11, 1945, Records of the USSR Branch (FEA), Box 95.

65. Hall, *North American Supply*, p. 460; Richard S. Sayers, *Financial Policy 1939-45*, History of the Second World War: United Kingdom Civil Series, Sir Keith Hancock, ed. (London: Her Majesty's Stationery Office and Longmans, Green and Co., 1956), p. 479.

66. Leahy, *I Was There*, pp. 435-36.

67. Record Group 160, "Records of Headquarters Army Service Forces," Box 3, "Lend-Lease as of September 30, 1945," 2:1049-50.

68. In a diary entry of August 16 Oscar Cox recorded that he learned of Truman's views on the curtailment of lend-lease from both Harry Dexter White and Jean Monnet (Cox Diary, FDR Library); Crowley's press conference was reported in the *New York Times*, Aug. 16, 1945, p. 26.

69. A proposed revised version of the JCS directives is in FEA Records, Box 794; a summary appears in *Foreign Relations 1945*, 6:103.

70. A draft of this directive, dated Aug. 13, with the accompanying memo for the president is in OWMR Records, Box 174; the final version is in *Foreign Relations 1945*, 6:102-3.

71. The account of this meeting is reconstructed from the following sources: President's Appointment Book, Papers of Harry S. Truman, Truman Library; Leahy Diary, Aug. 17, 1945, Leahy Collection, Container 12; *Philadelphia Inquirer*, Aug. 23, 1945, p. 1; Cox Diary, Aug. 17, 1945; Sayers, *Financial Policy*, p. 480; Leo T. Crowley, interview with the writer, Aug. 21, 1968.

72. Crowley's memos to FEA directors and branch heads are in Records of the USSR Branch (FEA), Box 89; copies of the six "types" of letters sent to lend-lease recipients are in Soviet Protocol Committee Records, Box 17 (the letter to Britain is printed in *Foreign Relations 1945*, 6:107-8); the FEA letters to department and agency heads are in FEA Records, Box 1173.

73. A copy of Martin's instructions is in WPB Records, Box 795; USSR Branch meetings are summarized in "Daily Reports," Records of the USSR Branch (FEA), Box 95; a summary of the Martin-Hicklin phone conversation is in Record Group 160, "Records of Headquarters Army Service Forces," Box 320, 400.318 Russia vol. 4.

74. Hazard, "Day Journal," Aug. 10, 1945.

75. WPB Records, Box 795.

76. A copy of Wesson's letter to Treasury Procurement is in ibid.; The WSA's instruction is in WSA Records, Box 61.

77. "Daily Reports," Records of the USSR Branch (FEA), Box 95; the following day Vinson's assistant, J. W. Pehle, wrote to him: "You will be interested to know that General Wesson of FEA has

informally requested the Procurement Division to 'drag its feet' on any further proposed commitments under Lend-Lease for the USSR. . . . Accordingly, no further purchases against Lend-Lease requisitions are being made for USSR requirements." Inter-Office Communication, Pehle to Vinson, Aug. 14, 1945, Frederick M. Vinson Papers, University of Kentucky Library, Lexington, Ky.

78. WPB Records, Box 795; Memos, Martin to Crowley, Aug. 17, 22, 1945, Records of the USSR Branch (FEA), Box 93.

79. Hazard, "Day Journal," Aug. 17, 1945.

80. WSA Records, Box 61.

81. Note dated Aug. 17, 1945, typed on bottom of Wesson to Harvey letter originally dated Aug. 11, 1945, Records of the USSR Branch (FEA), Box 154; memo by assistant chief, Division of Lend-Lease and Surplus War Property (Maxwell), Aug. 21, 1945, *Foreign Relations 1945*, 5:1032-33. Copies of numerous USSR Branch letters to various agencies make it clear that instructions were received around mid-day of Aug. 17, 1945 to take all steps regarding the cancellation of Russian lend-lease immediately and not to wait until the officially proclaimed V-J Day. This is also clear from an examination of the "Daily Reports" of this branch for Aug. 17, 1945 (Records of the USSR Branch [FEA], Boxes 154, 95, and 97).

82. A copy of this letter containing notations indicating its date and time of delivery is in FEA Records, Box 1173; its relevant paragraphs are quoted in *Foreign Relations 1945*, 5:1031-32.

83. Record Group 160, "Records of Headquarters Army Service Forces," Box 3, "Lend-Lease as of September 30, 1945," 2:1049-50; telegram, Cushing to Hutchins, Aug. 21, 1945, WSA Records, Box 61. According to entries in Hazard's "Day Journal" of Aug. 18, 1945, the Russians were aware as early as this date that lend-lease shipments to them were being discontinued, but they apparently were not aware until a few days later that the immediate cancellation applied only to them.

84. "Daily Report" for Aug. 25, 1945, Records of the USSR Branch (FEA), Box 95; memo, Aug. 25, 1945, ibid., Box 89.

85. Charles G. Ross to Arthur Krock, Oct. 17, 1945, Ross Papers, Truman Library; Henry Morgenthau, Jr., "The Morgenthau Diaries," *Collier's* 120 (Oct. 18, 1947):75; Acheson, *Present at the Creation*, p. 122.

86. Cox's efforts to modify the termination of lend-lease are described in his diary, particularly the entries for Aug. 13-24, 1945 (FDR Library), and are shown in the liberal draft revisions he proposed for directives on lend-lease termination to be submitted for

presidential approval (FEA Records, Box 794). Curiously, Cox was very discreet in his diary on this matter and used a code to conceal the names of those with whom he was talking. Thus, in his entry for Aug. 18, 1945, "Usvnbo" deciphers as Truman, "Czsoft" as Byrnes, and "Sptfonbo" as Rosenman.

87. Pritchard to the Secretary, Inter-Office Communication, Aug. 20, 1945, Vinson Papers.

88. Clayton's and Collado's exchange of messages with Washington on this matter is in *Foreign Relations 1945*, 6:79-108; a graphic description of their reaction to news of the termination is contained in Harrod, *Life of Lord Maynard Keynes*, pp. 595-96.

89. Raymond Dennett and Robert K. Turner, eds., *Documents on Foreign Relations*, vol. 8, *July 1, 1945-December 31, 1946* (Princeton, N.J.: Princeton University Press for the World Peace Foundation, 1948), p. 126.

90. Congressional sentiment is reported in the *New York Times*, Aug. 26, 1945, p. 27; the summary of correspondence to the FEA is recorded in the "History of Lend-Lease," part 1, chap. 11, p. 30, FEA Records, Box 3185; letters to the president on this subject are in Papers of Harry S. Truman, Official File, Truman Library; results of the *Fortune* poll of Dec. 1945 are in Cantril, *Public Opinion, 1935-1946*, p. 415.

91. *Foreign Relations 1945*, 4:292-93.

92. Ibid., 6:630-31, 670; Stimson Diary, vol. 52, Aug. 11, 1945.

93. *Foreign Relations 1945*, 2:1006-7.

94. Ibid., 5:1032-33; in an interview with the writer on May 28, 1969, Hazard stated that he had no clear recollection of this conversation. In his "Day Journal" for Aug 21, 1945, he noted the call but not the message recalled by Maxwell.

95. *Foreign Relations 1945*, 4:309-11.

96. The Truman-Stalin exchange concerning Japan is in ibid., 6:692, 698-99; the resolution of the Soviet request for UNRRA funds is in ibid., 2:1017-19, 1025, fn. 92.

97. While this explanation rejects the revisionist argument (Kolko, *Politics of War*, p. 500; Williams, *Tragedy of American Diplomacy*, p. 169; Alperovitz, *Atomic Diplomacy*, pp. 223-24) that the termination of lend-lease was a deliberate effort to use economic leverage, unlike the most careful orthodox account (Herring, *Aid to Russia*, pp. 231-36) it makes clear that Russia was treated in a distinctly different manner than other recipients and it argues that attitudes about Russia and the Russian aid program in particular did influence those who implemented the cutoff.

Chapter 6

1. *Foreign Relations 1945*, 5:942-44 (Harriman describes this meeting and his reaction to Molotov's proposal in *Special Envoy*, pp. 384-87).
2. *Foreign Relations* 1945, pp. 945-47.
3. Ibid., pp. 937-38.
4. Ibid., pp. 948-49.
5. Ibid., pp. 938-40.
6. Morgenthau's recollections of the day's conversations are in Blum, *From the Morgenthau Diaries*, 3:304-5, 394-95, and in Morgenthau Diary, vol. 808, pp. 310-11, 315-16. Stettinius's impression of Roosevelt's intentions is in a note to Hayden Raynor, Stettinius Papers, Box 243. Leahy's notes on his luncheon with Morgenthau are in Leahy Diary, vol. 11, Jan. 10, 1945.
7. *Foreign Relations 1945*, 5:956-58.
8. General Records of the State Department, 861.51/1-1845.
9. Calendar notes on meeting with the president, Jan. 18, 1945, Stettinius Papers, Box 243; memo, Clayton to Stettinius, Jan. 20, 1945, *Foreign Relations 1945*, 5:964-66.
10. Morgenthau's conversation with Clayton is summarized in Morgenthau Diary, vol. 812, pp. 207-10; the message to Harriman is in *Foreign Relations 1945*, 5:967-68.
11. Reston's article appeared in the *New York Times*, Jan. 26, 1945, p. 1; discussion of the story in the Treasury and State Departments, including Grew's unsuccessful efforts to make Reston "go slow" on it, is in *Morgenthau Diary (Germany)*, 2:908-9, Grew Papers, "Conversations," vol. 6, and General Records of the State Department, 861.51/1-2645 and 861.51/1-2945. Grew's instruction to Kennan, dated January 27, is in *Foreign Relations 1945*, 5:968-70.
12. *Foreign Relations: The Conferences at Malta and Yalta, 1945*, p. 324.
13. Stalin's remark to Roosevelt is quoted in Stettinius, *Roosevelt and the Russians*, p. 114; the Molotov-Stettinius exchange is in *Foreign Relations: The Conferences at Malta and Yalta, 1945*, p. 610.
14. Grew to Novikov, Feb. 2, 1945, *Foreign Relations 1945*, 5:971-72; aide-memoire to the Embassy of the Soviet Union, Mar. 24, 1945, ibid., pp. 991-93.
15. Roosevelt's message is in Goodrich and Carroll, *Documents on American Foreign Relations*, 7:516; Wallace wrote to the Bureau of the Budget on Mar. 15 and Apr. 2, 1945, endorsing legislation to

increase the lending authority of the Export-Import Bank and repeal the Johnson Act, specifically pointing out how this would improve relations between the United States and the USSR, Record Group 40, "Records of the Department of Commerce," General Correspondence, Box 823.

16. Cox to Crowley, Mar. 23, 1945, Cox Papers, Box 65; Reston's article is in the *New York Times*, Apr. 3, 1945, pp. 1, 3; Stettinius's speech is in Goodrich and Carroll, *Documents on American Foreign Relations*, 7:35.

17. *Foreign Relations 1945*, 5:817-20, 821-24.

18. Ibid., pp. 994-96.

19. Stettinius Papers, Box 233.

20. Truman, *Memoirs*, 1:14-17 for Stettinius's report; pp. 46, 98, for Truman's comments on means for financing reconstruction. Truman's disclaimer of "official" notification of the Russian credit request, made in a press conference on Dec. 7, 1945, is in *Public Papers of the Presidents of the United States, Harry S. Truman, 1945* (Washington, D.C.: Government Printing Office, 1961), p. 527.

21. *Foreign Relations 1945*, 5:832-38.

22. Ibid., pp. 997-98.

23. Ibid., pp. 839-46.

24. Ibid., pp. 256-58; Truman, *Memoirs*, 1:80.

25. Arthur H. Vandenberg, Jr., *The Private Papers of Senator Vandenberg* (Boston: Houghton Mifflin Co., 1952), p. 176.

26. Journal entry, Apr. 30, 1945, Joseph E. Davies Collection, Container 16, Library of Congress, Washington, D.C.

27. Kennan, *Memoirs*, pp. 266-70.

28. *New York Times*, May 13, 1934, p. 9; Memo, Cox to Crowley, May 28, 1945, Cox Papers, Box 65; Harriman to the Secretary of State, *Foreign Relations 1945*, 5:1008-9; *New York Times*, June 1, 1945, p. 10, June 3, 1945, sec. 4, p. 2.

29. Morgenthau's meeting is described in Morgenthau, *Presidential Diaries*, vol. 7, p. 1638; Bernstein's report is in *Morgenthau Diary (Germany)*, 2:1554-55.

30. Press and Radio Conference No. 11, June 9, 1945, Records of the White House Official Reporter, Harry S. Truman Library.

31. Grew to Harriman, *Foreign Relations 1945*, 5:1011-12; Harriman to the Secretary of State, June 12, 1945, ibid., p. 1022.

32. The test of the Spence Bill is in House, Committee on Banking and Currency, *Hearings*, Export-Import Bank of Washington (H.R. 3464 and H.R. 3490, superseded by H.R. 3771), July. 11-13, 1945, pp.

1-4; prior objections by Treasury and the bank are indicated in Memo, Cox to Crowley, June 12, 1945, Cox Papers, Box 63 and Cox Diary, entry of June 7, 1945.

33. Memo, Maffry to Taylor, June 7, 1945, "Russia" file, Export-Import Bank, Washington, D.C. (record in the bank's possession).

34. Memo (with enclosures), Angell to James R. Newman (assistant to deputy director for reconversion, OWMR), June 21, 1945, OWMR Records, Box 250.

35. Fred M. Vinson, draft of "Memorandum for the President," not sent, undated but apparently written in early July 1945, ibid., Box 185.

36. The administrative-congressional consultation that took place on the Export-Import Bank Bill is described in Memo, Vinson to the President, July 11, 1945, OWMR Records, Box 185; Collado's memo to Acheson (dated July 9, 1945) is in General Records of the State Department, 811.516 Ex-Im Bank/7-945.

37. House, Committee on Banking and Currency, *Hearings, Export-Import Bank of Washington* (H.R. 3464 and H.R. 3490, superseded by H.R. 3771), July 11-12, 1945.

38. *Congressional Record*, July 13, 1945, pp. 7535-48.

39. Senate, Committee on Banking and Currency, *Hearings, Export-Import Bank of Washington* (H.R. 3771), July 17-18, 1945, p. 5; *New York Times*, July 18, 1945, pp. 1, 25.

40. Senate, Committee on Banking and Currency, *Hearings, Export-Import Bank of Washington* (H.R. 3771), July 17-18, pp. 10-14.

41. *Congressional Record*, July 20, 1945, pp. 7827-41.

42. Memo, Cox to Crowley, July 17, 1945, Cox Papers, Box 63; Wallace to Crowley, July 24, 1945, Record Group 40, "General Records of the Department of Commerce," Box 957.

43. Crowley to Pepper, July 27, 1945, FEA Records, Box 1168.

44. Grew to Clayton, Aug. 7, 1945, *Foreign Relations 1945*, 2:1005-6. Harriman's Aug. 9 message to the State Department, referencing its instruction of Aug. 7, is in "Telegrams from Moscow," a microfilm of messages in the department's Records Service Division.

45. Records of the WPB, Box 795; Hazard, "Day Journal," Aug. 16, 1945.

46. Hazard, "Day Journal," Aug. 17, 1945; Weekly Newsletter no. 195, Aug. 18, 1945, Records of the USSR Branch (FEA), Box 154.

47. Martin to Crowley, Aug. 17, 1945, Records of the USSR Branch (FEA), Box 93.

48. Harriman to Secretary of State, Aug. 17, 1945, "Telegrams from

Moscow," microfilm in State Department's Records Service Division; Telephone Conversations, Aug. 20, 21, 1945, Krug Collection, Container 47; Taylor to Martin, Soviet Protocol Committee Records, Box 17.

49. Public Law 171, 79th Congress, Goodrich and Carroll, eds., *Documents on American Foreign Relations*, vol. 7, *July 1944-June 1945*, pp. 537-45.

50. Minutes of NAC Meeting No. 1 (Aug. 21, 1945), "Central Files," Office of Assistant Secretary for International Affairs, Treasury Department, Washington, D.C. (hereafter cited as Treasury Dept. Files).

51. Circular Telegram to Certain Diplomatic Officers, Aug. 30, 1945, *Foreign Relations 1945*, 5:878. This was the position that George Kennan, then chargé of the Moscow Embassy, was urging at the time (Kennan, *Memoirs*, pp. 269-70).

52. NAC Document 7 (Sept. 12, 1945), Minutes of NAC Meeting No. 2 (Sept. 13, 1945), Treasury Dept. Files.

53. Ibid., NAC Document 14 (Sept. 17, 1945), Minutes of NAC Meeting No. 3 (Sept. 18, 1945).

54. Memo for the President from the National Advisory Council, General Records of the State Department, Lot 60 D 137, Box 8.

55. Minutes of NAC Meeting No. 4 (Sept. 27, 1945), Treasury Dept. Files.

56. *Foreign Relations: The Conference of Berlin (Potsdam) 1945*, 1:714-15.

57. *Foreign Relations 1945*, 5:374-76, 388-90, 398-99.

58. Ibid., 4:49-65; 5:1252-53, 1289-91; 4:551.

59. Acheson to Harriman, Sept. 8, 1945, ibid., 2:1027 and Memo of Conversation, Sept. 24, 1945, General Records of the State Department, 861.51/9-2445; Memo, Oct. 9, 1945, Record Group 165, "Records of the War Department General Staff" Box 144, OPD 336TS sec 6 case no. 205.

60. *Foreign Relations 1945*, 5:1048 and General Records of the State Department, 861.51/11-2945.

61. U.S. Embassy in Moscow to the Secretary, Aug. 23, 1945, Records of the USSR Branch (FEA), Box 142; Harriman (conveying Page's report) to the Secretary, Nov. 15, 1945, *Foreign Relations 1945*, 5:916-18; Report by Attaché Thomas P. Whitney, *Foreign Relations 1946*, 6:824, fn. 97.

62. General Records of the State Department, 861.50/8-1545.

63. Harriman to Byrnes, Dec. 11, 1945, *Foreign Relations 1945*, 5:1049-50; memo, undated, Records of the USSR Branch (FEA), Box

94 (pencilled note at the top of this document reads: "Memo given to Secretary of State when he went to Moscow").

64. Memo of Conversation, Dec. 19, 1945, *Foreign Relations 1945*, 2:680; James F. Byrnes, *Speaking Frankly* (New York: Harper, 1947), p. 116. Benjamin V. Cohen, counselor of the State Department at the time, feels that Byrnes did not have in mind using a loan as a quid pro quo at the Moscow conference (interview with the writer, Mar. 27, 1970, Washington, D.C.).

65. Memo by Emilio G. Collado (addressed to H. Freeman Matthews, director of the Office of European Affairs, Assistant Secretary Clayton, Under Secretary Acheson and Secretary Byrnes), Feb. 4, 1946, *Foreign Relations 1946*, 6:823-25.

66. Byrnes's position on February 5 and his change of mind on February 8 are indicated in Hazard's "Day Journal," entries for Feb. 5 and 8, 1946.

67. Coordinating Committee Document 88a (an earlier version had been prepared on January 11), General Records of the State Department, Lot 122 (rev.) S/S-S, Box 60.

68. *Foreign Relations 1946*, 6:828-29. Evidence of Harriman's participation in the drafting of the note is given in Thomas G. Paterson, "The Abortive American Loan to Russia and the Origins of the Cold War, 1943-1946," *The Journal of American History* 46 (June 1969):86; Herbert Feis incorrectly states that the invitation to negotiate was not issued "until April 1946, when the crisis over Iran was past" (*From Trust to Terror: The Onset of the Cold War* [New York: Norton, 1970], p. 73).

69. *New York Times*, Mar. 2, 1946, p. 1.

70. Quoted in Myron Rush, ed., *The International Situation and Soviet Foreign Policy: Reports of Soviet Leaders* (Columbus, Ohio: Charles E. Merrill Pub. Co., 1970), pp. 116-23.

71. Quoted in Alfred J. Rieber, *Stalin and the French Communist Party, 1941-1947* (New York: Columbia University Press, 1962), pp. 255-56.

72. Byrnes, *Speaking Frankly*, pp. 295-96; Millis, *Forrestal Diaries*, pp. 134-35; Charles E. Bohlen, *The Transformation of American Foreign Policy* (New York: W. W. Norton, 1969), p. 75; *Foreign Relations 1946*, 6:695, fn. 39.

73. *Foreign Relations 1946*, 6:696-709. Kennan recollects that the message was inspired by a query for comment on Russia's unwillingness to adhere to the Bretton Woods institutions, but the editors of *Foreign Relations* identify it as a reply to a request for analysis of Stalin's speech (Kennan, *Memoirs*, pp. 292-95).

74. Acheson, *Present at the Creation*, p. 151.

75. Kennan, *Memoirs*, p. 295.

76. James F. Byrnes, *All in One Lifetime* (New York: Harper, 1958), pp. 349-50.

77. *Vital Speeches of the Day* 12, no. 11 (Mar. 15, 1946):329-32.

78. *Foreign Relations 1946*, 6:829-30.

79. Durbrow's and Collado's views and the preparation of the American message, dated April 18, are discussed in Hazard, "Day Journal," entries for Mar. 18, 19, 21, 22, 26 and Apr. 16, 18, 1946; the message itself is in *Foreign Relations 1946*, 6:834-37.

80. Gerschenkron comment in Hazard, "Day Journal," Apr. 4, 1946 (the extension of credits to France and China was announced a month later [*Christian Science Monitor*, May 9, 1946, p. 1]); Memo, H. W. Parisius to Wallace, Apr. 10, 1946, Record Group 40, "General Records of the Department of Commerce," Box 823; Minutes of NAC Meeting No. 23 and No. 24 (May 2, 6, 1946), Treasury Dept. Files.

81. A memo of Acheson's talk with Novikov is in *Foreign Relations 1946*, 6:838-39; the Russian note, dated May 17, is in ibid., pp. 841-42.

82. Sayers, *Financial Policy 1939-45*, p. 486.

83. Dennett and Turner, *Documents on Foreign Relations*, 8:132-34. William Clayton later wrote to financier Bernard Baruch: "We loaded the British loan negotiations with all the conditions that the traffic would bear" (quoted in LaFeber, *America, Russia and the Cold War*, p. 9).

84. Senate, Committee on Banking and Currency, *Hearings*, Anglo-American Financial Agreement (S. J. Res. 138), 6, 12, 13, Mar. 1946 pp. 62, 116, 265-71, 305-10.

85. Senate, Committee on Banking and Currency, *Report*, Implementation of Financial Agreement Dated Dec. 6, 1945 Between the United States and the United Kingdom, S. Rept. 1144, Apr. 10, 1946.

86. *Congressional Record*, Apr. 22, 1946, pp. 4079-82.

87. Debate and voting on the measure in the Senate took the better part of 16 legislative days over a three week period and filled more than 350 pages of the *Congressional Record*. The final vote is recorded on p. 4806.

88. Ibid., p. 4080.

89. Quoted in Richard N. Gardner, *Sterling-Dollar Diplomacy: The Origins and Prospects of Our International Economic Order*, 2nd ed. (New York: McGraw-Hill, 1969), p. 250.

90. House, Committee on Banking and Currency, *Hearings*,

Anglo-American Financial Agreement (H.J. Res. 311, S.J. Res. 138), May 15, 16, 23, 1946, pp. 53, 58, 68, 357.

91. House, Committee on Banking and Currency, *Report*, Implementation of Financial Agreement Dated Dec. 6, 1945 Between the United States and the United Kingdom, H. Rept. 2289, June 14, 1946.

92. Remarks of Rep. Brooks Hays (Dem. of Ark.), *Congressional Record*, July 8, 1946, p. 8431.

93. Quoted in McNeill, *America, Britain and Russia*, pp. 687-88.

94. *Congressional Record*, July 12, 1946, pp. 8823-24.

95. Memo, George Luthringer to William Clayton, May 23, 1946, *Foreign Relations 1946*, 6:842-43; Hazard, "Day Journal," June 6, 1946. It was also at this time that Byrnes first learned of former Treasury Secretary Morgenthau's January 1945 plan for a $10 billion loan to the USSR and, as he later wrote, had it placed in the "Forgotten File," Memo, HFM (H. Freeman Matthews) to the Secretary, May 22, 1946, transmitting Morgenthau's proposal, Byrnes Papers, Folder 637(2); Byrnes, *All in One Lifetime*, p. 310.

96. *Foreign Relations 1946*, 6:844-46.

97. *Public Papers, Truman, 1946*, p. 301.

98. Ibid., p. 351.

99. *Foreign Relations 1946*, 6:851-52.

100. *Public Papers, Truman, 1946*, pp. 381, 382-83.

101. Clayton to Byrnes, *Foreign Relations 1946*, 6:853-54; Clayton to Orekhov, ibid., pp. 854-55. After several more requests, each more strongly worded than the last, lend-lease settlement discussions between the United States and USSR finally began in 1947. These continued intermittently and without result until they were broken off in 1952. In 1960 they were resumed, but again no agreement was reached. In September 1972, new lend-lease settlement talks were initiated as part of a general trade agreement package between the two countries. This time the outcome was more successful. An agreement was signed on October 18, 1972, in accordance with which the Russians would pay between $722 and $759 million (a range very close to the sum of $800 million first requested by the United States) over a period of twenty-nine years as settlement for lend-lease goods and materials not consumed during the war and not returned to the United States (*New York Times*, Feb. 18, 1972, pp. 1, 10; Oct. 5, 1972, pp. 1, 8; and Oct. 19, 1972, pp. 1, 16). However, renunciation by the Russians of this agreement on January 14, 1975 once again stymied efforts to conclude a final Soviet-American lend-lease settlement (*New York Times*, January 15, 1975, pp. 1, 5).

Chapter 7

1. Kennan, *Memoirs*, p. 267.
2. Feis, *Churchill, Roosevelt and Stalin*, p. 647.
3. Herring, *Aid to Russia 1941-1946*, pp. 287-288.
4. Herz, *Beginnings of the Cold War*, pp. 166-167.
5. McNeill, *America, Britain and Russia*, p. 691.
6. Arthur Schlesinger, Jr., "Origins of the Cold War," *Foreign Affairs* 46 (Oct. 1967):44-45.
7. Williams, *Tragedy of American Diplomacy*, 1959 ed., p. 169.
8. Gardner, *Economic Aspects of New Deal Diplomacy*, p. 317.
9. Alperovitz, *Atomic Diplomacy*, p. 39, and *Cold War Essays*, p. 98.
10. LaFeber, *America, Russia and the Cold War*, p. 22.
11. Kolko, *Politics of War*, p. 499; Thomas G. Patterson, *Soviet-American Confrontation: Postwar Reconstruction and the Origins of the Cold War* (Baltimore: Johns Hopkins University Press, 1973), p. 34.
12. Graham T. Allison and Morton Halperin, "Bureaucratic Politics: A Paradigm and Some Policy Implications," *World Politics* (Supplement) 24 (Spring 1972):46.
13. Ibid., pp. 52-53. Illustrations of the influence of implementors on policy decisions are provided in Halperin, *Bureaucratic Politics and Foreign Policy*, chap. 13; a close study of such influence preventing implementation of presidentially approved policy is presented by Thomas R. Maddox in "United States-Soviet Naval Relations in the 1930's: The Soviet Union's Efforts to Purchase Naval Vessels," *Naval War College Review* 39 (Fall 1976):28-37.
14. The failure of lower-ranking foreign policy actors to formulate policy in another Cold War-related issue (the future of Eastern Europe) has been discussed by Lynn E. Davis in *The Cold War Begins: Soviet-American Conflict Over Eastern Europe* (Princeton, N.J.: Princeton University Press, 1974), especially pp. 370-88.
15. The alteration of goals that occurs during the implementation phase of policy making has been comprehensively discussed by Bardach, *The Implementation Game*, chap. 4.
16. Richard C. Snyder, H. W. Bruck, and Burton Sapin, *Foreign Policy Decision-Making: An Approach to the Study of International Politics* (New York: The Free Press of Glencoe, 1962), especially pp. 86-105.
17. Allison, *Essence of Decision*, p. 68.
18. Hoffman cites "direction, destruction, delay and deterrence" as four functions performed by Congress when it affects policy. "The

deterrent power of Congress," he writes, "may well be its most dangerous, although (or because) it is the most difficult to document and track down. Deterrence can be as effective in policy-making as it is in international strategy" (*Gulliver's Troubles, Or the Setting of American Foreign Policy* [New York: McGraw-Hill, for the Council on Foreign Relations, 1968] pp. 255, 258). The fate of foreign aid programs in the Congress illustrates this deterrent power.

19. The reassertion of Congress at the end of World War II has been shown by Bradford Westerfield, *Foreign Policy and Party Politics: Pearl Harbor to Korea* (New Haven, Conn.: Yale University Press, 1955). The writer is indebted to a former student, Andrew Polin, for pointing out in a seminar paper on Congress and the League of Nations how this same phenomenon occurred at the end of World War I. Even in the Vietnam conflict, which was less than a total war for the United States, it was several years before the Congress took an active role, independent of the executive branch, concerning the war.

20. Snyder, Bruck, and Sapin, *Foreign Policy Decision-Making*, pp. 100-2.

21. Joseph H. de Rivera, *The Psychological Dimension of Foreign Policy* (Columbus, Ohio: Charles E. Merrill, 1968), p. 21.

22. Robert Jervis, *Perception and Misperception in International Politics* (Princeton, N.J.: Princeton Univ. Press, 1976).

23. The extent to which this perception of an implacably hostile USSR had influenced all official analysis of Russian behavior can be seen in the following excerpts from a message from Ambassador to Moscow Walter Bedell Smith explaining what appeared to be conciliatory Soviet policy in Asia: "These disarming symptoms, in contrast to Soviet truculence in Europe, do not by any means indicate that USSR has abandoned predatory aims in Asia. They simply represent different tactical approach. . . . These tactics are more dangerous than more obvious ones employed in Europe and will bear close attention and reporting." Smith to the secretary of state, June 15, 1946, *Foreign Relations 1946*, 6:761-62.

24. The causes of delay in policy implementation are analyzed in detail in Pressman and Wildavsky, *Implementation*, pp. 113-124.

25. Yehezkel Dror, *Public Policy-Making Re-Examined* (San Francisco: Chandler, 1968), p. 193. The definitive discussion of the role of feedback in government is Karl W. Deutsch's *The Nerves of Government: Models of Political Communication and Control* (New York: The Free Press of Glencoe, 1963). Feedback as a component of implementation in the public policy process appears in the models of Smith ("The Policy Implementation Process") and

Van Meter and Van Horn ("The Policy Implementation Process: A Conceptual Framework").

26. John P. Lovell, *Foreign Policy in Perspective: Strategy, Adaptation, Decision Making* (New York: Holt, Rinehart and Winston, 1970), p. 222.

27. Other cases of inadequate feedback have been embarrassing to American policy makers, for example when President Kennedy learned only a year later (during the Cuban Missile Crisis) that his orders to remove obsolete missiles from Turkey had not been carried out. Roger Hilsman, *To Move a Nation: The Politics of Foreign Policy in the Administration of John F. Kennedy* (Garden City, N.Y.: Doubleday, 1967), pp. 202-4, 222.

Bibliography

Unpublished Sources

Records of Departments and Agencies of the United States

Record Group numbers are those assigned by the National Archives and Records Service for records in its custody.

Army, Department of the:

> Records of the Headquarters Army Service Forces (Record Group 160).
>
> Records of the War Department General Staff (Record Group 165).
>
> Reference Collection A762.

Commerce, Department of. General Records of the Department of Commerce (Record Group 40), Office of the Secretary, General Correspondence File.

Export-Import Bank of the United States. Miscellaneous correspondence from the files of the bank (1945-1946).

Foreign Economic Administration (Record Group 169):

> The "History of Lend-Lease" and supporting documents.
>
> Records of the Bureau of Areas (Office of the Executive Director and USSR Branch).
>
> Records of the Office of Economic Programs.
>
> Records of the Office of Administrator.
>
> Records of the Office of the General Counsel.
>
> Records of the Records Analysis Division.

Navy, Department of the. General Records of the Department of the Navy (Record Group 80).
Office of War Mobilization and Reconversion (Record Group 250):

General Records.

Records of the Office of the Director.

President's Soviet Protocol Committee. Records (FDR Library, Hyde Park, N.Y.).
State, Department of:

Central Decimal Files.

Office Files: "Record" of Edward R. Stettinius, Jr.; Records of the Coordinating Committee; Records of the Division of Research and Publication, Fennemore, George M. "The Role of the Department of State in Connection with the Lend-Lease Program." Records of the Office of Financial and Development Policy; Records of the Office of Foreign Liquidation (Record Group 59); Records of the Secretary's Staff Committee.

Treasury, Department of the. Minutes of Meetings, National Advisory Council on International Monetary and Financial Problems (in the possession of the Department).
War Production Board (Record Group 179):

Office File of Mose L. Harvey.

Policy Documentation File.

War Shipping Administration (Record Group 248). Records of the Russian Shipping Area.

Private Papers and Manuscripts

Arnold, Henry H. Library of Congress, Washington, D.C.
Barnes, James Martin. Library of Congress, Washington, D.C.
Baruch, Bernard Mannes. Princeton University Library, Princeton, N.J.
Byrnes, James F. Robert Muldrow Cooper Library, Clemson University, Clemson, S.C.
Cox, Oscar J. Franklin D. Roosevelt Library, Hyde Park, N.Y.
Davies, Joseph Edward. Library of Congress, Washington, D.C.
Forrestal, James Vincent. Princeton University Library, Princeton, N.J.
Grew, Joseph Clark. The Houghton Library, Harvard University, Cambridge, Mass.

Hazard, John N. "Day Journal" in the possession of Mr. Hazard, New York, N.Y.

Hopkins, Harry L. Franklin D. Roosevelt Library, Hyde Park, N.Y.

Hull, Cordell. Library of Congress, Washington, D.C.

Krug, Julius Albert. Library of Congress, Washington, D.C.

Leahy, William D. Library of Congress, Washington, D.C.

Morgenthau, Henry J. Franklin D. Roosevelt Library, Hyde Park, N.Y.

Patterson, Robert Porter. Library of Congress, Washington, D.C.

Roosevelt, Franklin Delano. Franklin D. Roosevelt Library, Hyde Park, N.Y.

Rosenman, Samuel I. Harry S. Truman Library, Independence, Mo.

Ross, Charles G. Harry S. Truman Library, Independence, Mo.

Smith, Harold D. Harry S. Truman Library, Independence, Mo.

Stettinius, Edward R., Jr. University of Virginia Library, Charlottesville, Va.

Stimson, Henry L. Yale University Library, New Haven, Conn.

Truman, Harry S. Harry S. Truman Library, Independence, Mo.

Vinson, Fred M. University of Kentucky Libraries, Lexington, Ky.

White, Harry Dexter. Princeton University Library, Princeton, N.J.

Interviews and Correspondence

Acheson, Dean. Letters to writer, March 19, 1969, July 17, 1969.

Arey, Hawthorne. Personal interview, Washington, D.C., April 2, 1969.

Bohlen, Charles E. Letter to writer, March 16, 1970.

Cohen, Benjamin V. Personal interview, Washington, D.C., March 27, 1970.

Crowley, Leo T. Personal interview, Chicago, Ill., August 21, 1968.

Durbrow, Elbridge. Letter to writer, August 18, 1972.

Hazard, John N. Personal interview, New York, N.Y., May 28, 1969.

Martin, William McChesney. Personal interview, Washington, D.C., April 2, 1969.

Sauer, Walter C. Letters to writer, July 3, 24, 1969.

Spalding, Sidney P. Letter to writer, March 22, 1970.

York, John Y. Letters to writer, March 8, 10, 1970; telephone conversation, March 31, 1970.

Published Sources

Official United States Documents

U.S. Congress. *Congressional Record*, 77th, 78th, 79th Cong., 1941-1946.

————. House of Representatives, Committee on Banking and Currency:

Export-Import Bank Act of 1945: Hearings. 79th Cong., 1st sess., July 11, 12, 1945.

Export-Import Bank of Washington, to Increase Lending Authority of: Report. H. Rept. 911, 79th Cong., 1st sess., July 12, 1945.

Implementation of Financial Agreement Dated December 6, 1945, Between the United States and the United Kingdom: Report. H. Rept. 2289, 79th Cong., 2d sess., June 14, 1946.

————. House of Representatives, Committee on Foreign Affairs:

Lend-Lease Bill: Hearings. 99th Cong., 1st sess., January 15-29, 1941.

Extension of Lend-Lease Act: Hearings. 78th Cong., 1st. sess., January 29–February 23, 1943.

Extension of Lend-Lease Act: Hearings. 78th Cong., 2d sess., March 1-9, 1944.

To Promote the Defense of the United States: Report. H. Rept. 18, 77th Cong., 1st sess., January 30-31, 1941.

Extending for One Year Provisions of Act to Promote Defense of the United States: Report. H. Rept. 188, 78th Cong., 1st sess., February 26, 1943.

. . . Extension of Lend-Lease . . . Report. H. Rept. 1316, 78th Cong., 2d sess., March 30, 1944.

————. Senate, Committee on Banking and Currency:

Export-Import Bank of 1945: Hearings. 79th Cong., 1st sess., July 17, 18, 1945.

Anglo-American Financial Agreement: Hearings. 79th cong., 2d sess., March 5-20, 1946.

Export-Import Bank of Washington, Increasing Lending Authority of: Report. S. Rept. 490, 79th Cong., 1st sess., July 19, 1945.

Implementation of Financial Agreement Dated December 6, 1945 Between the United States and the United Kingdom: Report. S. Rept. 1144, 79th Cong., 2d sess., April 10, 1946.

_____. Senate Committee on Foreign Relations:

Defense Aid Act of 1941: Hearings. 77th Cong., 1st sess., January 27–February 11, 1941.

Extension of the Lend-Lease Act: Hearings. 78th Cong., 1st sess., March 1, 2, 1943.

Extension of the Lend-Lease Act: Hearing. 78th Cong., 2d sess., April 26, 1944.

Extending for One Year Provisions of Act to Promote Defense of the United States: Report. S. Rept. 99, 78th Cong., 1st sess., March 10, 1943.

. . . Extension of Lend-Lease . . . Report. S. Rept. 848, 78th Cong., 2d sess., May 2, 1944.

_____. Senate, Committee on the Judiciary, Subcommittee to Investigate the Administration of the Internal Security Act and Other Internal Security Laws:

Morgenthau Diary (China), vol. 2. Washington, D.C.: U.S. Government Printing Office, 1965.

Morgenthau Diary (Germany), vols. 1, 2. Washington, D.C.: U.S. Government Printing Office, 1967.

_____. Senate, Special Committee to Investigate the National Defense Program. "Outlines of Problems of Conversion From War Production," *Additional Report No. 10, Pt. 12.* 78th Cong., 1st sess., November 5, 1943.

U.S. Department of Defense. "The Entry of the Soviet Union into the War Against Japan: Military Plans, 1941-1945." Mimeographed. 1955.

U.S. Department of State. *Foreign Relations of the United States:*

The Soviet Union, 1933-1939;

1941, vol.. 1;

1942, vol. 3;

The Conference at Cairo and Tehran, 1943;

The Conferences at Washington, 1941-1942, and Casablanca, 1943;

The Conferences at Washington and Quebec, 1943;

1943, vols. 1-3;

1944, vol. 4;

The Conferences at Malta and Yalta, 1945;

The Conference at Berlin (The Potsdam Conference), 1945, vols. 1 & 2;

1945, vols. 1-6;

1946, vol. 6.

————.*Peace and War: United States Foreign Policy, 1931-1941.* Publication 1983. 1943.

————.*Postwar Foreign Policy Preparation, 1939-1945*, prepared by Harley Notter. General Foreign Policy series 15. Publication 3580. 1949.

————.*Soviet Supply Protocols.* Publication 2759. 1947.

————. Office of Foreign Liquidation, Foreign Economic Section. *Report on War Aid Furnished by the United States to the USSR, June 22, 1941–September 20, 1945.* Nov. 28, 1945.

U.S. Export-Import Bank of Washington. *General Policy Statement.* 1945.

U.S. President. *Report to the Congress on Lend-Lease Operations.* 1941-1963.

————. *Public Papers of the Presidents of the United States: Harry S. Truman, 1945-1947.* 3 vols. Washington, D.C.: U.S. Government Printing Office, 1961-1963.

U.S. War Department, Army Service Forces, International Branch. *International Aid Statistics, World War II; A Summary of War Department Lend-Lease Activities Reported Through December 31, 1945.* 1946.

————. Finance Department. *Quantities of Lend-Lease Shipments: A Summary of Important Items Furnished Foreign Governments by the War Department During World War II.* 1946.

Unofficial Collections of Documents

Clayton, William. *Selected Papers of Will Clayton.* Edited by Frederick J. Dobney. Baltimore, Md.: Johns Hopkins Press, 1971.

Documents on American Foreign Relations. Vol. 7, *July 1944-June 1945.* Edited by Leland M. Goodrich and Marie J. Carroll. Princeton, N.J.: Princeton Univ. Press, 1947; Vol. 8, *July 1, 1945-December 31, 1946.* Edited by Raymond Dennett and Robert K. Turner. Princeton, N.J.: Princeton University Press, 1948.

Roosevelt, Franklin D. *The Public Papers and Addresses of Franklin Delano Roosevelt.* Edited by Samuel I Rosenman.

Rush, Myron, ed. *The International Situation and Soviet Foreign Policy: Key Reports by Soviet Leaders from the Revolution to the Present.* Columbus, Ohio: Charles E. Merrill, 1970.

Stalin's Correspondence with Roosevelt and Truman, 1941-1945. New York: Capricorn Books, 1965. (Translation of text issued by the Ministry of Foreign Affairs, USSR under the title, *Correspondence Between the Chairman of the Council of Ministers of the U.S.S.R. and the Presidents of the U.S.A. . . .)*

Stalin's Correspondence with Churchill and Attlee, 1941-1945. New York: Capricorn Books, 1965. (Translation of text issued by the Ministry of Foreign Affairs, USSR under the title, *Correspondence Between the Chairman of the Council of Ministers of the U.S.S.R. . . . and the Prime Ministers of Great Britain . . .)*

Truman, Harry S. *Addresses and Statements of Harry S. Truman, A Topical Record from January, 1935 to April, 1945.* Washington, D.C.: The United States News, 1945.

Diaries, Letters, Memoirs, and Participant Accounts

Acheson, Dean. *Present at the Creation: My Years in the State Department.* New York: W. W. Norton, 1969.

Blum, John Morton. *From the Morgenthau Diaries.* 3 vols. Boston, Mass.: Houghton-Mifflin, 1964-1967. Vol. 2, *Years of Urgency* (1965). Vol. 3, *Years of War* (1967).

Bohlen, Charles E. *The Transformation of American Foreign Policy.* New York: W. W. Norton, 1969.

———. *Witness to History, 1929-1969.* New York: W. W. Norton, 1973.

Byrnes, James F. *All in One Lifetime.* New York: Harper & Bros., 1958.

———. *Speaking Frankly.* New York: Harper & Bros., 1947.

Carr, Albert Z. *Truman, Stalin and Peace.* Garden City, N.Y.: Doubleday, 1950.

Churchill, Winston S. *The Second World War.* 6 vols. Boston: Houghton-Mifflin, 1948-1953.

Deane, John R. *The Strange Alliance: The Story of Our Efforts at Wartime Co-Operation with Russia.* New York: Viking Press, 1947.

Dennett, Raymond, ed., with Johnson, Joseph E. *Negotiating with the Russians.* Boston, Mass.: World Peace Foundation, 1951.

Eden, Anthony. *The Memoirs of Anthony Eden, Earl of Avon: The Reckoning.* Boston, Mass.: Houghton Mifflin, 1965.

Freedman, Max, annotater. *Roosevelt and Frankfurter: Their Correspondence, 1928-1945.* Boston, Mass.: Little, Brown & Co., 1967.

Grew, Joseph G. *Turbulent Era: A Diplomatic Record of Forty Years, 1904-1945.* Edited by Walter Johnson. 2 vols. Boston, Mass.: Houghton-Mifflin, 1952.

Harriman, W. Averell. *America and Russia in a Changing World.* New York: Doubleday, 1971.

———. *Special Envoy to Churchill and Stalin 1941-1946.* New York: Random House, 1975.

Hillman, William, ed. *Mr. President: The First Publication from the Personal Diaries, Private Letters, Papers and Revealing Interviews of Harry S. Truman, 32nd President of the United States of America.* New York: Farrar, Straus, & Young, 1952.

Hull, Cordell. *The Memoirs of Cordell Hull.* 2 vols. New York: Macmillan, 1948.

Kennan, George F. *Memoirs 1925-1950.* Boston, Mass.: Little, Brown & Co., 1967.

Kot, Stanislaw. *Conversations with the Kremlin and Dispatches from Russia.* London: Oxford University Press, 1963.

Leahy, William D. *I Was There; The Personal Story of the Chief of Staff to Presidents Roosevelt and Truman Based on His Notes and Diaries Made at the Time.* New York: Whittlesey House, McGraw-Hill, 1950.

Millis, Walter, ed., and Duffield, E. S., collaborator. *The Forrestal Diaries.* New York: Viking Press, 1951.

Morgenthau, Henry, Jr. *Germany Is Our Problem.* New York: Harper & Bros., 1945.

———. "The Morgenthau Diaries." *Collier's* 120(1947):75ff.

Nelson, Donald M. *Arsenal of Democracy: The Story of American War Production.* New York: Harcourt, Brace & Co., 1946.

Penrose, Ernest. *Economic Planning for the Peace.* Princeton, N.J.: Princeton University Press, 1953.

Roosevelt, Elliott, ed. *F.D.R.: His Personal Letters.* 4 vols. New York: Duell, Sloan & Pearce, 1947-1950.

Sherwood, Robert E. *Roosevelt and Hopkins: An Intimate History.* Rev. ed. New York: Harper & Bros., 1950.

Smith, Walter Bedell. *My Three Years in Moscow.* Philadelphia, Pa.: J. B. Lippincott Co., 1950.

Standley, William H. and Ageton, Arthur A. *Admiral Ambassador to Russia.* Chicago, Ill.: H. Regnery Co., 1955.

Stettinius, Edward R., Jr. *Lend-Lease: Weapon for Victory.* New York: Macmillan, 1944.

_____. *Roosevelt and the Russians: The Yalta Conference.* Edited by Walter Johnson. Garden City, N.Y.: Doubleday, 1949.

Stimson, Henry L. and Bundy, McGeorge. *On Active Service in Peace and War.* New York: Harper, 1948.

Truman, Harry S. *Memoirs.* 2 vols. Garden City, N.Y.: Doubleday, 1955-1956. Vol. 1, *Year of Decisions.* Vol. 2, *Years of Trial and Hope.*

Vandenberg, Arthur H., Jr., ed. *The Private Papers of Senator Vandenberg.* Boston, Mass.: Houghton Mifflin, 1952.

Welles, Sumner. *Seven Decisions that Shaped History.* New York: Harper, 1951.

_____. *The Time for Decision.* New York: Harper, 1944.

General Histories, Monographs, Articles, and Collections of Data

Alperovitz, Gar. *Atomic Diplomacy: Hiroshima and Potsdam; The Use of the Atomic Bomb and the Confrontation with Soviet Power.* New York: Random House, Vintage Books, 1965.

_____. *Cold War Essays.* Garden City, N.Y.: Doubleday, Anchor Books, 1970.

Arey, Hawthorne. *History of Operations and Policies of the Export-Import Bank of Washington.* Washington: U.S. Government Printing Office, 1953.

Baldwin, David A. *Economic Development and American Foreign Policy, 1943-1964.* Chicago, Ill.: University of Chicago Press, 1966.

Bernstein, Barton J., ed. *Politics and Policies of the Truman Administration.* Chicago, Ill.: Quadrangle Books, 1970.

Bernstein, Marvin D. and Lowenheim, Francis L. "Aid to Russia: The First Year," in *American Civil-Military Decisions: A Book of Case Studies,* edited by Harold Stein, pp. 97-152. Birmingham: University of Alabama Press, 1963.

Burns, James MacGregor. *Roosevelt: The Soldier of Freedom.* New York: Harcourt, Brace, Jovanovich, 1970.

Cantril, Hadley, ed. *Public Opinion, 1935-1946.* Princeton, N.J.: Princeton University Press, 1951.

Chadaev, I. E. *Economika SSSR v period velikoi otechestvennoi voiny* [The economy of the USSR in the period of the great fatherland war]. Moscow, 1965.

Cheklin, N. "K itogam lend-liza" [The results of lend-lease]. *Vneshiaia Torgovlia*, no. 10 (1945), pp. 8-13.

Coakley, Robert W. and Leighton, Richard M. *Global Logistics and Strategy, 1943-1945.* United States Army in World War II. Washington, D.C.: U.S. Government Printing Office, 1968.

Condliffe, J. B. "Implications of Lend-Lease: Economic Problems in the Settlement." *Foreign Affairs* 21 (1943):474-95.

Daniels, Jonathan. *The Man of Independence.* Philadelphia, New York: Lippincott, 1950.

Dawson, Raymond H. *The Decision to Aid Russia, 1941; Foreign Policy and Domestic Politics.* Chapel Hill: University of North Carolina Press, 1959.

Divine, Robert A. *Roosevelt and World War II.* Baltimore, Md.: Johns Hopkins Press, 1969. 3 vols.

Diplomaticheskii slovar' [Diplomatic Dictionary]. Moscow: Gosudarstvennoye Izadatel'stvo Politicheskoi Literatury, 1st. ed., 1948-1950; 2nd ed., 1960-1964.

Feis, Herbert. *Between War and Peace.* Princeton, N.J.: Princeton University Press, 1960.

————. *Churchill, Roosevelt and Stalin.* Princeton, N.J.: Princeton University Press, 1957.

————. *From Trust to Terror: The Onset of the Cold War, 1945-1950.* New York: W. W. Norton, 1970.

————. "Political Aspects of Foreign Loans." *Foreign Affairs* 23 1945):609-619.

Ferrell, Robert H. and Bemis, Samuel Flagg, eds. *The American Secretaries of State and Their Diplomacy.* Vol. 14, *James F. Byrnes* by George Curry; *E. R. Stettinius, Jr.* by Richard L. Walker. Vols. 12 & 13, *Cordell Hull* by Julius W. Pratt. New York: Cooper Square Publishers, 1964, 1965.

Fleming, D. F. *The Cold War and Its Origins.* 2 vols. Garden City, N.Y.: Doubleday, 1961.

Gaddis, John Lewis. *The United States and the Origins of the Cold War.* New York: Columbia University Press, 1972.

Gayer, Arthur D. "The Problem of Lend-Lease: Its Nature, Implications and Settlement," in *American Interests in the War and the Peace.* New York: Council on Foreign Relations, 1944.

Gardner, Lloyd C. *Architects of Illusion: Men and Ideas in American Foreign Policy.* Chicago, Ill.: Quadrangle Books, 1970.

————. *Economic Aspects of New Deal Diplomacy.* Madison, Wis.: University of Wisconsin Press, 1964.

Gardner, Richard N. *Sterling-Dollar Diplomacy: The Origins and the Prospects of Our International Economic Order.* 2nd ed. New York: McGraw-Hill, 1969.

Gladkov, I. A., ed. *Sovetskaia ekonomika v period velikoi otechetvennoi voiny, 1941-1945* [The Soviet economy in the period of the great fatherland war, 1941-1945]. Moscow: Izdatel'stvo "nauka," 1970.

Hall, Hessel Duncan. *North American Supply.* History of the Second World War, United Kingdom Civil Series, edited by Sir Keith Hancock. London: Her Majesty's Stationery Office & Longmans, Green, 1955.

Hancock, W. K. and Growing, M. M. *British War Economy.* History of the Second World War, United Kingdom Civil Series, edited by Sir Keith Hancock. London: His Majesty's Stationery Office & Longmans, Green, 1949.

Herring, George C., Jr. *Aid to Russia 1941-1946: Strategy, Diplomacy and the Origins of the Cold War.* New York: Columbia University Press, 1973.

————. "Lend-Lease to Russia and the Origins of the Cold War, 1941-1945," *Journal of American History* 46(1969):93-114.

————. "The United States and British Bankruptcy, 1944-1945: Responsibilities Deferred," *Political Science Quarterly* 86 (1971):260-280.

Herz, Martin F. *Beginnings of the Cold War.* Bloomington, Ind.: Indiana University Press, 1966.

Istoriia velikoi otechestvennoi voiny Sovetskogo Soiuza, 1941-1945 [History of the Great Fatherland War of the Soviet Union, 1941-1945]. 6 vols. Moscow: Voennoe izdatel'stvo, 1960-1965.

Jones, Robert Huhn. *The Roads to Russia: U.S. Lend-Lease to the Soviet Union.* Norman, Okla.: University of Oklahoma Press, 1969.

Kennan, George F. *Russia and the West Under Lenin and Stalin.* Boston: Little, Brown, an Atlantic Monthly Press Book, 1960.

Kimball, Warren F. *The Most Unsordid Act: Lend-Lease, 1939-1941.* Baltimore, Md.: Johns Hopkins Press, 1969.

Kolko, Gabriel. *The Politics of War: The World and United States Foreign Policy, 1943-1945.* New York: Random House, 1968.

Kuklick, Bruce. *American Policy and the Division of Germany: The Clash with Russia over Reparations.* Ithaca, N.Y.: Cornell University Press, 1972.

LaFeber, Walter. *America, Russia and the Cold War, 1945-1966.* New

York: John Wiley & Sons, 1967.

Langer, William Leonard and Gleason, S. Everett. *The Undeclared War, 1940-1941*. New York: Harper & Bros., 1953.

Leighton, Richard M. and Coakley, Robert W. *Global Logistics and Strategy, 1940-1943*. United States Army in World War II. Washington: U.S. Government Printing Office, 1955.

McNeill, William H. *America, Britain and Russia: Their Cooperation and Conflict, 1941-1946*. Survey of International Affairs, 1939-1946. London: Oxford University Press, 1953.

Morrison, Samuel E. *History of United States Naval Operations in World War II*. Vol. 1, *The Battle of the Atlantic, September 1939-May 1943*. Boston: Little, Brown, 1954.

Motter, T. H. Vail. *The Persian Corridor and Aid to Russia*. United States Army in World War II. Washington: U.S. Government Printing Office, 1952.

Ornatskii, I. *Eksportno-importnyi bank SShA* [Export-Import Bank of the U.S.A.]. Moscow, Institute of International Affairs, 1959.

Paterson, Thomas G. "The Abortive American Loan to Russia and the Origins of the Cold War, 1943-1946." *The Journal of American History* 46(1969):70-92.

————. *Soviet-American Confrontation: Postwar Reconstruction and the Origins of the Cold War*. Baltimore, Md.: Johns Hopkins University Press, 1973.

Pugh, Olin S. *The Export-Import Bank of Washington*. Columbia, S.C.: University of South Carolina, Bureau of Business and Economic Research, School of Business Administration, 1957.

Range, Willard. *Franklin D. Roosevelt's World Order*. Athens, Ga.: University of Georgia Press, 1959.

Roskill, S. W. *The War at Sea*. 2 vols. History of the Second World War, United Kingdom Military Series, edited by J. R. M. Butler. Vol. 1, *The Defensive*. Vol. 2, *The Period of Balance*. London: Her Majesty's Stationery Office, 1954, 1956.

Sayres, R. S. *Financial Policy 1939-1945*. History of the Second World War, United Kingdom Civil Series, edited by Sir Keith Hancock. London: Her Majesty's Stationery Office & Longmans, Green & Co., 1956.

Schlesinger, Arthur, Jr., "Origins of the Cold War." *Foreign Affairs* 46(1967):22-52.

Sherwin, Martin J. *A World Destroyed: The Atomic Bomb and the Grand Alliance*. New York: Alfred A. Knopf, 1975.

Shigalin, Grigorii I. *Narodnoe khoziaistvo SSSR v period velikoi otechestvennoi voiny* [The national economy of the USSR in the period of the great fatherland war]. Moscow: "Sotsegiz," 1960.

Starobin, Joseph R. "Origins of the Cold War: The Communist Dimension," *Foreign Affairs* 47(1969):681-696.

Ulam, Adam B. *Expansion and Coexistence: The History of Soviet Foreign Policy, 1917-1967.* New York: Frederick A. Praeger, 1968.

Val'kov, V. A. *SSSR i SShA (ikh politicheskie i ekonomicheskie otnosheniia)* [USSR and USA: their political and economic relations]. Moscow: "Nauka," 1965.

Voznesensky, Nikolai A. *The Economy of the USSR During World War II.* Washington: Public Affairs Press, 1948.

Werth, Alexander, *Russia at War, 1941-1945.* New York: Avon Books, 1964.

Westerfield, Bradford. *Foreign Policy and Party Politics: Pearl Harbor to Korea.* New Haven, Conn.: Yale University Press, 1955.

_____. *The Instruments of America's Foreign Policy.* New York: Crowell, 1963.

Williams, William A. *The Tragedy of American Diplomacy.* New York: Dell Publ. Co., A Delta Book, 1962.

Woodbridge, George, et al. *UNRRA, The History of the United Nations Relief and Rehabilitation Administration.* 3 vols. New York: Columbia University Press, 1950.

Young, Roland. *Congressional Politics in the Second World War.* New York: Columbia University Press, 1956.

Zhilina, P. A., ed. *Velikaia otechestvennaia voina, 1941-1945: kratkii nauchno-populiarnii ocherk* [The Great Fatherland War: short scientific-popular essay]. Moscow: Politizdat, 1970.

Policy Process and Theory-Related Studies

Allison, Graham T. and Halperin, Morton. "Bureaucratic Politics: A Paradigm and Some Policy Implications." *World Politics,* Supplement, 24 (spring 1972):40-79.

Allison, Graham T. "Conceptual Models and the Cuban Missile Crisis." *American Political Science Review* 63(1969):689-718.

_____. *Essence of Decision: Explaining the Cuban Missile Crisis.* Boston: Little, Brown, 1971.

Bardach, Eugene. *The Implementation Game: What Happens After a Bill Becomes a Law.* Cambridge, Mass.: MIT Press, 1977.

de Rivera, Joseph H. *The Psychological Dimension of Foreign Policy.* Columbus, Ohio: Charles Merrill, 1968.

Dror, Yehezkel. *Public Policymaking Reexamined.* Scranton, Pa.: Chandler, 1968.

Halperin, Morton H. *Bureaucratic Politics and Foreign Policy.* Washington: The Brookings Institution, 1974.

Halperin, Morton H. and Kanter, Arnold, eds. *Readings in American Foreign Policy: A Bureaucratic Perspective.* Boston: Little, Brown, 1973.

Hilsman, Roger. *The Politics of Policy Making in Defense and Foreign Affairs.* New York: Harper & Row, 1971.

Hoffmann, Stanley. *Gulliver's Troubles, or the Setting of American Foreign Policy.* The Atlantic Policy Studies Series, The Council on Foreign Relations. New York: McGraw-Hill Book Co., 1968.

————. "Restraints and Choices in American Foreign Policy," *Daedalus: Journal of the American Academy of Arts and Sciences,* fall 1962, pp. 668-704.

Jervis, Robert. "Hypotheses on Misperception," *World Politics* 20, no. 3 (April 1968):454-79.

————*Perception and Misperception in International Politics.* Princeton, N.J.: Princeton University Press, 1976.

Lindblom, Charles E. *The Policy-Making Process.* Englewood Cliffs, N.J.: Prentice-Hall, 1968.

Lovell, John P. *Foreign Policy in Perspective: Strategy, Adaptation, Decision Making.* New York: Holt, Rinehart and Winston, 1970.

Pressman, Jeffrey L. and Wildavsky, Aaron. *Implementation.* Berkeley, Calif.: University of California Press, 1974.

Robinson, James N. *Congress and Foreign Policy-Making: A Study in Legislative Influence and Initiative.* Rev. ed. Homewood, Ill.: Dorsey Press, 1967.

Rourke, Francis E. *Bureaucracy and Foreign Policy.* Studies in International Affairs no. 17, the Washington Center of Foreign Policy Research of the Johns Hopkins University School of Advanced International Studies. Baltimore, Md., 1972.

Schilling, Warner R., Hammond, Paul Y. and Snyder, Glenn H. *Strategy, Politics and Defense Budgets.* New York: Columbia University Press, 1962.

Smith, Thomas B. "The Policy Implementation Process," *Policy Sciences* 4(1973):197-209.

Snyder, Richard C., Bruck, H. W. and Sapin, Burton. *Foreign Policy Decision-Making: An Approach to the Study of International Politics.* New York: The Free Press, 1962.

Van Meter, Donald S. and Van Horn, Carl E. "The Policy Implementation Process: A Conceptual Framework," *Administration and Society* 6(1975):445-488.

Newspapers and Periodicals

After the War: A Bulletin Devoted to Problems of Postwar Reconstruction.

Baltimore Sun.

Christian Science Monitor.

Information Bulletin (Embassy of the USSR in the United States).

Izvestiia.

Journal of Commerce (New York).

New York Herald Tribune.

New York Times.

Philadelphia Inquirer.

Pravda.

Vital Speeches of the Day.

Wall Street Journal.

Washington Daily News.

Washington Post.

Washington Star.

Index

DATE DUE

NOV 2 0 1990			
			PRINTED IN U.S.A
GAYLORD			